GAMES
MAGAZINE

PRESENTS

THE GIANT BOOK OF GAMES

EDITED BY WILL SHORTZ

DESIGNED BY DON WRIGHT

TIMES BOOKS

All rights reserved under International and Pan-American Copyright Conventions. Published in
the United States by Times Books, a division of Random House, Inc., New York, and simultaneously
in Canada by Random House of Canada Limited, Toronto. All of the games that appear in this work
were originally published in *Games* magazine.

Library of Congress Cataloging-in-Publication Data

Games magazine presents the giant book of games / by Will Shortz, editor.
     p.   cm.
ISBN 0-8129-1951-3
1. Indoor games.   2. Puzzles.   I. Shortz, Will, 1952–   II. Games.   III. Title: Giant book of games.
GV1229.G1854   1991
793—dc20   91-26534

Manufactured in the United States of America
9 8 7 6

INTRODUCTION

GAMES magazine, the source of all the material in this book, has always had a bit of an identity problem. What kind of magazine is it?

The biggest portion of the magazine consists of puzzles, quizzes, and tests. As this book shows, these come in traditional and non-traditional formats, in color and in black-and-white. But it also publishes original two-player games, reviews of the latest commercial games and puzzle books, magic tricks, feature articles on playful subjects, contests, fake advertisements, and more.

Even newsstand dealers are puzzled. Some display GAMES in the crossword section, others next to the computer game magazines, and still others among the literary or science magazines like *The Atlantic*, *Omni*, and *Scientific American*.

All we know for sure is that whatever kind of magazine GAMES is, it's the only one of its kind.

Since GAMES was founded in 1977, it has published thousands of original puzzles, games, quizzes, tests, and things to do (we lost count long ago). This book is the magazine's latest compendium, containing 200 or so of our favorite doable features over the years.

A lot of people are responsible for the contents of this book, from the contributors (whose bylines appear over their works) to the magazine's many editors and designers, both past and present. I'd like to give special acknowledgment to Mike Shenk, who was the original editor of many of the puzzles in this book. I want to thank Mark Danna for his skill and care in preparing the book's contents for publication, and Don Wright for his expertise and professional eye in redesigning the material.

Now on to the games! Here's hoping that whatever category of mental challenge you like, you'll find it inside.

Will Shortz
Editor

CONTENTS

WARM-UP CALISTHENICS WITH WHICH TO STRETCH YOUR MENTAL MUSCLES

1

NO LEFT TURN

By Bob Stanton

On a scenic trip through Azalia, your route passes through an ancient walled village peopled by right-thinking folks—so right-thinking, in fact, they've completely banned left turns (and U-turns) within the village.

Using the map at left to guide you, can you get through the village without breaking the law?
Answer, page 173

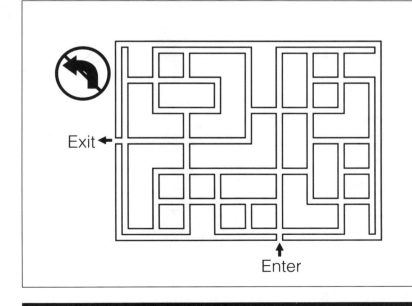

Exit ◄

Enter

LIMBERICKS

By Lola Schancer

A good limerick always ends with a twist, but a *limberick* ends every line with one. To solve, un-scramble the five words given in capital letters to complete each verse. A good sense of pun helps.

Answers, page 173

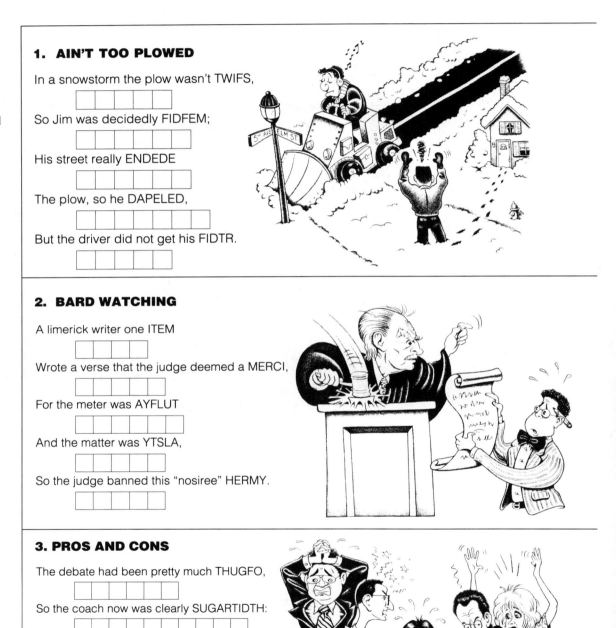

1. AIN'T TOO PLOWED

In a snowstorm the plow wasn't TWIFS,

So Jim was decidedly FIDFEM;

His street really ENDEDE

The plow, so he DAPELED,

But the driver did not get his FIDTR.

2. BARD WATCHING

A limerick writer one ITEM

Wrote a verse that the judge deemed a MERCI,

For the meter was AYFLUT

And the matter was YTSLA,

So the judge banned this "nosiree" HERMY.

3. PROS AND CONS

The debate had been pretty much THUGFO,

So the coach now was clearly SUGARTIDTH:

His squad GRADESIDE—

Press ahead or ONDECCE?—

Thus giving the team feud for HOGHUTT.

RICK TULKA

CAN IT!

By David Pope

No, this isn't the generic goods section at the supermarket. We've simply removed the labels from 12 cans of familiar products found at the grocery, pharmacy, hardware store, etc. Try to identify—just from the shape—the type of product or brand name associated with each. Can do? *Answers, page 173*

1._____
2._____
3._____
4._____

5._____
6._____
7._____
8._____

9._____
10._____
11._____
12._____

ILLUSTRATED EXCLAMATIONS!

Written and Illustrated by Robert Leighton!

Wowie kazowie! Look at all these exciting situations! But wait! Inside each of the exclamation balloons, there should be an appropriate word or sound! Choose the illustration of the correct word (labeled a–j) and place it in the appropriate balloon! Get 10 right and you can exclaim "Bravo!" for yourself!

Answers, page 173!

CHOICES

WANDERFUL

By Mike Shenk

The word search puzzle below has a twist. In fact, it has a number of twists, because it's also a maze. To solve, first find and circle the 39 maze-related words and phrases hidden in the grid. Each reads in a straight line forward, backward, up, or down (never diagonally). Then find a path through the unused letters, starting at the S indicated in the top row and ending at the X on the bottom. Only one route leads from start to finish. Watch out for dead ends!

Answer, page 173

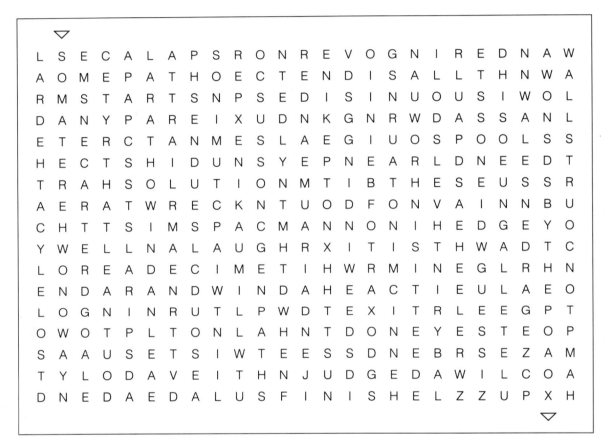

L S E C A L A P S R O N R E V O G N I R E D N A W
A O M E P A T H O E C T E N D I S A L L T H N W A
R M S T A R T S N P S E D I S I N U O U S I W O L
D A N Y P A R E I X U D N K G N R W D A S S A N L
E T E R C T A N M E S L A E G I U O S P O O L S S
H E C T S H I D U N S Y E P N E A R L D N E E D T
T R A H S O L U T I O N M T I B T H E S E U S S R
A E R A T W R E C K N T U O D F O N V A I N N B U
C H T T S I M S P A C M A N N O N I H E D G E Y O
Y W E L L N A L A U G H R X I T I S T H W A D T C
L O R E A D E C I M E T I H W R M I N E G L R H N
E N D A R A N D W I N D A H E A C T I E U L A E O
L O G N I N R U T L P W D T E X I T R L E E G P T
O W O T P L T O N L A H N T D O N E Y E S T E O P
S A A U S E T S I W T E E S S D N E B R S E Z A M
T Y L O D A V E I T H N J U D G E D A W I L C O A
D N E D A E D A L U S F I N I S H E L Z Z U P X H

ARIADNE	GOVERNOR'S PALACE	MEANDER	THESEUS
BENDS	GUESS	MINOS	TRAIL
CNOSSUS	HAMPTON COURT	MINOTAUR	TURNING
CRETE	HEDGE	MS. PAC-MAN	TWIST
DAEDALUS	LABYRINTH	PATHS	WALLS
DEAD END	LAWN	PUZZLE	WANDERING
ELY CATHEDRAL	LOOPS	RETRACE	WHITE MICE
EXIT	LOST	SINUOUS	WINDING
FINISH	MAZES	SOLUTION	
GARDENS		SPIRALS	
GOAL		START	

PICTURE IMPERFECT

By Tom Bloom

The spring scene at right is reproduced at the bottom of the page in 12 pieces. Three of the pieces, though, have something added to them, three have something deleted, three have something moved in them, and three are exactly the same as they are above. Studying the art closely, can you put each piece in its proper category?

Answers, page 173

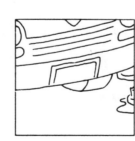

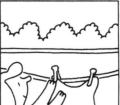

CRIME AND TREASON

By N.M. Meyer

Each pair of words below is a disguised rhyme of a familiar phrase. For example, the clue "White and gray" would lead to the answer NIGHT AND DAY, and the title of the puzzle would be a clue for RHYME AND REASON. How many of the following phrases can you unmask?   *Answers, page 173*

1. Sleuth and trail _____

2. Fork and greens _____

3. Draw and border_____

4. Ruts and jolts_____

5. Jars and pipes _____

6. Yak and gnu _____

7. Pride and chic _____

8. Stencil and scraper _____

9. Jamb and pegs_____

10. Spry and flighty_____

11. Grow and swell _____

12. Run and lames _____

13. Bops and clobbers_____

14. Swank and style _____

15. Prong and lance _____

16. Stein and brandy _____

THE SIGHS OF IT

By Shamlu Dudeja

This puzzle should elicit a number of sighs from you—14 of them, to be exact. That's because the answer to each clue is a word beginning with the *sound* SIGH. For example, the clue "Quiet state" would lead to the answer SILENCE, while "Coded message" would be CIPHER. If you have any trouble sizing any of these up, you'll find all the answers on page 173.

1. Police car sound _____

2. Ho Chi Minh City, formerly _____

3. Playwright Neil _____

4. Tornado-like storm _____

5. Apple drink _____

6. 1960 Hitchcock thriller _____

7. Thailand's old name _____

8. 1948 Triple Crown winner _____

9. Soviet exile site _____

10. Chemist or physicist, e.g. _____

11. Mideast peninsula _____

12. Mythical one-eyed monster_____

13. Agatha Christie poison _____

14. Grass-cutting tool _____

MISTAKEN IDENTITIES

By Nick North

Following the daring theft of thousands of dollars from the coffers of the Keen-Eyed Club, the detective in charge of the case was taking statements from four club members who were witness to this heinous crime.

"I saw him, all right," said one, "a guy with a pencil mustache, and dark hair, and a thick scarf around his throat."

"I saw him, too," said another: "He had an ugly-looking scar, and big, bushy eyebrows, behind thick glasses."

A third man spoke up: "He pushed me aside as he made for the door, so I saw him quite clearly. I'll agree he had a mustache, but he had thin eyebrows, and wasn't wearing a scarf."

A fourth man stepped forward: "Take no notice of them. The guy had blond hair, no glasses, and a scar on his left cheek."

As the detective had feared, none of the descriptions was altogether accurate. In fact, each witness had made one mistake in his description. Bearing this in mind, can you pick out the thief from the faces below?   *Answer, page 173*

FREDERICK WINKOWSKI

SCRAMBLED COMICS

Written and Illustrated by Robert Leighton

Some people like their comics over easy, but we prefer ours scrambled. The three comic strips on these pages have had their panels rearranged, with the unfortunate side effect of leaving their punch lines punchless. Can you put them sunny side up? There may be more

BEAUTY AND THE BUST

A   B   C   D

TOTALED RECALL

A   B   C   D

CHECKING OUT

A   B   C   D

than one way to arrange a set in a logical sequence, but—*prepare yourself*—only one solution leads to the yolk.   *Answers, page 173*

E

F

G

1. _____
2. _____
3. _____
4. _____
5. _____
6. _____
7. _____

E

F

G

1. _____
2. _____
3. _____
4. _____
5. _____
6. _____
7. _____

E

F

G

1. _____
2. _____
3. _____
4. _____
5. _____
6. _____
7. _____

LEFT AND RIGHT

By Will Shortz

There are only two directions to this puzzle—left and right. Each answer is a six-letter word, which is to be entered in the grid one letter per square according to the numbers. Half the answers will read from left to right, as in the example, BRAZIL (1–2). Half will read from right to left, as in the answer to 2–3, which begins LIZ-. Work both ways to complete the puzzle.

Answer, page 173

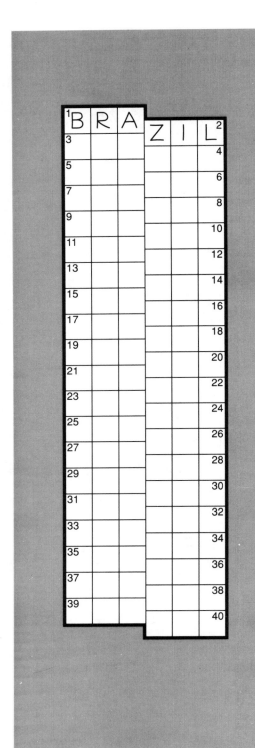

CLUES

1-2 Neighbor of Bolivia
2-3 Expensive shoe leather
3-4 Chinese New Year costume
4-5 Low-down dirty-rotten (hyph.)
5-6 '50s music style (hyph.)
6-7 Snow for skiing
7-8 Train porter
8-9 Green Bay player
9-10 Do more needlework
10-11 Xmas tree trim
11-12 Sappho's home in ancient Greece
12-13 Provided that, old-style
13-14 Cravat clip
14-15 It bites, as the RCA dog?
15-16 Cleared away, as a debt
16-17 Conversation
17-18 Played 18 holes
18-19 Render harmless, as a snake
19-20 Chewed
20-21 Fold of skin on the neck
21-22 Sign of fright
22-23 Retractable, as some window blinds (hyph.)
23-24 Preacher's stand
24-25 A-1
25-26 Three sheets to the wind
26-27 Military work group
27-28 Legally responsible
28-29 Where sweaters wear out first
29-30 Goes goo-goo over
30-31 Slept soundly?
31-32 Make fun of
32-33 Magazine VIP
33-34 Cheap liquor
34-35 One that pulls along
35-36 Jamaican blues-rock
36-37 One of Philly's teams
37-38 Rarely
38-39 Quick to blush from praise
39-40 African fly

PLAYER PIANOS

By James Forman

Never mind what this piano arrangement sounds like—all that counts is what it *looks* like. Below the 15 grand pianos disconcertingly arranged in the center of this page are four overhead views of the same pianos. But only one of the four exactly duplicates the arrangement in the center. If you're really sharp, you'll find it in nothing flat.   *Answer, page 173*

A   B   C   D

CONNECT-THE-DOTS EYEBALL BENDERS

By Robert Leighton

Fans of GAMES's regular Eyeball Benders page are familiar with the usual beguiling photographs of everyday items. But in this puzzle, you create your own Eyeball Benders by connecting the dots. When completed, each of the four pictures will reveal a close-up view of a different, common object. What are they?

Answers, page 174

A.

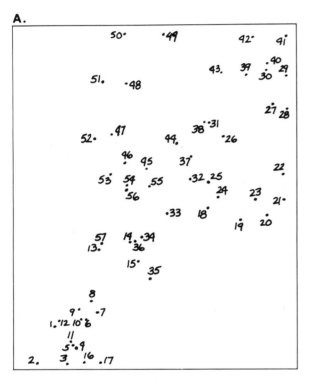

B.

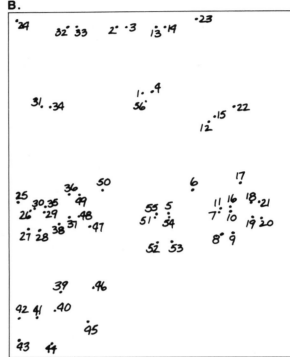

C.

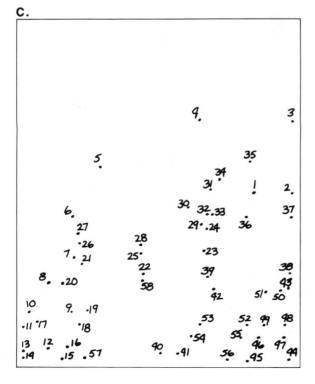

D.

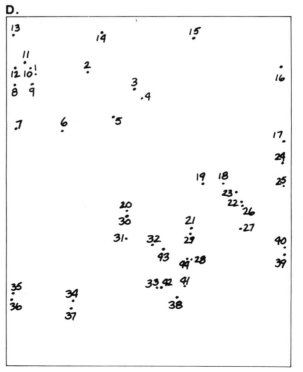

CAMERA SHY

By Todd McClary

Sheldon—that's him in the lower right corner—wants to walk to the stairs in the upper left, but the plaza is filled with tourists taking snapshots. Sheldon would hate to spoil anyone's picture, of course, so he doesn't want to step between a photographer and his or her subject. Using only your eyes, not a pencil, can you find the path Sheldon should take?

Answer, page 174

PHIL SCHEUER

CIRCULAR REASONING

From the GAMES Library

Of all the geometrical shapes, the circle encloses the greatest area with any given length of perimeter. Because of its perfect symmetry and aesthetic appeal, the circle is a fundamental element of art, architecture, religious symbolism, commercial design ... and puzzles, of course. On these two pages, we've rounded up six

1. FIGURE THIS

The numbers 1 through 7 can be placed into the seven compartments formed by the three interlocking circles below so that each circle will add up to the same total. The numbers 1, 4, and 6 have already been put in for you. Where do the other figures go?

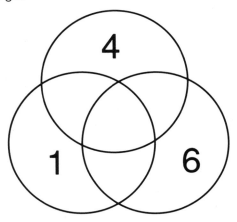

2. CENTRIPETAL ROUTES

Starting at A and travelling along the lines either radially toward the center or circularly in a clockwise direction, by how many different routes is it possible to arrive at the center? Note: Paths that include any segments running counterclockwise or away from the center don't count.

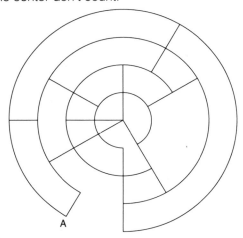

3. BRASS OR RUBBER?

This figure, designed by British puzzlist David Wells, shows five rings—four of brass and one of rubber—lying almost flat on a table. Naturally, the rubber ring is quite flexible, while the brass rings are flat and rigid. All we ask you to do is to say which of the rings is made of rubber.

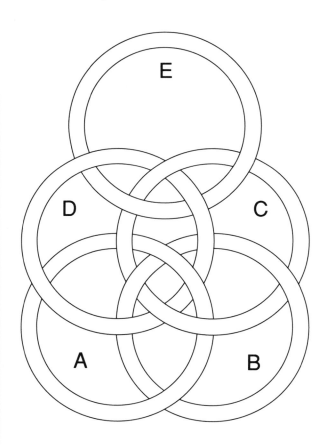

4. COMMON CENTS

Nothing to figure here—just make your best eyeball guess. What U.S. coin is the same size as the circle below?

classic problems based on circles, selected from the vast GAMES Library, along with one original brainteaser (#6) by GAMES Editor Will Shortz to round out the set.

None of the puzzles will throw you any curves—except, that is, in the literal sense.   *Answers, page 174*

5. THE PARIS MAZE

This picture, according to the turn-of-the-century American puzzle master Sam Loyd, is a correct diagram of the famous Ruchonnet puzzle-maze shown at the Paris Exposition. A person entering the maze held a ticket that was punched with the numbers of the different gates passed to reach the little house in the center. Over the entrance to the house were the large figures "136" and an announcement to the effect that anybody holding a card punched with six numbers adding up to 136 would be awarded a prize. Can you figure out the winning route through the gates to the center?

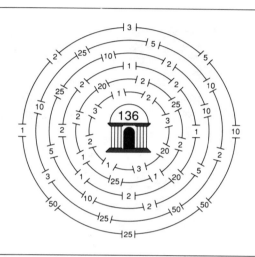

7. THE SIX COTTAGES

This puzzle is by Sam Loyd's great English rival, Henry Dudeney. It seems a circular road, 27 miles long, surrounds a tract of wild and desolate country. On this road are six cottages placed in such a way that every whole number of miles from 1 to 26 is the exact distance between at least one pair of cottages. Thus, Brown may be a mile from Stiggins, Jones two miles from Rogers, Wilson three miles from Jones, and so on. Of course, they can walk in either direction as required. Can you place the cottages at distances that will fulfill these conditions? The illustration is intended to give no clue as to the relative distances.

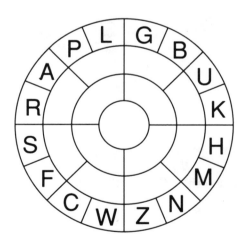

6. TARGET WORD

The bull's-eye target above has 16 different letters in the outer ring. Place 8 letters in the second ring that are all different from one another, 4 letters in the third ring that are all different from one another, and 1 letter in the bull's-eye in order to complete 16 four-letter words reading from the outer ring to the middle. Can you do it?

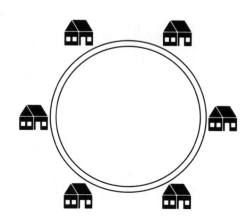

PRODUCT RECALL

By Robert Leighton

Advertising follows us all day long, from the moment we wake up ("Kellogg's—the best to you each morning") till the moment we go to bed ("Take Sominex tonight and sleep"). Some products' logos have become so familiar that we barely need to look at them to identify the items they're pushing.

We think you'll recognize all 15 logos on this page . . . but look again. Each has been altered in some small but important way. For example, the Playboy rabbit head (#2) is sporting the wrong bow tie. How many of the other changes can you spot? *Answers, page 175*

LOOK HERE!
VISUAL PUZZLES TO
TEST YOUR EYE-Q

2

TYPE CAST

By Mike Shenk

Is this your type of puzzle? We've taken a complete alphabet in the type style we use for GAMES's logo and cast it into the heap you see at left. Most of the letters, though somewhat obscured, are face up. Six of them, however, have landed face down on top of the pile. By a curious coincidence, these letters can be rearranged to form a word. To help you determine which letters are which, we've provided a copy of the complete alphabet at the bottom of the page. When you've identified the six face-down letters, unscramble them to spell an appropriate word.
Answers, page 175

ABCDEFGHIJKLM
NOPQRSTUVWXYZ

HANDIWORK

By Alan Robbins

One of the things that has given man the upper hand over other animals is our opposable thumb, enabling us to grasp, hold, and subtly manipulate objects such as tools. Not only that, we have the talent to *study* hands in action and guess what activities they are performing. Can you prove your mental and manual superiority to the rest of the animal kingdom by putting your finger on just what these 12 familiar activities are?

Answers, page 175

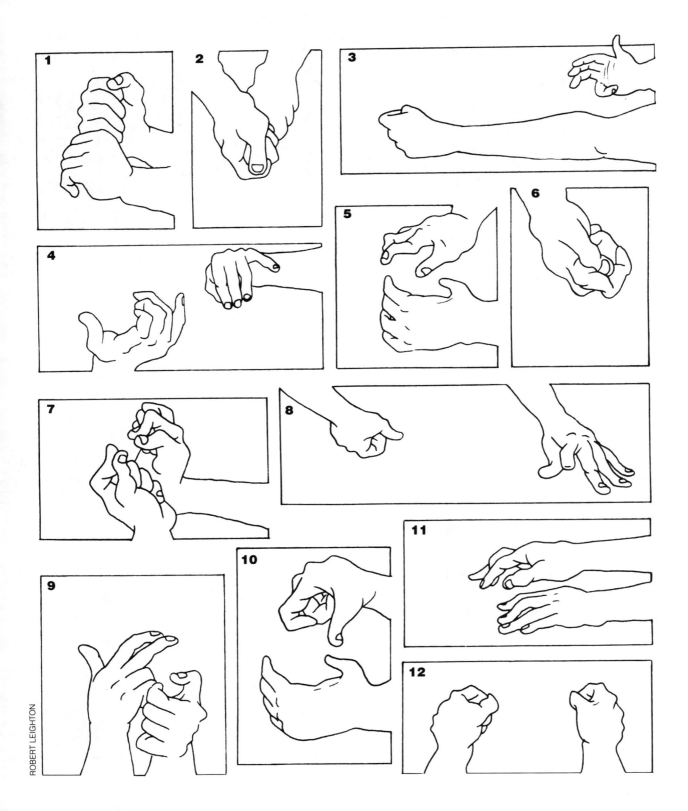

ROBERT LEIGHTON

BIT PARTS

By Steve and Caren Armstrong

When a computer goes to the movies, what does it see? Perhaps the images here. These six frames are from familiar film classics reduced to near abstraction by computer processing. Can you name the films?

Answers, page 175

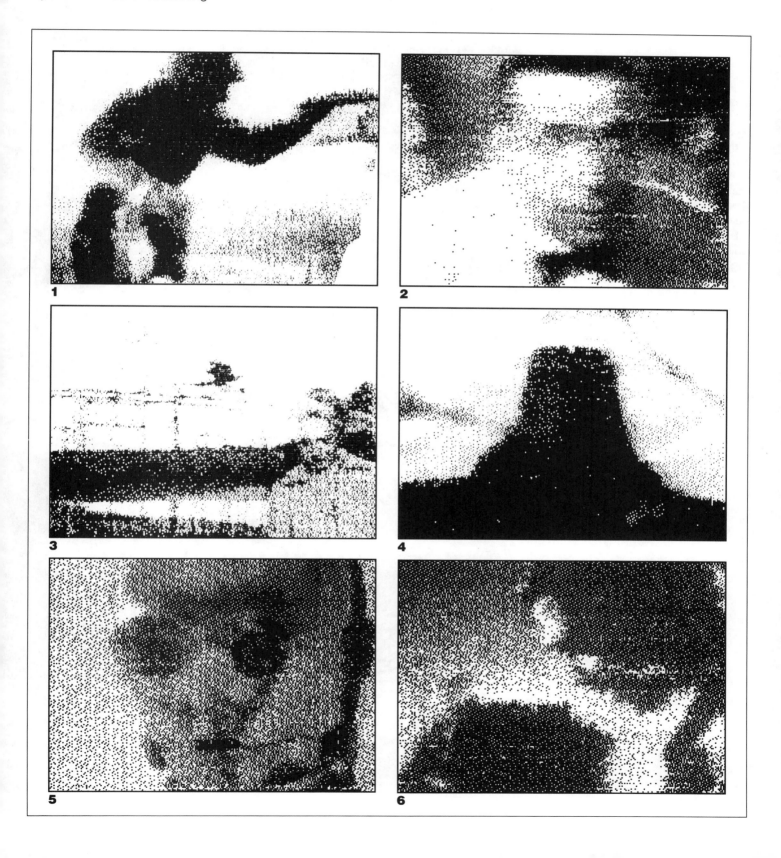

RANGEFINDER

Woodcut by Lars and Lois
Hokanson

The four rangers galloping across
these pages are in such a hurry,
they're oblivious to the 27 typically
Western objects to be be found in
the scene. Some are hidden in
plain sight and some are partially
concealed behind other objects.
See how many of these items you
can rustle up: an arrow, a boot,
a bow, a Bowie knife, a buffalo, a
bullet, a cactus, a canoe, a Conestoga wagon, a coyote, a derringer,
a guitar, a hangman's noose, a
horseshoe, an Indian headdress,
a jackrabbit, a peace pipe, a rifle,
a sheriff's star, a six-gun, a spur, a
tepee, Texas, a tomahawk, a totem
pole, a vulture, and a wagon wheel.
Luckily for you and the rangers,
there are no outlaws lurking here.
Answers, page 175

ICING ON THE CAKE

By Joy Baker

How odd. It's not your birthday, and your anniversary was months ago, yet someone has surprised you by sending you a cake. It looks like there's a message on top, but the baker absent-mindedly delivered the cake already in slices. Without moving the pieces around (except in your head), can you figure out the message—and the occasion?

Answer, page 176

PURTLE'S PLIGHT

By Robert Leighton

Some people have trouble suffering fools; others, like Purtle at right, have trouble suffering April Fools. As we all know, and as Purtle is about to find out, the best April Fools occur where you least expect them . . .

Answer, page 176

LEFTY AND RIGHTY

By Marvin Miller

Lavinia and Rosalinda are identical twin sisters who share an old house down the road. Even their best friends know only one sure way to tell them apart: Lavinia is left-handed, while Rosalinda is right-handed.

At right are six objects that were just used by the sisters. Study them carefully. Can you tell which ones were more likely to have been used by Lavinia and which by Rosalinda?

Answers, page 176

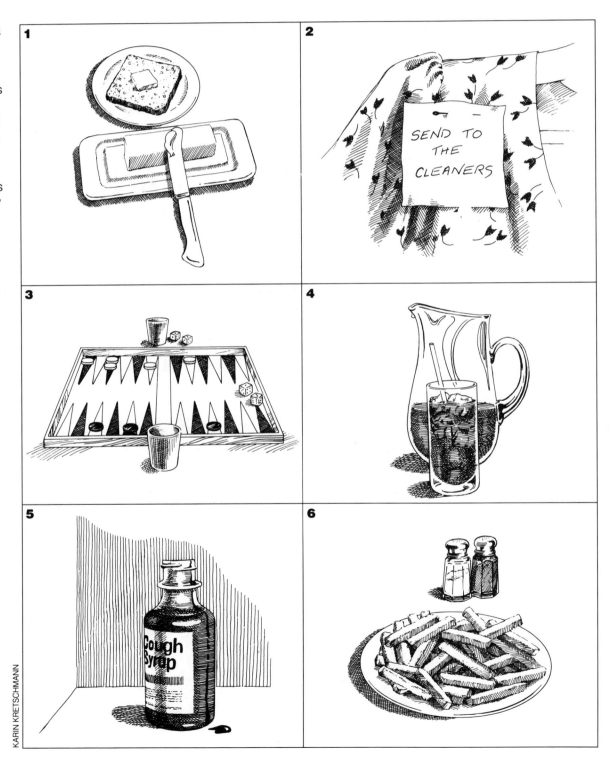

YOU ARE WHAT YOU ATE

By Robert Leighton

Prove the old saying true in this nouvelle quiz-ine. Each of these people just ate one of the food items shown at the bottom of the page. Can you match each with his or her chosen dish? You could try smelling their breath, but we recommend examining their outfits, conditions, and other visual clues.

Answers, page 176

FOODS

MIME'S THE WORD

Written and Illustrated by Robert Leighton

What are
these eight
people
doing?

*Answers,
page 176*

UFO'S

Photographs by Melissa Weiss

While on an excursion, our photographer had some strange encounters of a blurred kind, and she took these photos as evidence. Could it be that space visitors are so shy that they design their ships to look like familiar earthly objects? If so, what objects *are* they?

Answers, page 176

GONE BUT NOT FORGOTTEN

By Robert Leighton

Each of the twelve items on this page is missing one important element that makes it very difficult, if not impossible, to use.

Can you get a handle on just what's missing here?   *Answers, page 176*

ROUND TRIP MAZE

By Ulrich Koch

Connect the two
central circles.
Answer, page 176

SHADOW PLAY

Handy Puzzles from the
GAMES Library

Next to imitating birdcalls, perhaps the most popular form of parlor entertainment a century ago was making hand shadows. The performer would direct a strong light at a blank wall and, to the delight and amazement of the audience, use his or her hands to create shadows that looked like animals. The eight hand positions shown here are from the books *Hand Shadows* and *More Hand Shadows* by Henry Bursill, both published in the mid-19th century and reissued in the 1960s by Dover Publications. The puzzle is to identify the animal that each hand position will cast on the wall. Trying them yourself might shed some light on the tougher ones—and it could even help revive this old-fashioned hands-on game.   *Answers, page 176*

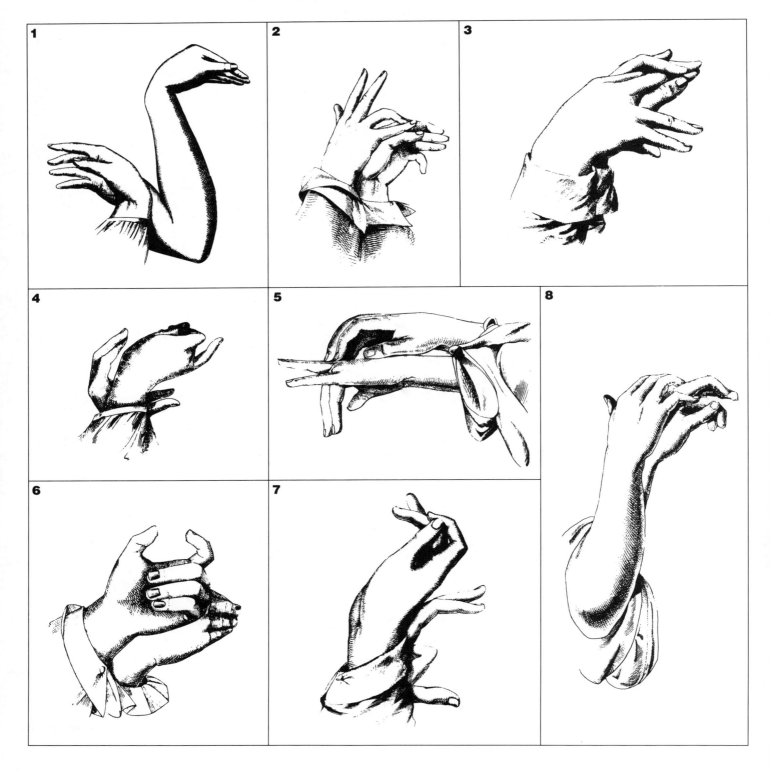

1

2

3

4

5

8

6

7

THE WONDERFUL WORLD OF WORDS

3

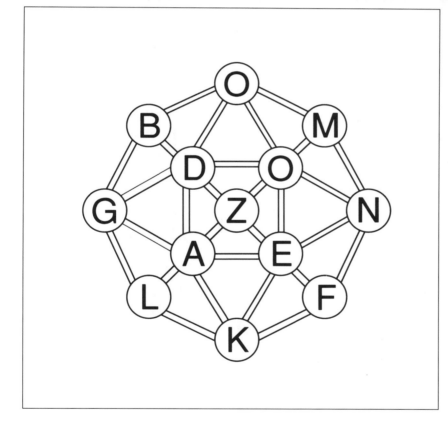

TRAIL-BLAZING

By George Bredehorn

How many words of three or more letters containing the letter Z can you spell out in the grid at left? You may start anywhere and move from letter to letter along the paths, but don't cross or retrace your path within a word. Only uncapitalized words are permitted. A score of 9 answers is good; 12 is excellent. Our solution lists 15 common words and one slightly less familiar word found mainly in crosswords.

Answers, page 177

SKETCHWORDS

By GAMES Readers

Ever notice that the scales of justice are in the shape of the letter T and that JUSTICE has a T in the middle? In response to a contest challenge, GAMES readers came up with many other examples of what we call Sketchwords. To solve them, first figure out what letter each picture represents; then fill in the blanks with other letters to form a word that's related in some way to those pictures.

Answers, page 177.

Ex. JUS___ICE

1. ___ ___ ___ ___ ___ ___ ___

2. ___ ___ ___ ___ ___ ___

3. ___ ___ ___

4. ___ ___ ___ ___ ___ ___

5. ___ ___ ___ ___ ___

6. ___ ___ ___ ___ ___

7. ___ ___ ___ ___ ___

8. ___ ___ ___ ___ ___ ___

9. ___ ___ ___ ___ ___

10. ___ ___ ___ ___ ___ ___

11. ___ ___ ___ ___ ___

12. ___ ___ ___ ___

13. ___ ___ ___ ___ ___

14. ___ ___ ___ ___ ___

15. ___ ___ ___ ___ ___ ___

16. ___ ___ ___ ___ ___ ___ ___

42

BUILDING BLOCKS

By Will Shortz

Three letters in each line of these puzzles are already in place. To solve, insert the "blocks" below each grid into the remaining squares—without rearranging any letters—to complete eight nine-letter words reading across. Each of the blocks will be used exactly once, so you may cross them off as you proceed. When all the squares in a puzzle have been filled, two of the columns reading down will spell some related words.   *Answers, page 177*

PUZZLE 1

S	C	H						
S	U	P						
J	A	Y						
P	O	L						
R	I	V						
T	R	E						
E	X	T						
C	R	O						

ACH	ERB	NAU	SSW
APH	ERN	OAT	WAL
ATE	ERY	OVA	YGR
AYS	KER	RIC	ZER

PUZZLE 2

						A	N	D
						N	C	E
						S	U	S
						A	T	E
						K	I	N
						A	R	D
						T	R	Y
						A	S	T

AGG	EVA	LAN	SEN
BRE	GAL	RED	SNA
CON	GRI	REG	TEL
COU	KES	RTY	WAS

VCR WORDS

By Bern Sharfman

While you were out … we taped this quick quiz. Every answer is a word that contains the letters V, C, and R in that order. How many of the 14 words can you identify with the help of the given clues?   *Answers, page 177*

1. Chapel leader   V __ C __ R

2. Loud, as a complaint   V __ C __ __ __ R __ __ __

3. Longtime English queen V __ C __ __ R __ __

4. Written receipt   V __ __ C __ __ R

5. Sell at an inflated price   __ V __ __ C __ __ R __ __

6. Popular cigarette brand V __ C __ R __ __

7. Of cars, trucks, etc.   V __ __ __ C __ __ __ R

8. Genial, like an uncle   __ V __ __ C __ __ __ __ R

9. Airplane's course direction V __ C __ __ R

10. Horror story author H.P.   __ __ V __ C R __ __ __ __

11. Word stock   V __ C __ __ __ __ __ __ R __

12. Everyday speech   V __ __ __ __ C __ __ __ R

13. Squeeze in too many   __ V __ __ C R __ __ __

14. Purely instinctive   V __ __ C __ R __ __

CRYPTO-MATES

By Dave Greenwald and Paul Rigby

Complete each Crypto-Mate cartoon caption with a pair (or in one case a trio) of anagrams (words with the same letters in different order). For example, a stirring tennis scene could be captioned "The tennis champion won the point with a LOVELY VOLLEY." The clues in the cartoons will help you

1

Private Snedge sounded reveille so loud today, he actually made his _____ _____!

nopqr noqpr

2

To hide buried treasure, how far will _____ _____?

efghijk ighfekj

3

While Bing Crosby moonlighted as a medic in the morgue, he was known as the _____ _____.

wxyyzax wyxyzax

4

If "Certain Sam" earns $1,000 for tossing ten knives, then how much is each _____ _____?

cdefg gfecd

solve. As an additional aid, the answers have been put in cryptogram form; if you can guess one word in a pair, you can automatically transpose its letters to get its mate. Each Crypto-Mate uses a new code, and no letter ever stands for itself. *Answers, page 177*

5

All the guests left early, except the one the _____ _____.

wxyz ywxz

6

How many thugs caught robbing that shoe store did the _____ _____?

efgghij ehfggij

7

I'll say this for "The Four Pancakes"—there are no _____ _____!

klmnoopq lmnqopok

8

If the king appears quite thirsty, serve him a _____ _____ _____.

mnopq oqpnm mnpqo

BLANKETY-BLANK

By Trip Payne

Originally, the 36 letters in the center of this word search, reading in order row by row, spelled a quip. But we've removed these letters and replaced them with shaded boxes. To discover the quip, solve the puzzle as you would any word search, finding and circling the words in the word list, with this difference: Some words cross into the shaded squares and need to have their missing letters filled in. Answers, as always, may read horizontally, vertically, or diagonally, but always in a straight line.

Answer, page 177

ANTIDOTE
BALANCED
"BALI HA'I"
BELFAST
BUCK HENRY
CARUSO
CARY GRANT
CHARCOAL
DECLARER
DENATURE
DEPTHS
DOORBELLS
DREADED
EGO-TRIPPING
EMPTY
EURASIA
FIR TREES
GEFILTE
GREAT DIVIDE
GREEN THUMB
GREMLINS
GUIDED MISSILE

HOLLYHOCKS
HOREHOUND
IMPEDED
INDISTINCT
"K-K-K-KATY"
MAI TAI
MALAWI

MILIEU
NEUFCHATEL
ON A ROLL
PENNY-A-LINER
POULTRY
REFRESH
RIP TORN

SCOREPAD
SCREEN TEST
SHE-DEVIL
SHEEPSHANK
SPARKLER
SQUASH
"SUITS ME"

TAIPEI
TENACITY
TIMOTHY
TOGETHER
TRAVEL
UNKEMPT
YUCATAN

```
Y  R  O  D  S  K  C  O  H  Y  L  L  O  H  U  G  V  E
F  E  I  A  O  U  A  O  N  S  L  L  E  B  R  O  O  D
G  N  I  P  P  I  R  T  O  G  E  T  H  E  R  D  E  T
H  I  E  E  T  E  Y  H  C  B  T  R  M  I  M  D  D  D
E  L  N  R  H  O  G  Y  A  M  L  L  F  I  A  E  G  S
S  A  A  O  G  E  R  L  R  S  I  I  L  E  N  B  R  T
U  Y  U  C  A  T  ▓  ▓  ▓  ▓  ▓  ▓  R  T  R  E  E  S
E  N  H  S  L  N  ▓  ▓  ▓  ▓  ▓  ▓  E  V  I  L  E  K
D  N  K  U  C  E  ▓  ▓  ▓  ▓  ▓  ▓  L  E  U  F  N  N
I  E  O  E  U  S  ▓  ▓  ▓  ▓  ▓  ▓  K  K  A  T  Y
V  P  D  S  M  P  ▓  ▓  ▓  ▓  ▓  ▓  R  C  H  S  H  T
I  E  E  E  P  P  ▓  ▓  ▓  ▓  ▓  ▓  A  S  U  T  U  I
D  I  N  D  I  S  T  I  N  C  T  Q  P  L  O  B  M  C
T  D  A  A  L  L  A  E  R  F  E  S  M  A  P  B  A
A  T  T  R  T  A  R  M  A  A  E  U  I  E  E  M  R  N
E  S  U  B  B  O  U  V  T  H  S  T  E  D  O  W  H  E
R  E  R  A  L  C  E  D  S  C  R  E  E  N  T  E  S  T
G  A  E  L  E  L  I  S  S  I  M  D  E  D  I  U  G  T
```

MISSING LINKS

By Gary Disch

In both puzzles below, the crisscross grid on the right has been left unfinished. Insert the 16 missing letters, listed on the left, into the appropriate squares to complete a pattern of common words reading across and down. You may cross off the missing letters as you solve, because none will be used more than once. *Answers, page 177*

PUZZLE 1

Missing Letters

A A C D
K L M N
N O P R
S S U Y

PUZZLE 2

Missing Letters

A A A B
C E E E
H I M R
R S S U

COMMON ELEMENTS
By Gary Disch

PRESTO CHANGO
By N.M. Meyer

The answer words in each pair below have two things in common: Both are members of the same category (like trees, actors, etc.), and both contain an identical three-letter sequence. Fill in the blanks in each pair with the same three letters in the same order to get the words. For example, given the pair CAB___E and RUTA___A, you'd add BAG to get CABBAGE and RUTABAGA, both vegetables. How many of the following common elements can you identify?   *Answers, page 177*

Change one letter in each of the three words in each line below to get three new words that are members of the same category. For example, given BIRTH, YAK, and PINT, you could change a single letter in each to get BIRCH, OAK, and PINE. No rearrangement of letters is necessary.   *Answers, page 178*

1. S W E ___   ___ M A R K

2. ___ L   T ___ Z

3. S U P ___ O R   ___ E

4. S ___ N   E L ___ N

5. S ___   ___ D O C K

6. S ___ P I O   C A P R I ___ N

7. ___ C E   P ___ D

8. B ___ Z E   I ___

9. S ___ M   R ___ I G H

10. V E ___   U R A ___

11. ___ S S   ___ C K E R S

12. G ___ T S   I N D ___ S

13. ___ C H   ___ R

14. C ___ E R   ___ H U R

1. AMPLE   DEMON   GRANGE
_____

2. SQUIRE   OPAL   ECLIPSE
_____

3. PORCH   HEARING   TUNE
_____

4. CROCKS   PHONY   DAILY
_____

5. BRIDLE   WAIST   HEARTH
_____

6. PARROT   PAISLEY   RAVISH
_____

7. COOPER   ICON   CRANIUM
_____

8. SCORCH   GUN   WHISKER
_____

9. ANGLE   KNEW   GRIST
_____

10. TICKLE   CANTER   FALLBACK
_____

11. TANGY   BUSTLE   LITTERBUG
_____

12. COLOR   DISH   BRACKEN
_____

MIX WELL

By Robert Leighton

This Thanksgiving kitchen scene is also home to 19 pairs of items whose names are anagrams of each other. For instance, the HOSE seen through the window contains the same letters as the SHOE worn by any of the people in the picture. All of the anagrams have four or more letters. How many of them can you find? Getting 12 or more is good; 15 is excellent. Find all 19 and you deserve a turkey dinner with all the trimmings.

Answers, page 178

INGENIOUS INVENTIONS AND SNAPPY CONTRAPTIONS

By Mark Mazut

Remember the commercial about the peanut butter truck that collides with a truck full of chocolate? The result was a great new product combining both tastes.

The bizarre items seen here were formed through similar chance encounters, but with decidedly more dubious results. That's because the two items combined have nothing in common but a part of their names. In the example below, a corkscrew was combined with a screwdriver to form the thoroughly useless corkscrewdriver. Before you rush out to buy the others, how many of them can you identify?

Answers, page 178

Ex.

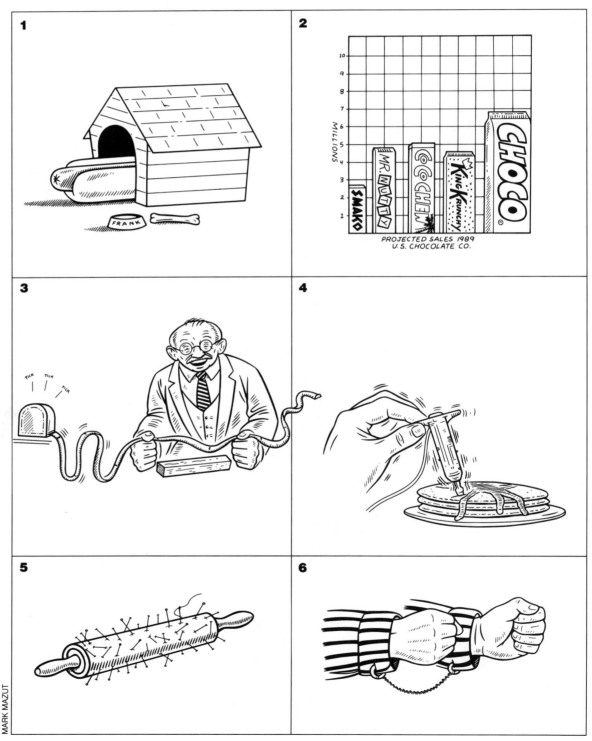

MARK MAZUT

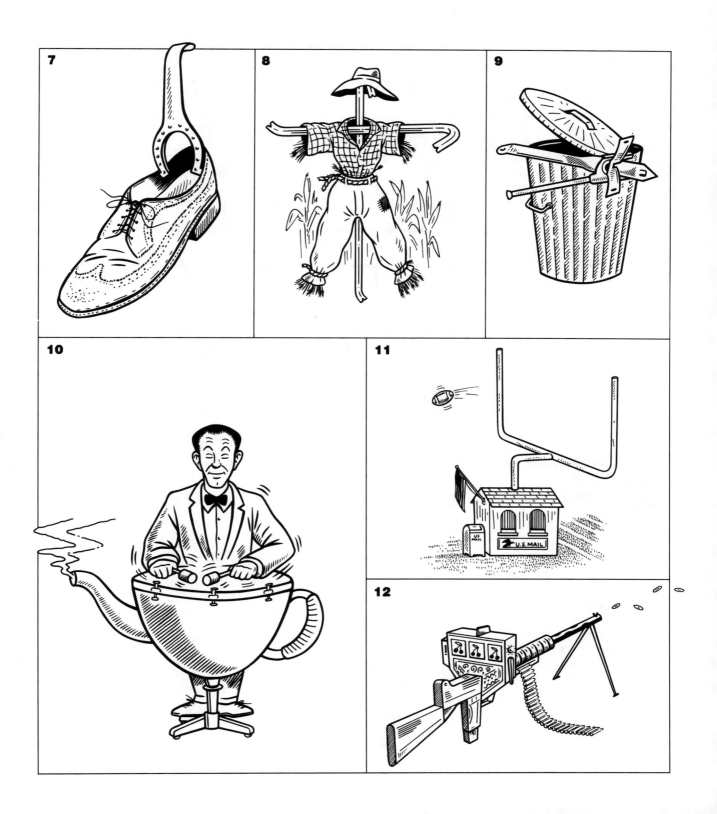

LETTER LOGIC

By Lawrence Graber

Fill in the empty squares in each grid at right to complete four five-letter words reading across. What's the catch? The four words in each completed grid must contain 10 different letters, each used exactly twice. For example, in grid #1 the letter E already appears twice, so it can't be used again. The letter Q, however, appears only once so far. Think of a word in which the second Q will fit, and proceed from there. It may take you several tries to find the right combination of words— so keep your eraser handy.

Answers, page 178

1

Q			F
S	E		T
W		I	T
E			P

2

T			P
A	U		E
O	L		R
T			Z

3

T			O
C	U		B
S	A		R
M			C

4

U			P
P	A		E
H	B		T
T			E

5

N			H
S	U		T
P	N		H
S			F

6

L			L
S	A		E
R	S		Y
G			E

TOPS OFF

By Fraser Simpson

Each set of letters at right started as a two-word phrase in which both words began with the same letter (like *soft soap* or *jumping jacks*). We removed the initial letters of the words, and then removed the space between them. How many of the original phrases can you identify?

Answers, page 178

1. umboet _____

2. aselosed _____

3. astergg _____

4. oodrief _____

5. elferve _____

6. ndiank _____

7. appyour _____

8. estind _____

9. fterll _____

10. aperlates _____

11. astood _____

12. open _____

13. liveil _____

14. atchold _____

15. oveetter _____

16. ruitly _____

SPLIT DECISIONS

By George Bredehorn

The only clues in this crossword are the letter pairs provided in the grid. Each answer across and down consists of two words, which share the letters to be entered in the empty squares. In the example below, the empty squares are filled with the letters O-R-Y to make GLORY and IVORY. Note: A few of the combinations in the grid may have more than one possible answer, but only one will fit with the crossing(s).

Answer, page 178

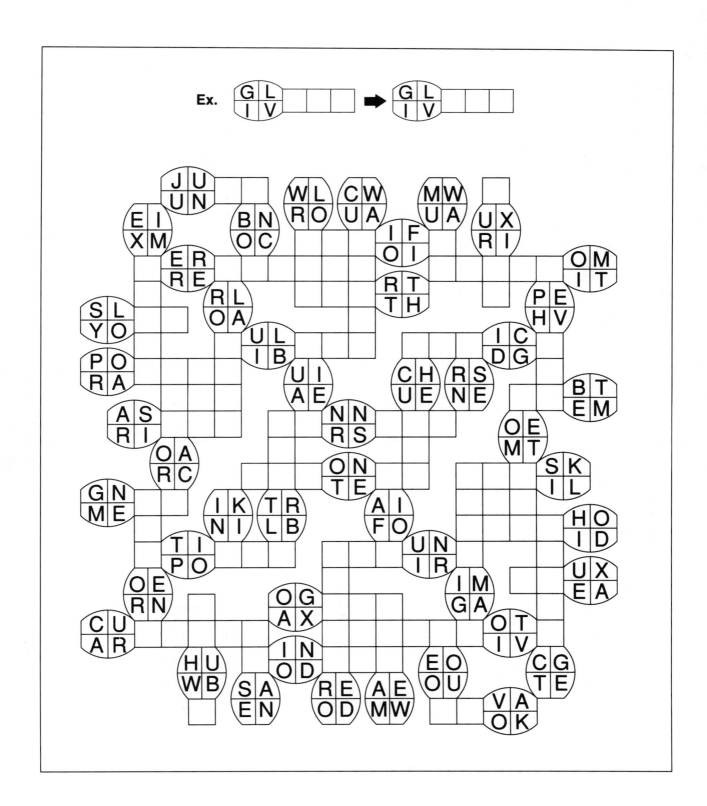

ALTERED EGOS

By Adam Sumera

Plenty of celebrities have had their names changed before making their debut in the pictures— but never quite this way. We've taken the first and last names of six well-known people, changed one letter in each name, and illustrated the results at right. Can you identify the original celebrity names? For example, pictures of a TUNA and a BURNER might represent TINA TURNER.
Answers, page 178

CONSTELLATIONS

By Doug and Janis Heller

By the time you've solved these three constellation puzzles, you may be seeing stars—movie stars, that is. That's because each answer is the title of a well-known film. To solve, begin at the "star" indicated by the arrow and pro-ceed from letter to letter in any direction via the connecting lines to spell the film title answer. Every line and letter will be used one or more times in each constellation.

Answers, page 178

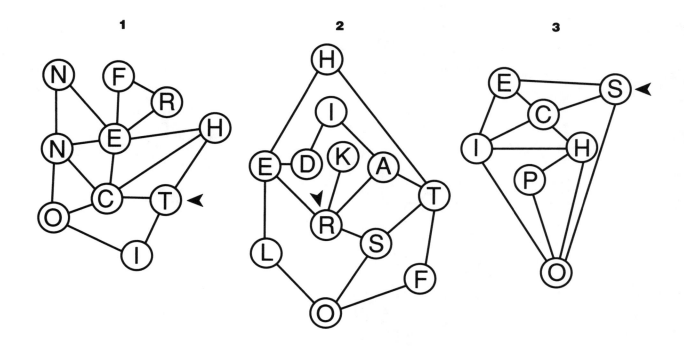

SHORT CHANGES

By Don Wulffson

Add one letter to each word below—at the front, at the end, or somewhere inside—so that each numbered pair becomes two words of opposite meanings. For example, adding P and L to PLUM and SENDER in #1 makes PLUMP and SLENDER.

Answers, page 178

1. PLUM	SENDER	PLUMP, SLENDER	9. ORATE	PLAN	
2. VIOLET	CAM		10. SOLD	RAISE	
3. FLAT	SIN		11. COMPETE	LACING	
4. BONY	WHIT		12. MOON	GENUS	
5. MARRED	SINGE		13. PLAID	STORY	
6. RAID	SOW		14. TACT	SATED	
7. KID	MAN		15. BUGLER	EXERT	
8. STALE	SHAY		16. UNIFORMED	LEANED	

ILLUSTRATED HINKY-PINKIES

Written and Illustrated by Robert Leighton

If the snakes that slithered onto the Ark were "Noah's boas," and a bearded gnome is a "hairy fairy," then can you tell what pair of rhyming words is suggested by each of the following drawings? The length of the words in each answer is indicated by the number of dashes.

Answers, page 178

1. _ _ _ _ _ _   _ _ _ _

2. _ _ _ _   _ _ _ _ _

3. _ _ _ _ _ _   _ _ _ _ _

4. _ _ _ _ _ _ _   _ _ _ _ _ _

5. _ _ _ _ _ _ _ ' _ _ _ _ _ _ _ _

6. _ _ _ _ _ _   _ _ _ _ _

7. _ _ _ _ _ _ _ _ _   _ _ _ _ _ _ _ _

8. _ _ _ _ _   _ _ _ _ _

9. _ _ _ _ _ _ _ _ _ '   _ _ _ _ _ _ _ _ _

10. _ _ _ _ _   _ _ _ _ _ _

11. _ _ _ _ _ _ _ _ _   _ _ _ _ _ _ _

12. _ _ _ _ _ _ _   _ _ _ _ _ _

FRACTURED PHRASES

By the GAMES Staff

What familiar phrase or title does each of the following series of words represent? For example, "Butch, harmony, weigher, Mao, this" is "Put your money where your mouth is." Hint: Saying the words out loud *slowly* sometimes helps.
Answers, page 179

1. Egg, no, rinses, blitz _____

2. Dusk, harlot, ladder _____

3. Loam, Anne, undertow, tamp, hole _____

4. Whimper, data, tuba, data _____

5. False, Peter, Ed _____

6. Up, pig, visional, lid, help, bond _____

7. Commie, eerie, spawn, sibyl _____

8. Radar, softer, law, stark _____

9. Dues, calm, penny, tree, sauerkraut _____

10. Heap, lorry, bassoon, hymn _____

11. Raw, cop, pipe, hay, peon, Audrey, daub _____

12. Essay, mad, tariff, hacked _____

13. Nudge, arch, fair, older, Asians _____

14. Depict, sheriff, Torah, yank, ray _____

15. Force, currents, heaven, yes, hag, hoe _____

16. Hate, Pauline, decide, park, head _____

17. Thick, gray, dust, Joe, wan, hurt _____

18. Ultra, stop, hen, knob, plastic, hoe _____

19. Echo, redig, curried, hog _____

20. Apple, latch, her, leech, hence, toothy, fleck _____

21. Charleston, done, hick, cough, dime _____

22. Abe, eyesore, kill, belt, fat, who _____

23. Specks, awfully, hank, Harry, up, hex, tech _____

24. Snob, crag, hull, lamp, hop _____

25. Dad, mental, note, ales _____

BULL'S-EYE 20 QUESTIONS

By Will Shortz

Here's a test of your word "marksmanship." The answer to each of the 20 questions in the puzzle is one of the 25 words in the bull's-eye target. Each answer scores a "hit," which you may cross off in the target since no answer word is used more than once. When all the clues have been answered, the five unused words can be arranged to form a comment by the sportswriter Roger Kahn. *Answers, page 179*

WHICH WORD...

1. is concealed in the first sentence of the instructions?

2. can have two different meanings, depending on its pronunciation?

3. is an anagram of a state's name?

4. consists solely of letters written in three straight strokes?

5. would sound like the name of a famous movie if you said its second syllable first?

6. would become a new word if a Q were substituted for one of its letters?

7. has every letter in it exactly twice?

8. would spell the name of a headache remedy if you put the letter T at the end and reversed it?

9. consists of the names of two consecutive articles of clothing?

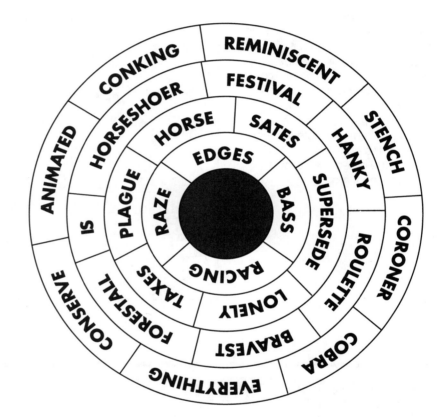

10. would become a new word if you changed its R's to L's?

11. would form a word meaning "binge" if you crossed out every other letter?

12. would form a synonym of itself if you dropped its last letter and rearranged the remainder?

13. would become a new word if you interchanged its fourth and seventh letters?

14. completes this sentence in a punny way: "Hurricane Hugo _____ the beachfront homeowners to flee." ?

15. sounds the same as a word that means its opposite?

16. consists of a word meaning "'60s dresses" inside "up-to-date"?

17. would become a phrase meaning "emaciated" if you dropped its first and last letters?

18. contains the letters of five consecutive chemical symbols (aluminum, iron, sulfur, titanium, and vanadium, not necessarily in that order)?

19. would become the name of a famous person if you shifted each of its letters three letters down the alphabet?

20. is an anagram of the last letters of the other remaining five words?

MENTAL BLOCKS

By Frederic Kock

In each stack of blocks below, jockey the letters of the horse-racing word in the top row, repeating any of the letters as needed, to complete the words in the seven rows beneath it. Each letter in the top row must be used at least once in each of the other rows in the stack, and no additional letters may be used. To get you off to a fast start, the letters T I P in #1 can complete the word INEPT in the next row down. Can you get the others? All answers are common words.

Answers, page 179

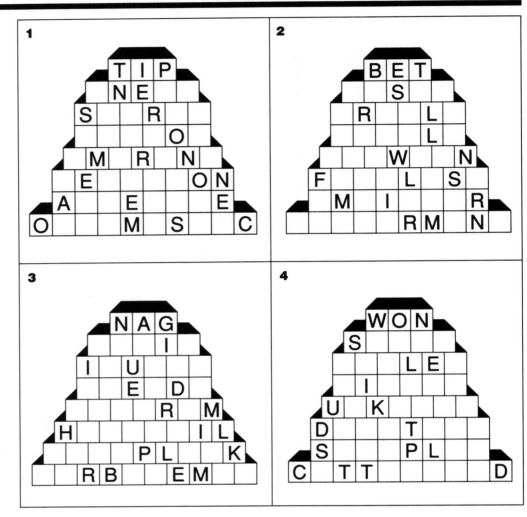

AROUND THE WORLD

By Shamlu Dudeja

By putting one letter in each blank below, you can change the name of the country into a word that fits the clue. For example, the clue "Seller of vegetables" with blanks "G R E E _ _ _ _ C E _" would lead to the answer GREENGROCER. If any of the clues stump you, there's no need to travel around the world to find the answers; they're in the back of the book.

Answers, page 179

1. At first   I _ _ T _ A L _ Y

2. Boeing vehicle   _ I R _ _ A N _

3. Chewing gum flavor   S P _ _ A _ _ I N _

4. Tramp   _ _ G A B O N _

5. Sweet smell   F R A _ _ _ _ N C E

6. Sweet smell   P E R _ U _ _

7. Group of fruit trees   _ _ C H A _ D

8. Louisiana flower   M A _ _ _ _ L I _

9. Sit on eggs   _ _ C U B A _ _

10. Too-close feeling   _ _ A U S T R _ _ _ _ _ _ I A

11. He's light-headed?   _ _ R O M A N I A _

12. Fur-yielding rodent   C H I N _ _ _ _ _ _ A

13. Clear from guilt   _ I N D I _ A _ _ _

14. Causing shame   _ I S _ R A _ E _ _ L

CRYPTO-FUNNIES

By Robert Leighton

In this comic strip, all the dialogue has been converted into a cryptogram. That is, every letter of the alphabet has been consistently replaced by another letter throughout the cartoon. For example, if G represents V in one word, it will represent V in every word. Look for distinctive letter patterns and punctuation to help you get started.

Answer, page 179

CARTOON REBUSES

By GAMES Readers

After years of solving GAMES's Cartoon Rebuses, readers finally got the chance to demonstrate their skill in making them—for prizes. Our "Cartoon Rebuses" contest drew more than 600 readers, who, in turn, created more than 3,000 individual rebuses. Displayed on these two pages are the 12 winning entries, all of which were redrawn by Kimble Mead, our regular rebus cartoonist.

HOW TO SOLVE

The answer to a cartoon rebus is found by combining any or all of the following elements:

- Words or synonyms of words spoken by the characters or found elsewhere in the picture;

- Names of prominent objects in the picture;

- Isolated letters in the picture;

- Words implied by the cartoon's action or scene.

These elements are combined *phonetically* to form a name fitting the category and the number of letters given as clues above the cartoon.

For example, the answer to cartoon #2 at right (Novel: 3,5,6) is THE GREAT GATSBY. It is found by combining THE, given in the dialogue; GRATE, the drain cover in the picture; GATS, the robber's guns; and the letter B, on the robber's sweater. Put them together phonetically and you get THE-GRATE-GATS-B.

Answers, page 179

1. Magazine: 10,5

2. Novel: 3,5,6

3. Newscaster: 6,8

4. Bay: 10

5. Pop Singer: 7,5

6. World Leader: 5,6

7. Goddess: 9

8. Tourist Attraction: 3,5,3

9. TV Character: 7,4

10. Asian City: 3,5

11. Movie: 4,4,4

12. Singer: 5,4

SEASONAL DOUBLE CROSS

By Anne Brown

Answer the clues for words to be entered on the numbered dashes. Then transfer the letters on the dashes to the correspondingly numbered squares in the puzzle grid to spell a quotation reading from left to right. Black squares separate words in the quotation.

Work back and forth between grid and word list to complete the puzzle. When you're done, the initial letters of the words in the word list will spell the author's name and the source of the quotation.

Answer, page 179

1C	■	2J	3H	4U	5R	■	6L	7O	8M	9P	10A	11N	■	12B	13G	14R	15F	16Q	17L	18E	■	19J
20D	■	21C	22N	23P	24T	25O	26B	27R	28G	29M	30I	31H	32A	33V	■	34N	35Q	■	36S	■	37F	38M
39U	40K	■	41A	42D	43H	44E	■	45P	■	46T	47B	48L	49Q	■	50K	51M	52R	53G	54L	55E	56B	57N
58H	■	59R	60B	61G	62D	63P	64Q	65A	66S	67E	68L	■	69P	70V	71B	72H	73N	74A	75R	76O	■	77F
78G	79C	80E	■	81L	82B	83U	■	84Q	85F	86R	87H	■	88S	89I	90O	91C	■	92P	■	93D	94E	95A
96V	■	97N	98Q	■	99U	100B	■	101O	102E	103H	■	104G	105J	106A	107B	■	108D	109N	110M	111Q	112H	113A
114V	115G	■	116O	117K	■	118P	119J	120B	■	121V	122S	123H	124U	■	125M	126A	127Q	128G	■	129F	130L	131C
■	132H	133M	134U	■	135H	136B	137R	138D	139P	■	140Q	141V	142F	143N	■	144U	145I	■	146Q	147H	148R
149I	150J	151T	152A	153K	154U	155N	■	156L	157R	■	158P	159M	160O	161B	■	162N	163D	164E	165O	166T	■	167L
168J	169Q	170R	—	171K	172P	■	173C	174O	175S	176H	177B	178G	■	179Q	180K	181D	182R	183A	184C		

A. Poet and author of *A Child's Christmas in Wales* (2 wds.)
113 10 183 65 106 41 126 95 32 74 152

B. "The hopes and fears of all the years/Are met ___" (3 wds.)
47 100 26 60 71 120 12 136 161 56 107 82 177

C. Entryway for Santa Claus
21 173 1 79 131 91 184

D. "And Mama in her ___, and I in my cap..."
93 181 62 108 163 42 138 20

E. Day the "pipers piping" were given
80 67 44 55 164 94 18 102

F. Spice used in eggnog
85 15 77 129 142 37

G. *Lost Horizon*'s magic land (hyph.)
178 13 28 128 53 115 78 104 61

H. Popular Christmas carol (4 wds.)
123 135 3 87 31 147 72 43 132 112 58 103 176

I. "It's Christmastime in the ___" ("Silver Bells")
149 89 30 145

J. Santa's cry (3 wds.)
168 19 2 150 119 105

K. With a fringe of neckfeathers, as some grouse
180 171 50 117 153 40

L. Where the Christmas star shone (3 wds.)
54 48 156 17 68 130 6 167 81

M. Winter road-clearing vehicle
29 133 38 125 159 110 51 8

N. Cartoonist who first drew Santa as we know him today (2 wds.)
155 22 97 143 34 11 57 109 73 162

O. Christmas kisser's plant
90 165 25 76 7 160 101 116 174

P. Marley's Ghost, for example
9 69 172 45 23 63 118 92 158 139

Q. Christmas entree, in Merrie Olde England (2 wds.)
140 64 169 98 179 111 49 16 84 146 35 127

R. Author of "A Visit From St. Nicholas" (2 wds.)
59 86 5 27 148 75 170 137 14 157 52 182

S. Decrease in force
175 66 36 88 122

T. Ice-skating site
166 24 151 46

U. North American warbler that nests on the range?
39 4 83 154 144 99 124 134

V. Margin for error
70 33 141 96 114 121

A COLORFUL JOURNEY THROUGH THE PAGES OF GAMES

4

WALTER WICK

IT'S A PIP!

By Mike Shenk

And it's also a maze. By moving alternately between odd- and even-numbered faces, can you get from the red pip at the center to the two-pip die that's breaking away at the upper right? You may move horizontally or vertically, but not diagonally, along any of the cube's three visible sides.

Answer, page 180

1. Laurel. . .

Amos and Andy, Kate and Allie, Daryl Hall and John Oates. All are well-known pairs—and you'll probably recognize all the pairs we show below. But do you re-

WHICH IS WHICH?

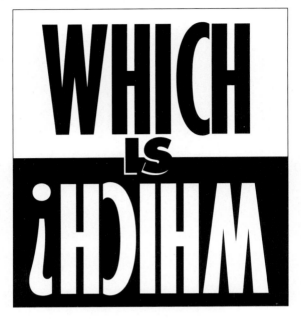

. . .& Hardy

member, for example, which is Starsky and which is Hutch? Dynamic solvers will be able to identify 10 duos; get all 14 right, and you're a doubles champ.

By Evie Eysenburg

Answers, page 180

2. MacNeil & Lehrer

3. Cagney & Lacey

5. Alligator & Crocodile

4. Chinese & Japanese

6. Siskel & Ebert

7. Vivien Leigh & Janet Leigh

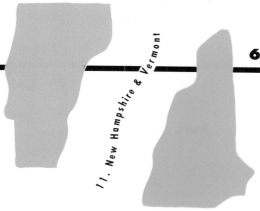

8.
Bert
&
Ernie

12. Abbott

&

Costello

9. BIG MAC®

13. Zsa Zsa   & Eva Gabor

& WHOPPER®

14. Starsky & Hutch

10.
Manet
&
Monet

MIRROR LAKE

Everything seems perfect out here—the fish are biting, the sky is blue, and there's just the right mild breeze in the air. Only one thing mars the setting: the 30 mistakes in Mirror Lake's reflection of the surrounding scene. Pitch your tent hereabouts and see

Illustrated by Greg Harlin

how many differences you can find between the real world and its mirror image in the lake. *Answers, page 180*

REFLECTIONS ON THE GREAT OUTDOORS

NUMBERS, PLEASE

Photographed by
Keith Glasgow

Can you figure out where you would find each of these 20 numerical images? If you're counting on the answers, see page 180.

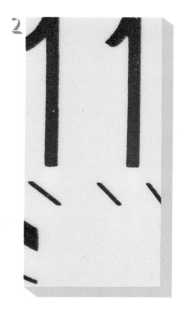

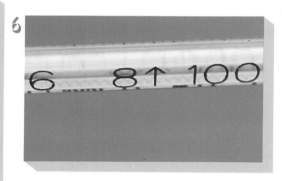

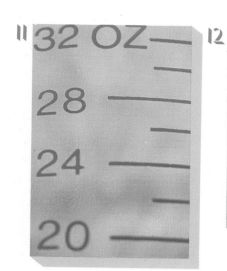

POP PARTY

Illustrated by David Gordon

You're invited to the rock 'n' roll party of the year. Attending are 32 of pop history's greatest performers, both groups and individuals. Give your invitation to the portly man checking tickets at the door (yes, that's Chubby Checker!), and then try to identify the rest of these superstar musicians.

LAKE MICHIGAN

Answers, page 180

FAMILY FOOD

A PALATABLE SEQUENCE PUZZLE

By Keith Glasgow

A

B

C

G

H

I

We've opened the most popular door in the house—the one on the refrigerator—to give you a peek at one family's shelves over the course of a day. The first photo, A, was taken just before breakfast; the other 11 photos (B–L) have been mixed up. Can you place them in their proper order, thereby reconstructing the day's meals, ending with a midnight snack?

Answer, page 180

THE SAGA OF SUBWAY SAM

A Logic Puzzle by Stephanie Spadaccini

Subway Sam has pulled a heist in South Ferry, and has been spotted entering the subway system there. We can be sure that he's planning to hide out with either his mother, his girlfriend, his bookie, or his lawyer, each of whom lives in a different borough. To throw the police off his trail, he's going to ride through each borough (except Staten Island, which is not on the subway system) at least once.

According to his police file, Sam knows the New York subway system like you know the back of your hand. He never backtracks or rides the same line twice in the same borough, though he will cross over lines already traveled. Also, he will not leave the subway system until he has reached his destination.

Other information available to the police follows:

By the end of the day, reports from all boroughs are in. The reports include the direction in which Sam was traveling, but not the time at which he was seen. From the above information and the police reports below, can you deduce the location of Sam's hideout? Can you also discover the quickest way for him to have gotten there if he'd "gone straight"?   *Answers, page 181*

1. The four people with whom he might be hiding live in Jackson Heights, Queens; Parkchester, the Bronx; Sheepshead Bay, Brooklyn; and the vicinity of Rockefeller Plaza, Manhattan.

2. His lawyer was raised in Queens, but hasn't been back in 20 years.

3. The bookie's subway stop is nearest the water.

4. His mother lives on 177th Street.

5. His last ride goes just one stop.

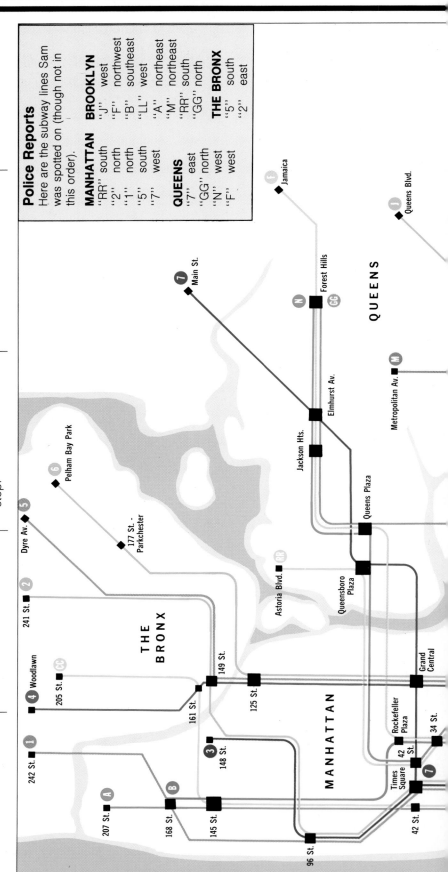

Police Reports

Here are the subway lines Sam was spotted on (though not in this order).

MANHATTAN		BROOKLYN	
"RR"	south	"J"	west
"2"	north	"F"	northwest
"1"	north	"B"	southeast
"5"	south	"LL"	west
"7"	west	"A"	northeast
		"M"	northeast
QUEENS		"RR"	south
"7"	east	"GG"	north
"GG"	north	**THE BRONX**	
"N"	west	"5"	south
"F"	west	"2"	east

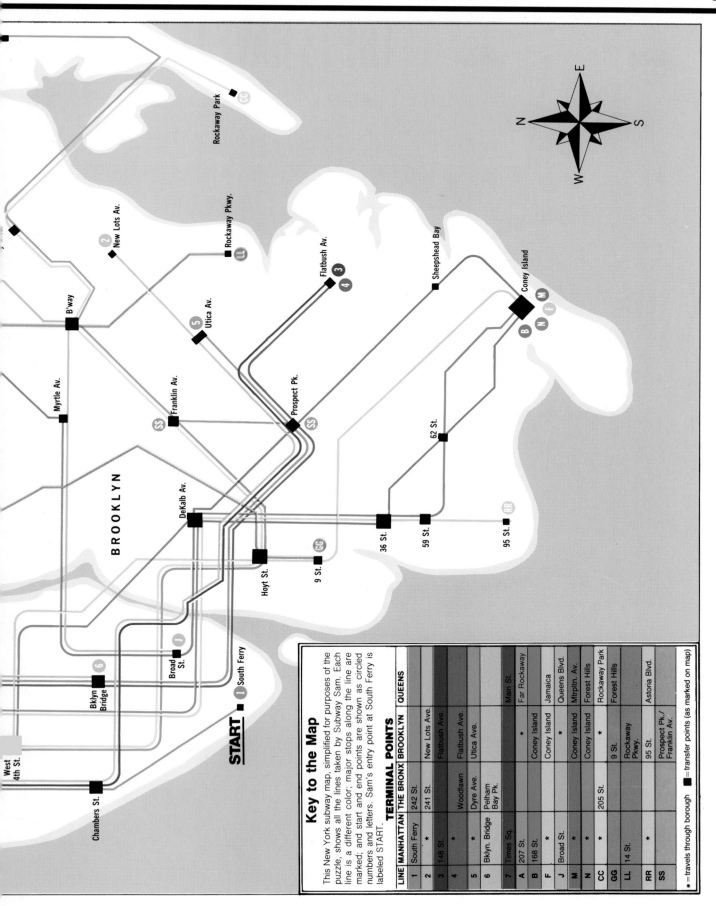

Key to the Map

This New York subway map, simplified for purposes of the puzzle, shows all the lines taken by Subway Sam. Each line is a different color; major stops along the line are marked; and start and end points are shown as circled numbers and letters. Sam's entry point at South Ferry is labeled START.

TERMINAL POINTS

LINE	MANHATTAN	THE BRONX	BROOKLYN	QUEENS
1	South Ferry	242 St.		
2	*	241 St.	New Lots Ave.	
3	148 St.		Flatbush Ave.	
4	*	Woodlawn	Flatbush Ave.	
5	*	Dyre Ave.	Utica Ave.	
6	Bklyn. Bridge	Pelham Bay Pk.		
7	Times Sq.			Main St.
A	207 St.		*	Far Rockaway
B	168 St.		Coney Island	
F	*		Coney Island	Jamaica
J	Broad St.		*	Queens Blvd.
M	*		Coney Island	Mtrpltn. Av.
N	*		Coney Island	Forest Hills
CC	205 St.			Rockaway Park
GG			9 St.	Forest Hills
LL	14 St.		Rockaway Pkwy.	
RR	*		95 St.	Astoria Blvd.
SS			Prospect Pk./ Franklin Av.	

* = travels through borough   ■ = transfer points (as marked on map)

Rockaway Park

New Lots Av.

Rockaway Pkwy.

Flatbush Av.

Sheepshead Bay

Coney Island

B'way

Utica Av.

Myrtle Av.

Franklin Av.

Prospect Pk.

62 St.

BROOKLYN

DeKalb Av.

36 St.

59 St.

95 St.

Hoyt St.

9 St.

START ■ ① South Ferry

Broad St.

Bklyn Bridge

Chambers St.

West 4th St.

THE I's HAVE IT

By John Craig

This "I"-Q test tests just one thing: your knowledge of I. How many of the 52 images whose names begin with the letter I can you identify? *Answers, page 180*

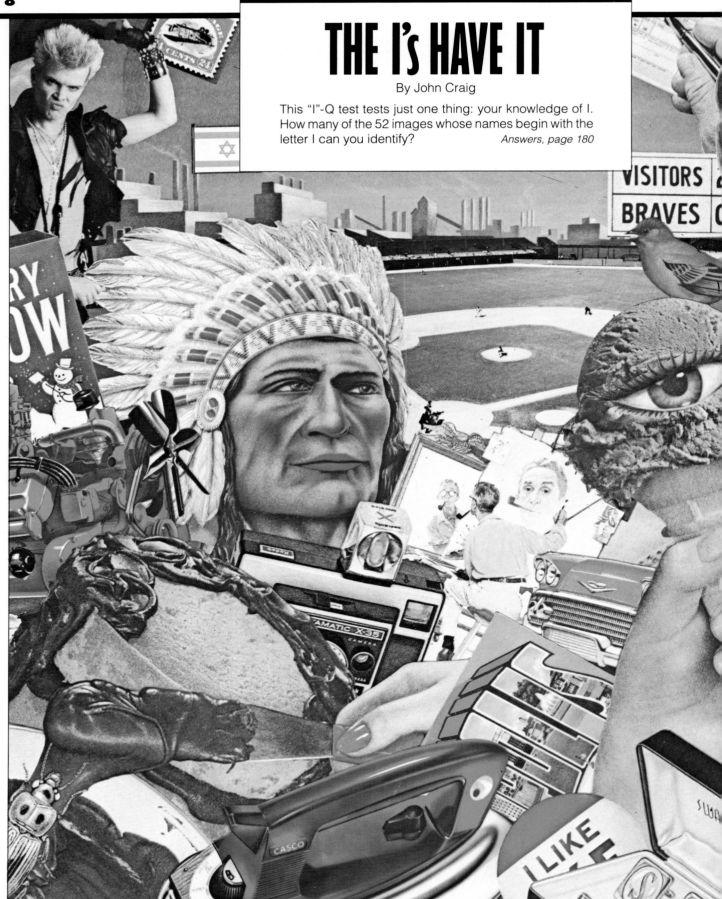

PHOTO FINISH

14

15

16

17

A PICTURE PUZZLE
BY ARLENE ALDA

Can you find the theme that unites all the photos and then name the one image that's missing from the set?

Answers, page 180

18

19

20

21

22

23

24

25

FOOD, GLORIOUS FOOD

A CULINARY TRIVIA QUIZ

By Curtis Slepian

Famished for a food quiz? This smorgasbord of questions should satisfy your appetite. We've served up the subject in many aspects (but no aspics)—from gourmet to junk. You're invited to nosh buffet-style, or sit down and devour the entire feast at once. The material won't seem so tough if you chew over it for a while.

Answers, page 181

EATING IN

1. There's nothing like a home cooked meal (depending on the home, of course). Though many amateur chefs improvise in the kitchen, most still depend on cook-books. Which is the best-selling American cookbook of all time?

a) *The Joy of Cooking*
b) *The Fannie Farmer Cookbook*
c) *The Betty Crocker Cookbook*
d) Julia Child's *Mastering the Art of French Cooking*

2. The recipe for success here is to guess what familiar food is made from each set of ingredients.

a) 4 packages active dry yeast
   1 quart tepid water
   12 cups whole-wheat flour
   2 Tbs. sugar
   5 tsp. salt
   2 Tbs. shortening
b) ½ head white cabbage, finely
   shredded
   1 large carrot, coarsely grated
   5 Tbs. salad dressing or
     mayonnaise
   1 tsp. sugar
   salt/pepper
   few drops of vinegar or lemon
     juice
c) ¼ cup short-grain rice
   2 Tbs. sugar
   2 cups milk
   butter
   1 tsp. ground cinnamon
   1 tsp. vanilla

3. Cookbooks aren't the only place one finds recipes. Which literary work contains usable recipes?

a) *Naked Lunch* by William Burroughs
b) *Heartburn* by Nora Ephron
c) *A Moveable Feast* by Ernest Hemingway
d) *Goodbye Mr. Chips* by James Hilton

EATING OUT

4. Ballpark fare for hungry baseball fans is no longer limited to peanuts and Cracker Jacks. Match the regional specialties (a–e) to the baseball teams (1–5) that serve them at their home parks.

a) Crab cakes   1. New York Mets
b) Bratwurst   2. San Francisco Giants
c) Knish
d) Alameda wine   3. Texas Rangers
                 4. Baltimore Orioles
e) Nachos   5. Milwaukee Brewers

5. Fast food is as American as Mrs. Smith's frozen apple pie. In this lack-of-taste-test, can you tell which is a McDonald's Big Mac, a Burger King Whopper, a Wendy's Single, and a White Castle?

a   **b**

c   **d**

6. Any food fanatic worth his imported sea salt knows the latest culinary fads. In the last 15 years, there have been three such major trends. Can you define each?

Nouvelle cuisine
a) Lighter, fresher, more inventive food artfully presented
b) Food quickly prepared with the newest, most high-tech kitchen equipment

Cuisine minceur
a) The French notion that all foods should be minced for easier digestion
b) Low-calorie food

Grazing
a) A menu for the health-conscious that serves a series of vegetarian dishes high in roughage
b) A menu that includes many smaller "tasting" courses, instead of a few large courses

7. Several years ago, a Gallup poll listed 34 food items and asked people which they preferred to eat at a salad bar. Can you arrange these eight foods from the list in the correct order of preference?

a) Raw green beans
b) Iceberg lettuce
c) Coleslaw
d) Hard-boiled eggs
e) Tomato
f) Bacon bits
g) Fresh fruit
h) Cucumbers

8. They don't throw banquets like they used to. Which one of the following dinners never took place?

a) Nineteenth-century gourmand Grimod de la Reynière held a dinner with a funeral theme: Invitations read like obituaries, the centerpiece of the table was a catafalque, and a coffin stood behind each diner's seat.
b) During a four-day eating marathon held by the Duke of Burgundy in the 15th century, 28 musicians performed inside a giant pie.
c) Despite a local taboo against eating horsemeat, a London gentleman held an equine feast in 1864. Its menu included horse consommé, terrine of horse liver, roast filet of Pegasus, and a 280-pound baron of horse.

d) In 1833, President Andrew Jackson had a banquet catered by the Iroquois Indians; the spread included 20,000 pieces of fried Buffalo chicken wings, 3,000 ears of corn-on-the-cob, and 5,000 sticky buns.

WEIRD AND WONDERFUL FOODS

9. First, it was the mango, then the kiwi. Thanks to jet transport, more foods than ever before are available to jaded palates. Can you match the exotic fruits (a–f) to their names (1–6)?

1. Carambola
2. Cactus pear
3. Cherimoya
4. Kumquat
5. Pomelo
6. Papaya

10. These tidbits are tastier than they sound. Be adventurous and give 'em a try... match the food (a–j) to its definition (1–10).

a) Haggis   f) Tabbouleh
b) Gnocchi   g) Blintz
c) Jerky   h) Vichyssoise
d) Cornichons   i) Scrapple
e) Hush puppies   j) Flan

1. Midget pickled cucumbers
2. Crepe rolled around a cheese filling
3. Breakfast dish made with scraps of left-over pork
4. Leek and potato soup
5. Pasta dumpling
6. Salad made of steamed cracked wheat
7. Air-dried beef
8. Sausage made of animal innards in cow guts
9. Deep-fried corn meal balls
10. Custard dessert

WHERE IN THE WORLD?

11. While Europe has sent to the Americas such classics as French fries and pizza, it's not a one-way street. Which of these foods *wasn't* introduced to the Old World by the New?

a) Eggplant
b) Vanilla   e) Tomato
c) Turkey   f) Bell pepper
d) Potato

12. Viva the world's culinary Thomas Alva Edisons! Match each food (a–e) to the country (1–5) in which it was invented.

a) Croissant   1. China
b) Doughnut   2. United States
c) Ice cream cone   3. Italy
d) Spaghetti   4. Austria
e) Pretzel   5. Holland

YOU ARE WHAT YOU EAT

13. For every book about the joys of eating, there's a killjoy volume on how to stop eating. Which of these diets has never been proposed in print?

a) *The Eat-All-You-Want Diet*
b) *The Sex Diet*
c) *The Drinking Man's Diet*
d) *The Couch Potato Diet*

14. No wonder Nutrasweet is so popular. The average American eats about how many pounds of sugar a year?

a) 10   b) 55   c) 128   d) 175

15. Which food contains the highest percentage of fat?

a) Pancakes   d) Devil's-food cake
b) Avocados   and chocolate icing
c) Buttermilk   e) flank steak

16. Recent findings show that some foods reduce the amount of cholesterol in the blood. Which of these won't?

a) Oats   c) Bananas
b) Salmon   d) Olive oil

17. In each of the following pairs, which has more calories:

a) A cup of pasta cooked al dente or a cup cooked tender?
b) The white or the yolk of an egg?
c) 10 pitted dates or 10 unpitted dates?

GLUTTONS FOR PUNISHMENT

In Roman times, Epicureans gave gluttony a bad name. But when it comes to excess, the 20th century holds its own. According to *The Guinness Book of World Records...*

18. Per pound, what is the most expensive foodstuff in the world?

a) Black Perigord truffles
b) Spanish saffron
c) Beluga caviar
d) Chinese wild ginseng

19. In 1983, champion eater Peter Dowdeswell of England ate 100 yards of spaghetti in how many seconds?

a) 5.1   b) 21.7   c) 61   d) 122.4

20. Which is the all-time best-selling cookie?

a) Mallomars   c) Oreos
b) Chips Ahoy!   d) Fig Newtons

FINAL COURSE

21. This quiz covers food from soup to nuts. Speaking of which, here's the question about nuts: Only one of the following is a true nut. Which one?

a) Pecan   c) Peanut
b) Brazil nut   d) Almond

NICK KOUDIS

TIME OUT

FIVE PUZZLES THAT RUN LIKE CLOCKWORK
By Scott Marley

Time is relative, said Einstein. It all depends on how you view it. So it is with these puzzles. Can you solve them?

BREAK TIME

This antique pocket watch has been broken into three pieces, the numbers of which add up, respectively, to 25, 26, and 27. Suppose another watch is broken differently into a certain number of pieces, with the totals on the segments again adding up to consecutive numbers. Assume that none of the numbers is damaged (for example, the 12 isn't split into the digits 1 and 2), and that there are at least two numbers on each clock segment. How many pieces are there, and what are the numbers on each piece?

FLIBBERTY-DIGITS

One morning a digital clock shows the readout at top left, which is surprising since it's well before noon. Nearly two hours later, the clock displays the second readout shown. What is the likely cause of the incorrect displays?

DOUBLE TROUBLE

The two clocks below were correctly set at noon, but both now show the wrong time. That's because one is running at twice the normal speed, while the other is running at the correct speed, but in reverse. What time is it?

PHOTOGRAPHS BY STAN FELLERMAN

A STICKY SITUATION

All the numbers but the 12 and the 3 have been removed from the clock above. Suppose the other 10 numbers are glued back on, but every one is placed in the wrong position. If the three numbers between 10 and 4 total 13, the three numbers between 9 and 5 total 18, and the three numbers between 6 and 11 total 26, how are the numbers arranged?

MINUTE MYSTERY

A British lord invited four friends—a Frenchman, a German, a Spaniard, and an Italian—to his country house. The house was securely locked at night, so only these five men, along with the lord's British butler and maid, could have been inside.

One morning the maid discovered her employer's corpse on the library floor. In his dying moments, he had crawled to the five nonworking clocks on the mantel and moved their hands, apparently to leave a message about his killer's identity. Who was the murderer?

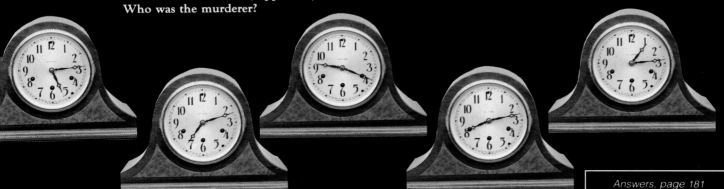

Answers, page 181

AH, WILDERNESS!

A ZOOM-IN MAPPIT PUZZLE

By Robert Leighton

If you like to travel with all the comforts of home, here's a relaxing way to take a trip to our National Parks.

The four rows of maps and photos at right offer different perspectives on five U.S. National Parks. They progress from the macro scale of state or regional maps in the top row (A–E); to the more detailed area maps of the second row (F–J); down to the micro scale on the parks maps in the third row (K–O). The bottom row zooms in further with photos of particular landmarks detailed in each park map.

By carefully examining state landmarks, town names, interstate highways, and other features from a map in the top row, can you zoom in on the map in the second row that logically follows it? Continue your journey through the appropriate park map and on to the photo of your destination … then breathe in that clean air, enjoy the silence, and take off for the next scenic wonder.   Answers, page 181

A

B

F

G

K

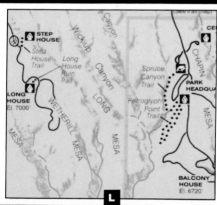

L

P

Q

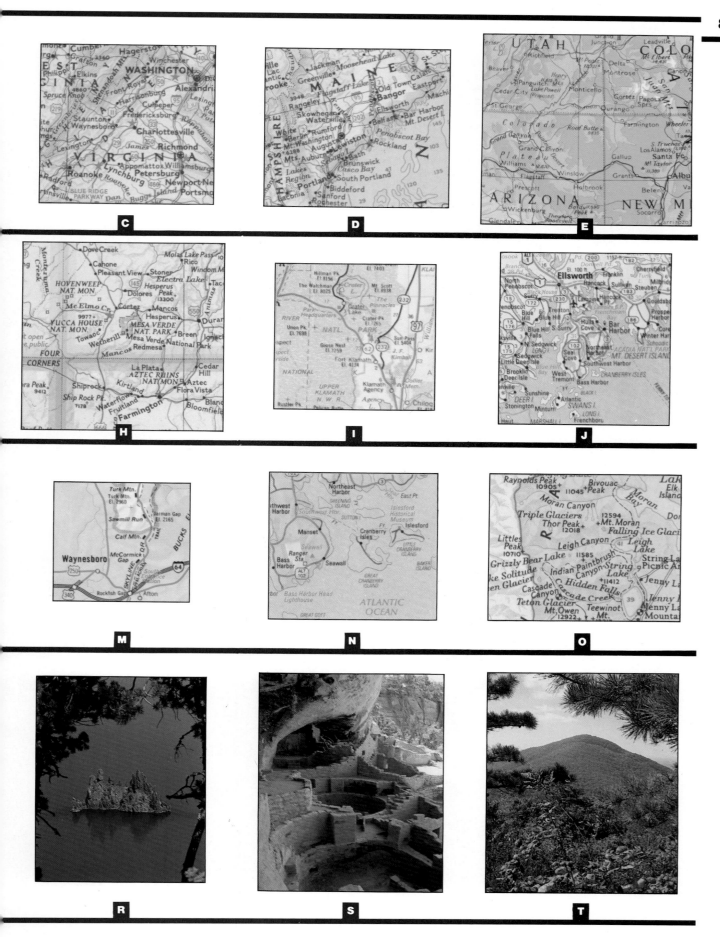

BEMUSEMENT PARK

WHAT'S WRONG WITH THIS PICTURE?

The really amusing thing about this amusement park
is the mistakes scattered throughout it. Can you find all 37 of them?

Answers, page 181

MITCH HYATT

DRAWN & QUARTERED

A Rebus Puzzle Illustrated by Peter de Sève

This puzzle will help you see common phrases in a most uncommon way. Each picture represents an everyday expression, but because the expression is depicted very literally, its usual idiomatic meaning isn't readily apparent. For example, the ungainly creature attached to the mast of the boat at left suggests a "white elephant sale" (sail). Can you puzzle out the others?

Answers, page 182

Example:
White Elephant Sale

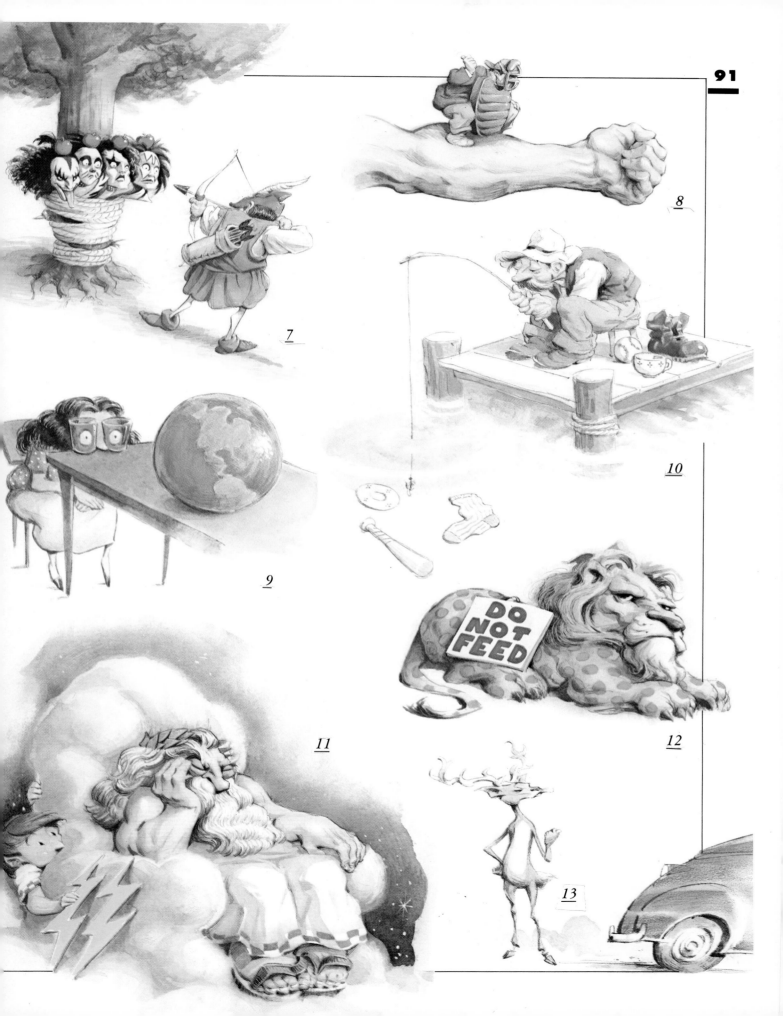

MISSION:IMPROBABLE

A TIME-WARP SEQUENCE PUZZLE

By Stephanie Spadaccini and Water Wick

Suicide missions were Captain Rocky Cragg's specialty, and this qualified as one—in spades. At first it didn't sound so risky: The Nova Ore Corporation wanted Cragg to collect samples of glowing crystals from the planet Verdanta and perform experiments on them before they faded. The crystals lose their glow outside the planet's atmosphere, and the NOC wanted to know why.

But that "why" had cost the lives of 12 men on eight failed missions. Those who had made it past Verdanta's radioactive quasar rings and survived its flesh-melting teflon storms had to deal with the Verdantans. And nobody in his right mind wanted to deal with the Verdantans.

Except Rocky Cragg. He volunteered.

Cragg made the voyage in his rusty space-bucket, the *S.S. Doberman*, and he lived to tell about it. But the trip had taken its toll on pilot and ship. When Cragg landed at the Cleveland Spaceport, he was suffering from such a bad case of space lag that he refused to leave the *Doberman*'s sick bay. And since he had neglected to keep a ship's log (again), the job of reconstructing the mission fell (again) to Ground Commander "Ground" Chuck Jones. Usually Jones based the log on tape recordings of inflight radio transmissions. But on this trip, the radio had gone dead right after Cragg reported activating the ship's cooling system because of an overheated engine.

So the only record of the trip was the composite photograph seen here which, by means of warp-drive photography, recorded various problems Cragg encountered along the way. Each section of the cockpit window represents a different time period during the round trip between Earth and Verdanta, and thus the photo enabled "Ground" Chuck to logically reconstruct the entire journey. Can you do the same?

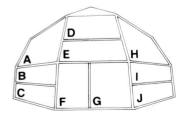

Arrange the sections of the cockpit window (labeled A–J in the diagram) in chronological order to discover what took place aboard the *S.S. Doberman*. *Answer, page 182.*

SELL MATES

Characters on product packages are often as memorable as the names of the products they help to sell. Can you identify these familiar faces by naming the products on which they appear? *Answers, page 182*

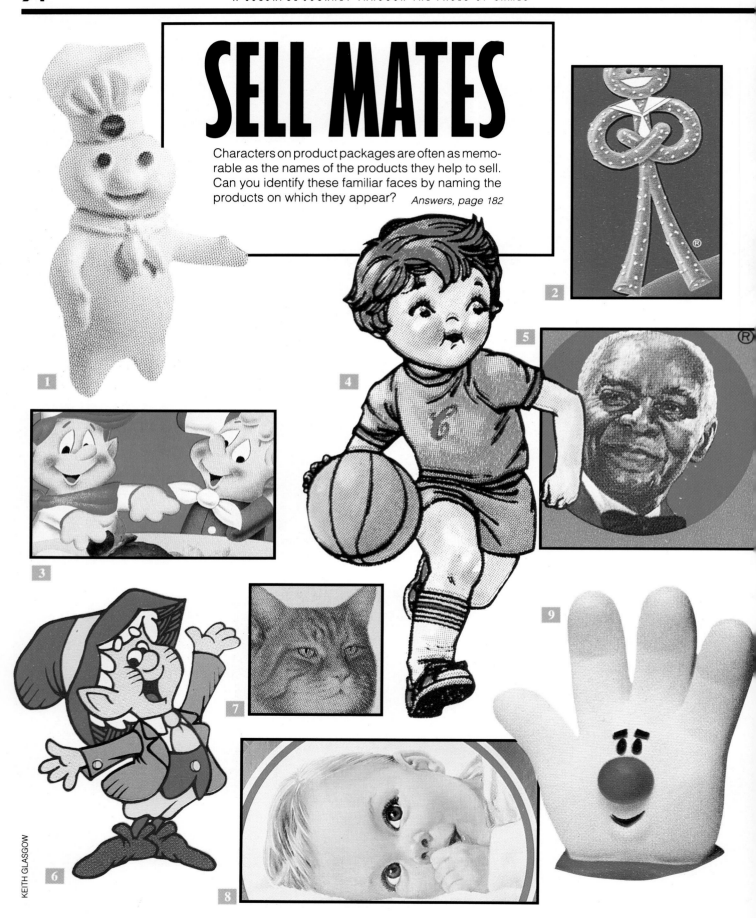

KEITH GLASGOW

COLOR CROSSWORD

By Peter Gordon

Who says crossword puzzles aren't colorful? In this one, every letter and black square has been replaced by a color, according to the chart below. Thus, if the word WORD were in the grid, it would appear as violet-blue-red-green. Black squares can be represented by any of the four colors that ap-pear above them in the chart. When the puzzle is correctly completed, the black squares will be arranged symmetrically (that is, the grid will look the same upside-down as right-side-up). Clues are provided, but not in their regular order.   *Answer, page 182*

CLUES

Autograph

Breakfast item (2 wds.)

Child's toy that "walks" down stairs

Children ride them down snowy hills

Clothes buyer's concern

Colorful arc in the sky

Daffy or Donald, for example

Decorates a cake

Dodge, as the draft

Elegant, as a ship's quarters

Evening TV fare

Fibber

Ford flop

Gift-giving wise men

Greenish blue

Living being

1975 shark horror film

Not urban

Outline for a meeting

Philadelphia basketballer, for short

Runs away to wed

Scream

Shakespeare's theater

Strange happening

Therefore

Wax maker that lives in a hive

What a copy is made from

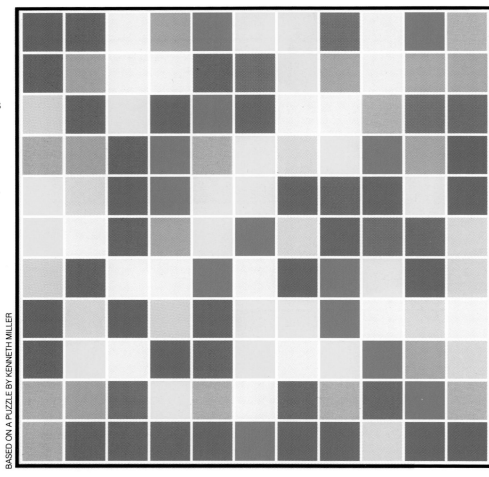

BASED ON A PUZZLE BY KENNETH MILLER

COLOR CHART

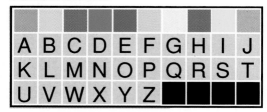

A	B	C	D	E	F	G	H	I	J
K	L	M	N	O	P	Q	R	S	T
U	V	W	X	Y	Z				

MATH, LOGIC, AND A LITTLE MYSTERY

5

KNIGHT TRAIN

By Marek Penszko

A knight has made a complete tour of the 6 x 6 board at left (jumping as in standard chess), beginning at the 1 in the upper left corner and returning to the 1 at the finish. The squares have been numbered consecutively as the knight landed on them (2, 3, 4, etc., up to 36), but only a few of the numbers are revealed. Can you logically determine the missing numbers for the other squares? Every square (except #1) was visited exactly once. *Answer, page 182*

DIGITITIS

By Peter Gordon

We've removed most of the digits from the four long-division problems below. Can you replace the numbers, one digit per dash, so that each completed division is mathematically correct? Each puzzle has a unique solution.

If you've never tried a Digititis puzzle before, it may look baffling at first. But don't panic—the solution requires nothing more than logic and basic arithmetic. Hint: The puzzle's bottom is often the best place to start. *Answers, page 183*

1. WARM-UP

2. CHALLENGING

3. HARD

4. WHEW!

I'VE GOT A SECRET

By Susan Zivich

Miss Baer arrived at Dyer High School one morning with an exciting secret—she was engaged. During the morning coffee break she shared her secret with Greg and the Chemistry teacher. At lunch, these two each told two other people. And during their afternoon coffee break, the four people who had heard the secret at lunch each told two others. With that, all 14 of Miss Baer's fellow teachers—who themselves formed seven married couples—knew about her engagement. From the following clues, can you determine each teacher's full name, the subject each teacher teaches, and who told whom of Miss Baer's engagement? *Answers, page 182*

CLUES

1. Each person who shared the secret told one man and one woman, though no one told his or her spouse or another member of his or her own department.

2. Although no department is all male or all female, no one is in the same department as his or her spouse.

3. Jon, who heard the secret from a woman, told Mr. Lotak and the Literature teacher.

4. Carol and one of the Science teachers heard the secret from the same person.

5. The Spanish teacher, who heard the secret from Sally, told Dick and the Geometry teacher.

6. Steve, Mr. Martin, and Mary are all members of the same department.

7. Bill teaches German.

8. Paul's wife told Mr. Lee.

9. Gail, who heard the secret from a man, told Mrs. Wiseman and the Creative Writing teacher.

10. Carol's husband teaches Poetry.

11. Mrs. Lotak teaches Botany.

12. Marcia told Mrs. Fedirka.

13. Paul is the only man in the Art department.

14. Debbie is the youngest of the 15 teachers.

15. Mr. Redeagle teaches Algebra.

16. The French teacher's husband teaches Calculus.

17. Mr. Schwartz, who heard the secret from one of the Mathematics teachers, told Mrs. Lee and the Sculpture teacher.

18. Marge teaches Ceramics.

19. Al and Patrice are married.

20. The departments and subjects taught are as follows:
Art: Ceramics, Painting, Sculpture; **English:** Creative Writing, Literature, Poetry; **Language:** French, German, Spanish; **Mathematics:** Algebra, Calculus, Geometry; **Science:** Biology, Botany, Chemistry.

FLOATING STOCK

By Nick North

The year is 2192, and space technology has moved on apace. Space resorts are opening up every-where, for that once-in-a-lifetime get-away-from-it-all vacation, with their garish neon lights lighting up vast expanses of the void.

Here we see a typical family preparing to pack their space-station-wagon for the long trek out to the Milky Way Motel, where they have booked a stay. They have laid out what

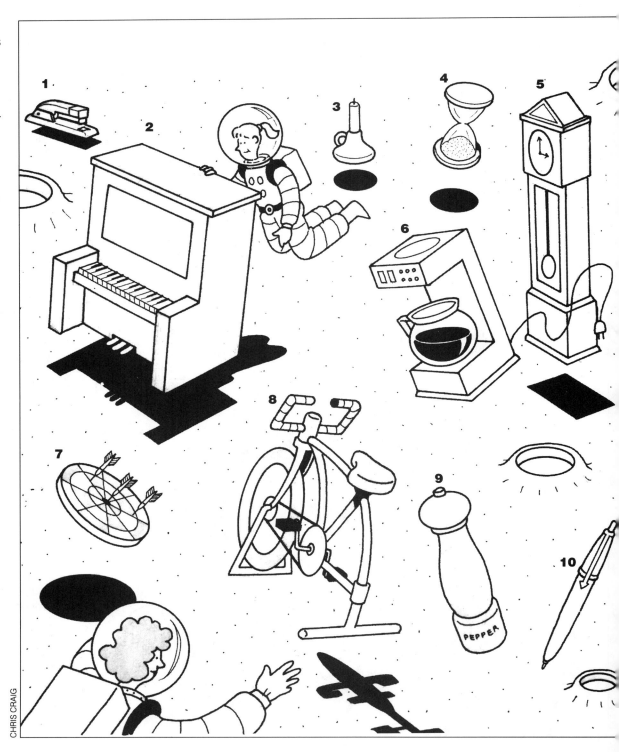

CHRIS CRAIG

they want, or think they may need, during the month-long journey. Can you help them pack their bags, bearing in mind that there will be no gravity in the space-wagon during the journey? Just determine which items pictured on these two pages would function properly in a weightless, zero-gravity atmosphere. You should have room for about a third of the things.

Answers, page 183

CAN YOU THINK UNDER PRESSURE?

By Nick North

This test measures your ability to follow directions and think clearly under pressure. Test pilots, gun-fighters, and short-order cooks may have a slight advantage. You have exactly 14 minutes to read and answer the following questions. Have a pencil ready, and a clock or a stopwatch handy to time yourself. When the 14 minutes are up, stop working, whether or not you have come to an end.

On your mark, get set, go!
Answers and ratings, page 183

The letter that occurs most in this sentence is _____. Now write out the second month of the year backwards here: _____. Pay no attention to the next question, unless the first sentence of this quiz begins and ends with the same letter. From January to December, which two consecutive months have 31 days? _____ _____ Assume that all boys like toys, and that all girls have curls. Roy is a boy, and Pearl has curls. Yes or no: Must Roy like toys? _____ Must Pearl be a girl? _____ How many rectangles, of any shape or size, are there in the diagram (''A'') at right? _____ Do you know exactly which two letters of the alphabet are missing from this sentence of the quiz? _____ Sitting down to eat, Jon has three more won tons than Ron, Ron has twice as many won tons as Don, and Jon has one more won ton than Don and Ron together. How many won tons has Jon? _____ Name two countries whose names begin with the letter J. _____ _____ Start at the 2 on the push-button phone at right (''B''). Move one button at a time horizontally or vertically, traveling to six other numbers, but not 1 or 7, and not using any number twice. Write the resulting seven-digit phone number here _____, unless there are two Ps in ''the pod,'' in which case write NOTHING. Think of four words, each starting with the letter E and containing two more Es, unless you think you can't, in which case be sure not to omit the answers: _____ _____ _____ _____. Consider the die shown at right (''C''). How many spots on it cannot be seen? _____ Circle the one that does not belong: acehp, enpru, aegpr, ilptu. Make sure that you avoid not reading the next sentence, unless the previous sentence does not have an odd number of words. Leave this space blank _____, unless a ton of feathers weighs more than a ton of coal, in which case write BLANK in the preceding space. Ignore the next sentence. Try not to think how little time you have left. Circle the circle in the figure at right (''D'') that is two counterclockwise from the circle opposite the circle that is four clockwise from the circle shaded black. Take three score and ten, divide it by the number of Snow White's dwarfs, and add the number of wings on a dove. Now subtract the number that is the same as the answer to this subtraction, and write that number here: _____. If there is a nationality that sounds like the point that you've reached in this quiz, write it in this blank: _____. If not, write the word FINISH.

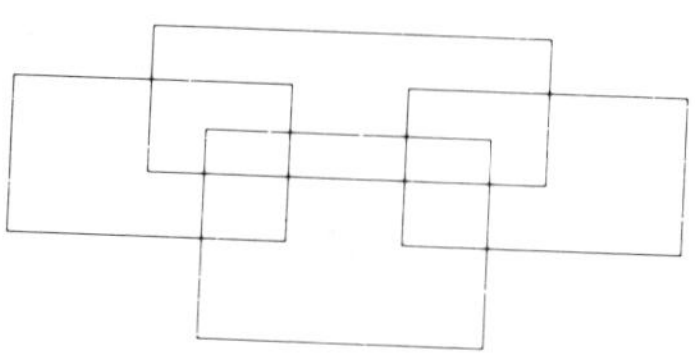

A.

B.

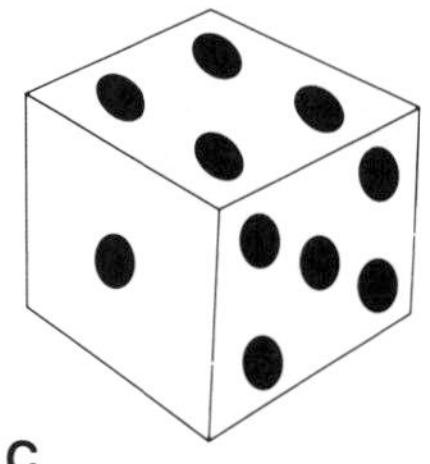

C.

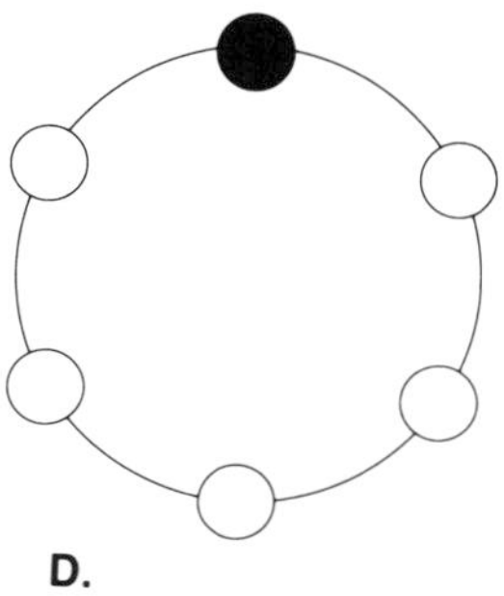

D.

ANIMAL CRACKERS

By Ulrich Koch

Each illustration below represents an animal cracker that a friend wants to break in half and share with you. Can you divide each shape into two identical pieces by making a single cut along the lines of the grid? The two pieces may be rotated but not reflected (as in a mirror image) to look alike. Ignore the shaded three-dimensional sides which appear only for artistic effect. Solving hint: Study the irregularities of the borders of the crackers and see if you can determine where they can be duplicated inside. The puzzles get harder as you go. *Answers, page 183*

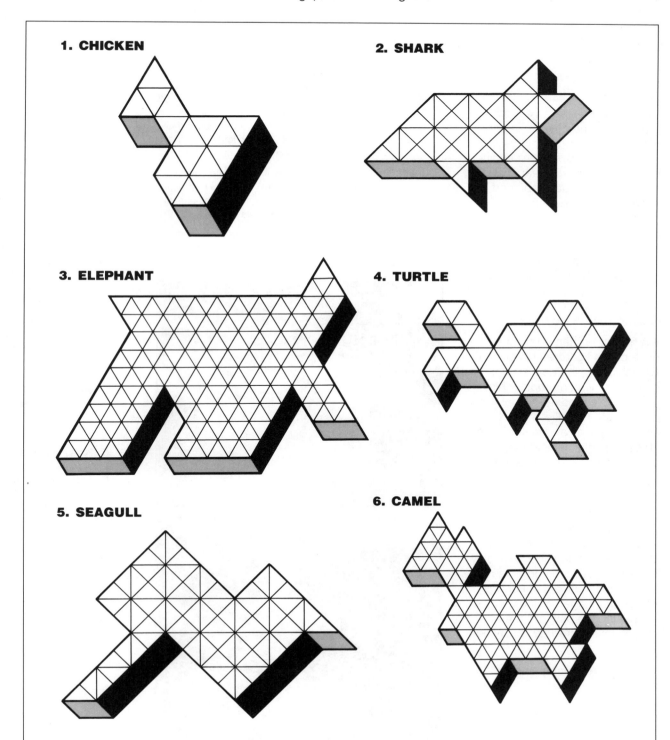

1. CHICKEN

2. SHARK

3. ELEPHANT

4. TURTLE

5. SEAGULL

6. CAMEL

EXTRASENSORY DECEPTION

THE STRANGE STORY OF THE PROFESSOR AND THE PSYCHIC

By The Amazing Randi

Quentin Shillip was an assistant professor in the physics department of Luckbridge University. At 28, he was an exceptionally gifted physicist, a man of great, though diffident, charm, tall, taut, and spare of body. His character, however, belied all this apparent efficiency. Shillip wore mismatched socks, drove his car ineptly, and often was late for his classes because he had gone to the wrong room. When a package said OPEN THIS END, he could be counted on to struggle with the other.

But he was a talented teacher, so none of this bothered his boss, Dr. Gottinhimmel, the department chairman. What did bother him was Shillip's readiness—not to say eagerness—to believe in extrasensory perception and clairvoyance. This unscientific attitude cast a shadow over Shillip's chances for promotion.

One day, fate threw Professor Shillip into the path of The Great Crispin, who described himself as "the world's foremost mentalist." Crispin was scheduled to display his powers at a college fund-raiser in the auditorium at Luckbridge, and Shillip, eager for the chance to observe the psychic at close range, volunteered as faculty host for the day.

That is, if the great man ever showed up.

Shillip, accompanied by his assistant, Judy, who was overseeing the details of the evening's entertainment, had driven like a madman to the airport, arriving, typically, a little late. Leaving Judy to park the car, he rushed into the terminal. But although Crispin's flight had arrived 20 minutes earlier, the psychic was nowhere to be seen. Then Shillip felt a tap on his shoulder. It was Crispin. "Sorry I'm late. A little trouble with the luggage." Shillip found it odd that Crispin recognized him, since they had never met.

The oddness continued. As they were walking to the parking lot, Crispin stopped in his tracks with a mysterious, faraway look in his eyes. "Is your pretty red-haired assistant waiting for us in the car?" he asked. Dumbfounded, Shillip nodded his head. How could Crispin know that Judy was there or what she looked like?

Driving them downtown, Shillip began to explain that Crispin's hotel reservation has been changed at the last minute and he was now going to stay at …

"No, don't tell me!" Crispin broke in. "I get the name … Dorset … no, wait a moment … it's Dorchester."

Shillip nearly veered off the highway. Regaining his composure, he smiled. "Gottinhimmel will never believe this. Judy, you're my witness."

What an airhead, she thought. Judy, who looked as though she could be bruised by brushing against a magnolia blossom, was as tough-minded and practical as Shillip was wide-eyed. And she wasn't overjoyed at having to spend her day off baby-sitting Crispin, whom she had seen in Las Vegas and considered a sideshow swami. Her response to this apparent clairvoyance was characteristically caustic: "That's amazing, Crispin. And can you tell, oh great mystic, what *I'm* thinking?"

Crispin answered testily: "Reading minds may not be hard-hat work, young lady, but it isn't easy. However, the tone of your voice tells me what you're thinking, so I needn't bother with a mind probe." For the rest of the short trip, he read the local newspaper he found on the back seat.

At the Dorchester, while Crispin was signing in, the desk clerk tried to hand him an envelope containing a message. Crispin waved it away. "It's from my mother in Kansas City. She says my brother's wedding has been postponed." He didn't even look up from the register.

Shillip grabbed the envelope from the clerk and tore it open. Crispin had been exactly right. The professor's eyes shone. "What extraordinary precognitive abilities!" he said. Under her breath, Judy muttered, "Then why didn't his mother save money by sending Dr. Marvelous the message telepathically?"

Shillip was too buoyed up to argue. He grinned at Judy and told her to keep the mentalist company for an hour while he drove home to change clothes and fetch Crispin's pay for his night's work—a check for $7,500. But when he had gone, the two avoided each other, Crispin at the bar recharging his psychic batteries with a few bottles of beer, Judy in the lobby arcade letting off steam playing Pac-Man.

When Shillip returned on time and wearing matching socks and an anticipatory smile, he found he had forgotten Crispin's check. "Not to worry," Crispin said. "We'll pick it up on the way to the campus." Shillip agreed—but how had Crispin known that his house *was* on the way to the campus?

The drive to Shillip's house continued the magical mystery tour. At one point, Crispin correctly guessed that they were five miles from the house. Then, when they were pulling into the driveway, Crispin knew that the phone would be ringing. Shillip went in to get the check, and Judy went along to check the phone, afraid that her bedazzled boss would hear it ringing even if it wasn't. But it was. Judy sank into a chair, looking bemused. "You know," she said, "I could use a drink. It's really too early to go to the auditorium anyway. Why don't you invite the swami in for a quick brew—witch's, of course."

When Crispin entered the living room he went straight to a photograph on a table. "This must be your fiancée, Marilyn," he said. "I hope you'll have a lovely wedding next month." While Shillip's mouth was still wide open, Crispin said, "I think I'll not have a drink. I've had more than enough beer already. But I'd like to use your bathroom."

"Then you *are* human," Judy said. The professor gave her a reproving look and showed Crispin through his bedroom to the bathroom.

On the way to the auditorium the mentalist advised Shillip against buying a

motorcycle—something Shillip had been planning secretly for months. Although Judy was delighted that the professor wouldn't be threatening life and limb on campus, she was frustrated by her inability to prove Crispin a fake. "If you're so smart," she exploded, "why don't you make a million dollars on the stock market?"

Unconsciously patting his wallet, which contained the check for the evening's performance, Crispin replied loftily, "I don't use my God-given powers for personal gain."

That night The Great Crispin lived up to his billing with an astounding psychic display, and he brought down the house with a climactic mind-reading feat. After a volunteer from the audience blindfolded him, Crispin asked her to roll three dice until three different numbers came up. She finally threw 6 5 3 and, as instructed, wrote the numbers on a blackboard center stage. Following Crispin's orders, she reversed the numbers and subtracted the smaller from the larger. The board read:

$$653 \\ -356 \\ \overline{297}$$

Turning to page 297 of the local telephone directory (which had been brought on stage after Crispin was blindfolded), she concentrated on the first phone number listed, which Crispin had announced he would guess by reading her mind. The psychic broke into a sweat as he strained to get the first digit. His guess was wrong. "My dear," he said kindly, "the image is fuzzy. Let me hold your hand." Again he strained, and finally offered another number—the right one. Starting slowly, then gathering speed, he repeated the next six digits without a miss. This was his final trick, and the crowd left happily mystified, none more mystified or happier than Shillip.

On the drive back to Crispin's hotel, Shillip's admiration was unbounded. (Judy had declined the honor of accompanying them.) As Crispin got out at the Dorchester, he said, "By the way, Shillip, you know that special class you're teaching tomorrow? For a change, you'll be early."

When Shillip woke up the next morning, he saw that the great man had missed his final prognostication. He was actually running late. He threw on his clothes, skipped breakfast, and careened insanely off to campus. As the car screeched into the parking lot, Shillip glanced at the clock on the auditorium tower and saw that he

was, in fact, more than a half-hour early. His eyes still glued to the clock, he ran right into the taillight of Dr. Gottinhimmel's Mercedes. With a sinking feeling, Shillip knew he could kiss his promotion goodbye. If only the mentalist had warned him.

Well, Crispin can't predict everything.

IS IT LOGIC OR ESP?

The four illustrations on these pages show—through Crispin's eyes—everything that was germane to his total performance. Crispin had no confederates. He had never been to Luckbridge and had never seen Shillip or Judy or a photograph of either. The Dorchester was one of 20 hotels in the city, and there was no Dorset Hotel. Neither Shillip nor Judy had let slip any information about themselves. So how did Crispin know …

1. who Shillip was when he met him at the airport?

2. that Judy was a redhead and was waiting in the car?

3. that he'd be staying at the Dorchester?

4. the contents of his mother's message?

5. that Shillip's house was on the way to the campus?

6. the distance to Shillip's house?

7. that Shillip's phone would be ringing?

8. that Shillip was engaged to a girl named Marilyn?

9. that Shillip was planning to buy a motorcycle?

10. the correct telephone number, in his act's finale?

11. that Shillip would get to school early the next day?

Are there logical explanations, or was it ESP?   *Answers, page 184*

PUZZLES FROM THE POLE VAULT

From *Sam na Sam*

Foreign countries are a rich source of interesting puzzles—especially ones involving logic or math. Over the years GAMES has published braintwisters from England, France, Hungary, Australia, the Soviet Union, and elsewhere around the world. Some time ago we discovered a treasury of original problems in a popular Polish magazine called *Sam na Sam*. (The title translates roughly as "all by oneself.") For ingenuity and execution, these 10 puzzles are hard to beat. Some are fairly easy; others, pretty tricky. Not many solvers, we dare say, will master them all.

Answers, page 184

1. PAINT BOX

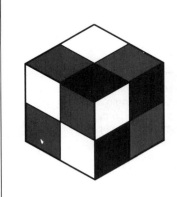

Each face of the cube at left has been divided into four sections, which have then been painted red, yellow, or black. No two sections of the same color meet along an edge anywhere on the cube. Three faces of the the cube are shown. How many sections of each color appear on the entire cube?

2. BICYCLE RACE

When Adam reached the finish line of a 50-kilometer race, Bogdan was two kilometers behind him. The next day they decided to race again. To even up the contest, Adam started two kilometers behind Bogdan, while Bogdan began at the starting line as usual. Assuming they cycled at the same speeds as the day before, which cyclist won the second day's race?

3. SUM WAY OR OTHER

Complete the following equation (one number per dash)

3 ___ ___ ___ + ___ ___ ___ ___ = ___ ___ ___ 0

by moving along the lines from circle to circle below, starting at the 3 and ending at the 0. You may return to any circle as often as you wish, but may not stand on a circle to use it twice before proceeding. Every circle must be used at least once in your answer.

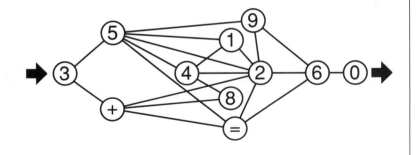

4. EIGHTEEN HOLES

Can you arrange the numbers from 1 to 9 in the circles so that each straight line of three numbers totals 18?

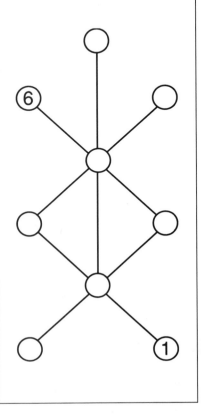

5. FOLLOW THE FOLDS

Which of the six cubes below *cannot* be folded from the pattern?

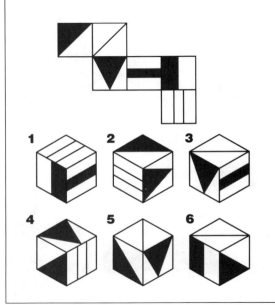

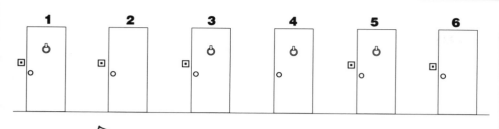

6. PUZZLED POSTMAN

Mr. Kowalski was expecting a package, so he tacked the following note to his door:

"The doorbell on my apartment doesn't work. If you want to leave a package, use the knocker.

"If nobody answers, ring the doorbell of my neighbor next door.

"If no one answers there, try my sister's at apartment 2."

When the postman arrived with the package, he found the note had fallen to the floor, and he couldn't tell which door it had been pinned to. Nevertheless he was able to deliver the package correctly.

Which apartment is Mr. Kowalski's?

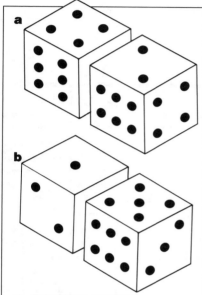

7. TAKING SIDES

The two dice in each pair above are identical. As usual, the numbers on opposite sides of each die add up to seven. On each pair, what is the total of the two hidden sides that face each other?

9. TUNNEL VISION

A train passes through a long tunnel in the mountains. The train is 125 meters long, and travels at 40 kilometers per hour.

Just as the last car is is completely inside the tunnel, a man begins walking from the end of the train to the front. He walks at 5 kilometers per hour and reaches the front of the train just as it emerges into the daylight.

How long is the tunnel?

10. RANK AND FILE

Nine soldiers are in a trench too narrow for them to pass by each other. Each space in the trench, as shown below, is just large enough for one soldier. However, there are three niches into which a man can fit, allowing another to squeeze by.

Sergeant A (space 10) has just received orders to go to the front of the trench (space 1) while moving the other soldiers as little as possible. What is the smallest number of moves it can take him to reach the front and return the other soldiers to their original positions? Moving a soldier counts as one move no matter how many spaces he travels.

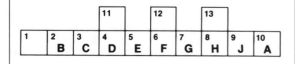

8. LABYRINTH

Can you find a route out of the labyrinth, starting in the center room and passing through each of the pointers in the direction indicated? Do not pass through any corridor or intersection more than once.

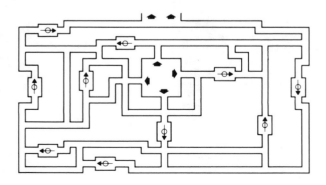

MY LITTLE GAMBLE

By Marek Penszko

Every week millions of Poles spend their hard-earned zlotys on state-organized games of chance, similar to some American state lotteries. Coupons may be bought or sent to offices of the firm organizing the game any day from Monday to Saturday. The drawing takes place on Sunday.

The most popular Polish lottery game is called toto-lotek. In its simplest form, the game is to cross out six of the 49 numbers printed on one of the coupon squares. (The shading around the 42, 45, and 49 plays no part in this version of the game.) A players wins money if he or she correctly guesses three or more of the numbers drawn on Sunday.

I am a toto-lotek addict. For the past few years I've crossed out the same six numbers every week—so far, I might add, with little success. Each digit from 0 through 9 appears exactly once in my set of numbers, and no two of my numbers appear in the same row or column in the square.

What are the six numbers that I cross out every week?

Answer, page 184

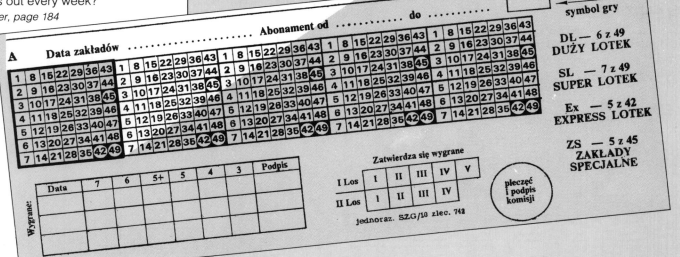

MURDER ON THE ALPINE EXPRESS

By Carol Eastman

At ten minutes to eight, the first-class dining car of the Alpine Express held its six most distinguished passengers: the world-famous diva, Mme. Ciandi; an American business tycoon named Mr. Watterson; Mrs. Frothingham, the widow of an English publisher; a Hungarian nobleman named Count Zathmary; a young American heiress named Miss Lindsay; and M. Duval, the French actor.

To the rear of the dining car was the deluxe sleeping car in which the six had accommodations. The car's six compartments were numbered, from the front of the train to the rear, No. 10, No. 11, No. 12, No. 13, No. 14, and No. 15.

M. Duval was the first to leave the dining car for his compartment, which was No. 10. At precisely 8:42, a shot rang out—and the number of distinguished passengers was reduced to five. M. Duval lay dead in his berth.

By a fortuitous coincidence, Dr. Whitneedle, the renowned private investigator, was a passenger in the next sleeping car. Having determined that the five remaining passengers were the only possible suspects, he proceeded with his investigation. Dr. Whitneedle discovered that it took two minutes to return to the sleeping car from the dining car, and that the only person who could have committed the crime was the person who left the dining car at 8:40.

Dr. Whitneedle questioned the dining car steward, the sleeping car porter, and the five suspects, and received the following comments:

Dining car steward: "Sorry, but I was too busy to notice in what order the passengers left the dining car. I do know that after Duval left at 8:00, the others departed singly at 10-minute intervals. Oh, yes—the two other men did not leave one right after the other."

Sleeping car porter: "Aside from Duval, who came to the sleeping car shortly after 8:00, I saw only the woman in No. 15 returning and, afterward, the man in No. 12."

Mr. Watterson: "I don't know if anyone other than the poor victim left before I did. I know that the woman who has No. 13 and the other man were still in the dining car when I left."

Mme. Ciandi: "The person whose compartment is immediately rearward of mine returned after I did. I heard the door open and shut, and then I heard movement within the room."

Mrs. Frothingham: "I didn't see whether anyone was still in the dining car when I left. I saw the man who had No. 12 leave before me. And before he left, a woman left. She has the compartment next to his."

Miss Lindsay: "Of course, I recognized Mme. Ciandi; she left the dining car before I did. I am sure that the man whose compartment is immediately frontward of mine was still in the dining car when I left."

Count Zathmary: "I did not notice the others. They are peasants and are of no interest to me."

As Dr. Whitneedle pondered these statements, he realized that if all were true, they would enable him to name the person who left the dining car at 8:40. Proceeding on this assumption, he confronted the murderer and soon had a confession.

Can you match Dr. Whitneedle's detective prowess by placing the five suspects in their correct compartments, telling what time each person left the dining car, and naming the murderer?

Answer, page 185

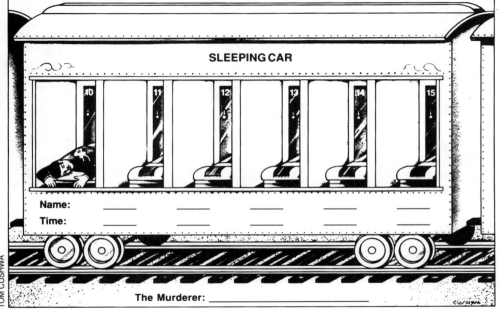

SLEEPING CAR

10　11　12　13　14　15

Name: ___ ___ ___ ___ ___ ___
Time: ___ ___ ___ ___ ___ ___

The Murderer: _____

FROM THE DESK OF...

By Scott Marley

Tiberius Wumble, president of Wumble's Candy Company, looked at the papers scattered on his desk and swore under his breath. When this proved ineffective, he swore over his breath, and began to feel a little better.

"Look at the time wasted by those egocentric nincompoops I employ," he hollered, "sending memos back and forth when they should be working!" And with a violent, impulsive sweep of his

From: The Vice President
To: All Employees

Good news! That dull old equipment room is being repainted in exciting new colors--Cotton Ball White with Peach Fuzz Beige trim! Employees using any of the three connecting rooms should keep the connecting doors closed to prevent fumes from spreading.

From: The Vice President
To: All Employees

The reason the conference room and the women's room are hot in the mornings is because of their eastern exposure. I've spoken once again with the air conditioning repairman and he assures me that this time he really will be able to get the temperatures adjusted properly. Please continue to be patient.

From: The President
To: The Assistant to the President

No, you incompetent moron, we are not going to raise all the ceilings in the building. Your ridiculous "improvements" would have us bankrupt in six months. Meanwhile, the door between the kitchen and the lounge still squeaks. See that it gets oiled.

From: Bookkeeping
To: The President

The wall safe in the bookkeeping department should be installed between the two doors in the paneled wall. Since we'll need to buy a picture to camouflage it with, we took a vote and agreed on the one with all the dogs playing poker.

From: The Assistant to the President
To: The President

Okay, then, if you don't want to raise the ceilings, here's an even better idea. We should put in some new doors, like between my office and the display room. As it is now, I have to walk through at least two other rooms to get there from my office.

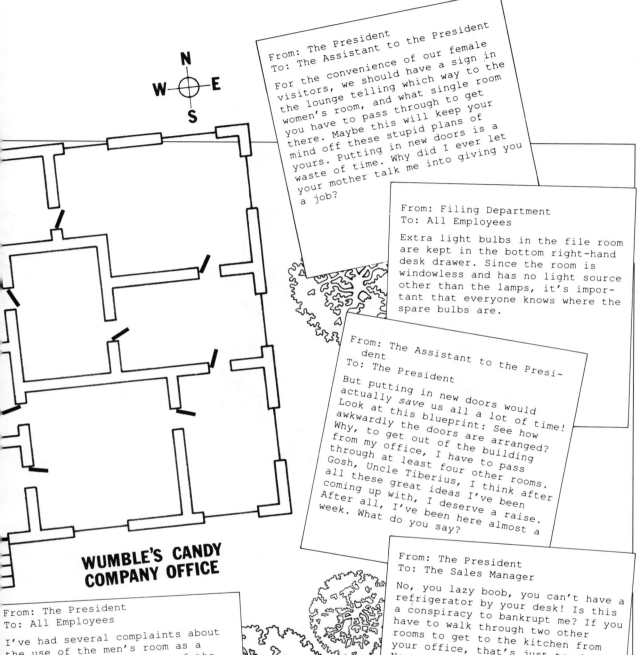

WUMBLE'S CANDY COMPANY OFFICE

From: The President
To: The Assistant to the President

For the convenience of our female visitors, we should have a sign in the lounge telling which way to the women's room, and what single room you have to pass through to get there. Maybe this will keep your mind off these stupid plans of yours. Putting in new doors is a waste of time. Why did I ever let your mother talk me into giving you a job?

From: Filing Department
To: All Employees

Extra light bulbs in the file room are kept in the bottom right-hand desk drawer. Since the room is windowless and has no light source other than the lamps, it's important that everyone knows where the spare bulbs are.

From: The Assistant to the President
To: The President

But putting in new doors would actually *save* us all a lot of time! Look at this blueprint: See how awkwardly the doors are arranged? Why, to get out of the building from my office, I have to pass through at least four other rooms. Gosh, Uncle Tiberius, I think after all these great ideas I've been coming up with, I deserve a raise. After all, I've been here almost a week. What do you say?

From: The President
To: The Sales Manager

No, you lazy boob, you can't have a refrigerator by your desk! Is this a conspiracy to bankrupt me? If you have to walk through two other rooms to get to the kitchen from your office, that's just too bad. Now get back to work or I'll fire you and the rest of the staff as well!

From: The President
To: All Employees

I've had several complaints about the use of the men's room as a route between the offices of the sales manager and the vice president. A recent incident involving fifteen visiting representatives, six of them women, so upset an employee who was using the facilities at the time that he had to lie down the rest of the afternoon. The men's room, I'd like to remind you all, is not the only room that connects with both offices, and I would like to suggest that in the future, going through the bookkeeping department would be more appropriate.

arm, he sent papers flying in the general direction of the wastebasket.

Had Mr. Wumble been more of a puzzler, he might have noticed that the memos just happened to form a logic problem. Can you match each room in the Wumble's Candy Company offices (listed at bottom right) with its position on the floor map shown?

Answer, page 185

ROOMS:

Assistant to the President's Office	Kitchen
Bookkeeping Department	Lounge
Conference Room	Men's Room
Display Room	President's Office
Equipment Room	Sales Manager's Office
File Room	Vice President's Office
	Women's Room

THE STATE VS. JOSEPH HILL

By Roy Post

Ladies and Gentlemen of the Jury: There were no eye-witnesses to the murder of Clinton Bragg. Not even the murderer was there to see him die. And three persons with motive to murder him had opportunity to commit the crime.

He was not a lovable character, Ladies and Gentlemen. He was a misanthrope, a miser, a loan shark. He had been crippled for years, unable to move from his bed unassisted, and this had embittered him until he seemed to take vicious delight in inflicting pain on those who fell into his clutches.

Now, Ladies and Gentlemen, the first of the trio with both motive and opportunity to murder Clinton Bragg was his landlady, the widow Susan Ball.

When her husband died 13 years before, Mrs. Ball found that the only thing he had left her was their new home, a modern place which she was able to keep only because she turned it into a superior rooming house. Bragg was her first tenant. Because of his miserliness he would not hire a nurse to attend to his wants, but paid Mrs. Ball to take care of him, to wait on him hand and foot, by promising to make her daughter his heir.

On the evening before his body was found, he quarrelled with Mrs. Ball because she kept her daughter in a boarding school. He called it a waste of money. He reviled her, mocked her, and others heard him shout that the next morning he'd have his lawyer come to change his will so neither she nor her daughter would ever get a cent of his money to squander.

The State Versus
JOSEPH HILL
Exhibit A

The other two with motive and opportunity to commit the murder were Burton Meek and Joseph Hill, who shared a suite of two rooms on the floor above Bragg's room with Thomas Lane, like them a clerk in a brokerage office.

Though neither Hill nor Meek knew of the other's plight, both had borrowed from the old loan shark to repay small thefts from their offices. And after making payments to Bragg every week for almost four years, each still owed the old man five to six times as much as the original loan, a situation not at all unusual in loan shark dealings.

On the afternoon before the body was found, Bragg had called them in separately and ordered each to pay the money the next day, even

if they had to steal it from their offices. Neither had the money. He told them if they didn't pay, he would inform their employers of their peculations.

We come now to the night before the body was found. We are fortunate in having as a witness Mrs. Hunter, who spent the night in the room nearest the old man's, sitting up with a sick friend, Mrs. Wayne, another paying guest. As it was a warm August night, Mrs. Hunter kept the door open. So from her chair she was able to keep a watch on Bragg's door. I submit State's Exhibit A to make clear this point by showing the relationship of the rooms. No. 1 is Bragg's room, No. 2 is Mrs. Wayne's.

At 11 P.M., as she did every night, Mrs. Ball went to Bragg's room, arranged his bed, opened the window some six inches, lowered the

A CLASSIC JURY BOX PUZZLE FROM THE GAMES LIBRARY

The State Versus
JOSEPH HILL
Exhibit B

blind to within eight inches or so of the sill, and went downstairs to her own room. She did not lock Bragg's door. He had a horror of being locked in.

At 12:30 A.M., while Mrs. Hunter was sitting with the light out until her patient went to sleep, Mrs. Ball came quietly up the stairs and entered Bragg's room. She was there about five minutes and then as silently went down again, not knowing that Mrs. Hunter was watching her. Mrs. Ball told you she went to plead with Bragg to keep his promise, but found him asleep, and so left.

At 1:55 A.M., Joseph Hill came home from a party. Mrs. Hunter heard his step on the stairs, but did not see him because at that moment her patient became restless and she went to the bed. So she is unable to testify whether he went into Bragg's room or whether, as he testified, he went directly upstairs.

At 7 A.M., Mrs. Hunter left her chair for the second time during her vigil. No one else had come up or downstairs all night. Her patient awoke, and Mrs. Hunter closed the door so no one could hear the sick woman.

At 7:05 A.M., Burton Meek left his room and started for work, having tasks at his office he had to do before it opened. This is verified by his roommates and by his office manager. Meek says he walked directly downstairs without stopping and that he saw no one.

At 7:10 A.M., her patient having fallen asleep again, Mrs. Hunter reopened the door. She pulled down the shade so that the bright sunlight would not disturb her patient. She sat down to wait for another friend, who was to relieve her.

At 9:35 A.M., as was customary, Mrs. Ball came up with Bragg's breakfast. She saw Mrs. Hunter and said, "I hope the old skinflint has decided not to change his will." She opened the door to Bragg's room, and gas gushed out into the corridor. Someone had gone into the room as Bragg slept, closed the window, turned on the gas heater and left Bragg to die.

Police with gas masks dragged out the old man; doctors said he had been dead anywhere from two to ten hours. Nothing was out of order in the room except on the window sill, which is shown as police found it in State's Exhibit B. As Detective Casey told you, "There were some wilted flowers in the vase on the sill and that sill was a regular morgue for flies and mosquitoes. The only ones in the room were dead, killed by the gas, I guess. There was also a cigarette and Bragg's pipe."

And this cigarette was of the unusual brand, which testimony proves was smoked by Hill, and Hill alone of those in the house. He has admitted it was his cigarette, but he had said he crushed it out the day before while talking to the old man.

Now, Ladies and Gentlemen, even though Bragg was a despicable character and probably worthy of no better fate, I ask you, as Jurors sworn to do your duty, to find Joseph Hill, defendant at the bar, guilty of murder in the first degree.

All the facts necessary to solve this crime and reach the correct verdict are contained in the story and exhibits. Please reach your decision and mark your jury ballot below.

Answer, page 184

I find the defendant, Joseph Hill:
___ Guilty   ___ Not guilty

HIROIMONO

Presented by John Fairbairn

Logic puzzles like the six on this page date back at least as far as 14th-century Japan, where, some experts believe, they originated as subjects of wagers. Known as *hiroimono* (hee-roh-ee-moh-noh), or "things picked up," they are traditionally set up with the stones used for the Oriental game of go, and played by removing the stones one at a time. But they can be played just as easily with pencil and paper.

The object in each puzzle is to fill the circles with the counting numbers (1, 2, 3, etc., in order) according to specific rules and without having any unfilled circles left over.

To start, pick a circle (the choice is important) and put the number 1 in it. Then move left, right, up, or down to a new circle and put a 2 in it. Continue moving to unfilled circles and filling them with numbers while observing these restrictions:

1. You may move only horizontally or vertically—never diagonally.

2. You may not pass over unfilled circles. (You may, however, pass over filled circles or any empty space between circles.)

3. You may not retrace any part of your most recent move. For example, if you just moved from left to right, your next move cannot be from right to left.

Below is an example configuration solved correctly and incorrectly.

CORRECT   **INCORRECT**

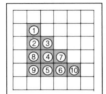   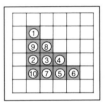

Note that in the second grid, the move from 1 to 2 illegally passes over an unfilled circle, and the move from 6 to 7 illegally retraces the move from 5 to 6.

Some *hiroimono* puzzles have more than one solution, but finding *any* solution is sometimes surprisingly tricky.   *Answers, page 185*

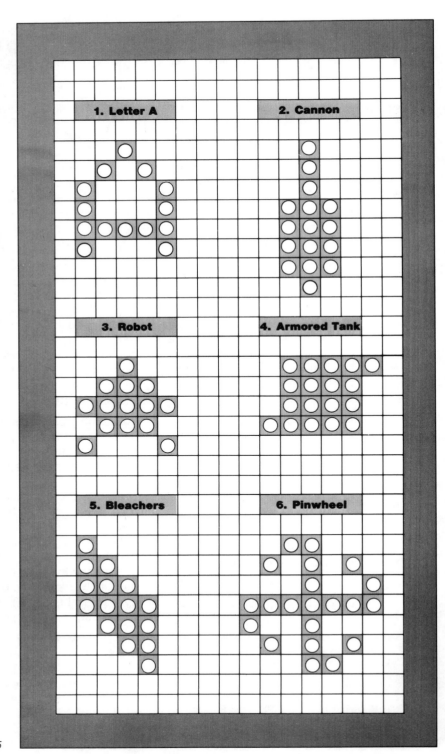

WELL, WHAT DO YOU KNOW?

A QUIZ FOR (ALMOST) EVERY OCCASION

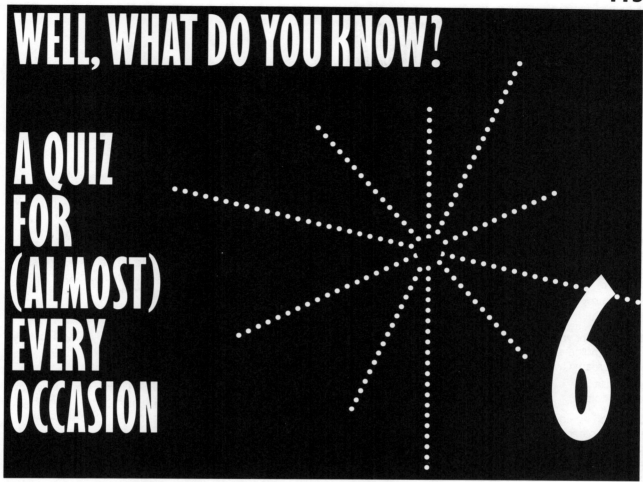

6

SAY CHEESE!

By Manny S. Miles

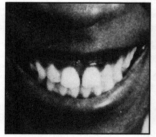

1

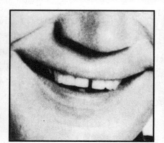

2

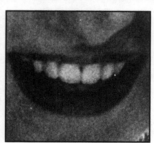

3

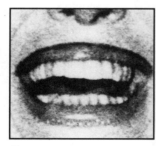

4

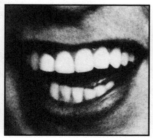

5

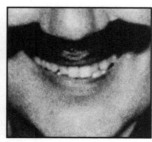

6

Why are these famous people smiling? We don't know. What we do want to know is, who are these famous smiling people?
Answers, page 185

ICE CREAM, YOU SCREAM

By Burt Hochberg

No one knows for sure where and when ice cream originated—but who cares? The important thing is that it's cool and sweet and comes in umpteen flavors. Before you eat some, see if you can lick these questions about America's favorite dessert.

Answers, page 185

1. Year after year, sales figures and surveys indicate that the most popular ice cream flavor is

a) vanilla   c) coffee
b) chocolate   d) strawberry

2. Which age group consumes the most ice cream, eating it an average of 56 times a year? And which group consumes the least?

a) 6-12
b) 13-18
c) 19-34
d) 35-54
e) over 55

3. On average, according to a recent study, those who consume the most ice cream

a) are well educated and well paid
b) live in a warm climate
c) own pets

4. The region with the highest per capita ice cream consumption is

a) the South   c) the West coast
b) the Midwest   d) New England

5. According to the *New York Times*, the average American consumed how much ice cream, including sherbets and ices, in 1987?

a) 22 pints   c) 22 gallons
b) 22 quarts   d) 22 tons

6. Häagen-Dazs, as you know, is manufactured right here in the U.S. The words, however, mean

a) "frozen dessert" in Swedish
b) "good humor" in Danish
c) "happy days" in Norwegian
d) nothing

7. Another rich ice cream brand with an odd name is Frusen Glädjè, which means

a) "frozen delight" in Swedish
b) "happy freshness" in Danish
c) "ice cream" in Finnish
d) nothing

8. Without using your tongue, arrange the following fruit flavors in the order of their popularity in sherbet:

lime   lemon
orange   pineapple
raspberry

9. Eskimo Pie, a name trademarked in the 1920s, was the first

a) ice cream sandwich
b) chocolate-covered ice cream bar
c) ice cream manufactured in Alaska
d) ice cream made from whale blubber

10. Frank Epperson accidentally left a glass of lemonade with a spoon in it overnight near an open window in the middle of winter. In the morning, he found he had discovered

a) the frozen daiquiri
b) the Popsicle
c) a great way to cool his kitchen

11. The ice cream cone, according to the best evidence, came into being at the 1904 St. Louis World's Fair, when an ice cream concessionaire ran out of serving dishes and, in a panic, borrowed a supply of these from a neighboring concession:

a) hamburger buns
b) éclair shells
c) rolled-up newspapers
d) Syrian waffles

12. He began his career in 1925, making high-quality ice cream in a Massachusetts basement and selling it in a store bearing his name. Local businessmen soon began buying supplies from him and paying him for the right to use his name. As a result, he became the acknowledged father of the U.S. franchising industry. His name?

a) Louis Sherry
b) Wentworth ("Wendy") McDonald
c) Howard Johnson
d) F.W. Woolworth

13. The Good Humor Corp. was founded by a man named Harry Burt, who chose the name Good Humor because

a) he believed that "the humors of the mind are regulated by the palate"
b) before emigrating to the U.S. from his native Germany, his family name was Gutjuhmer
c) he thought the phrase would put customers in a good mood so they would want to buy ice cream
d) it was the name of the restaurant where he had been given his first job

14. If you keep ice cream tightly covered in your freezer and maintain a temperature of zero degrees Fahrenheit, how long will the ice cream stay fresh, according to the National Dairy Council?

a) 2 days   c) 2 months
b) 2 weeks   d) 2 years

15. According to federal law, ice cream must contain at least 20 percent

a) vitamin D   c) butterfat
b) sugar   d) ice

16. Federal law also requires that, to be labeled "French," ice cream must contain

a) eggs
b) brie
c) milk from French cows

17. History tells us that Washington, Jefferson, and other fathers of our country loved ice cream just as much as we do. But who do you think was the first First Lady to serve it at a White House state dinner?

a) Lucretia Garfield
b) Mary Todd Lincoln
c) Dolley Madison

18. Richard Nixon, in addition to his other problems, had to have his favorite ice cream flavor flown in from Hawaii because it was unobtainable in Washington. That flavor?

a) poi and pineapple
b) mahimahi mint chip
c) macadamia nut

19. During the Vietnam conflict, U.S. military leaders came up with a stroke of generalship rarely equaled in the annals of war—"Operation Deep Freeze," which was a plan to

a) demoralize the North Vietnamese by using thermal bombs to melt their ice cream supplies
b) send tainted ice cream into enemy-held areas
c) install 30 ice cream plants near Pleiku to boost U.S. servicemen's morale

20. U.S. airmen in Britain during World War II would stow ice cream mix in the rear gunners' compartments of their B-52s because

a) ice was scarce, and this was the fastest way of transporting the mix before it soured
b) the combination of high-altitude freezing and aircraft vibration made the ice cream especially smooth
c) the creamy mix formed a perfect buffer for the live ammunition kept there, preventing it from detonating if hit by enemy fire

21. The famous violinist Jascha Heifetz once had his lawyer swear out a complaint against Good Humor because

a) the stick in a Popsicle splintered in his mouth and injured his gums
b) the ice cream melted too quickly and dripped on his Stradivarius
c) the bells on the Good Humor trucks prowling his neighborhood made too much noise

22. The ice cream sundae originated around 1890, give or take a few minutes. Although evidence about its origin is both sketchy and contradictory, the most commonly accepted theory is that

a) blue laws in the Midwest prohibited the sale of soda on Sunday, so on that day fountain owners served "soda-less sodas," consisting of ice cream, syrup, fruit, etc.
b) fountain owners received ice cream fresh from local dairies on Mondays, and on preceding Sundays they got rid of the week's leftovers by serving combinations of random flavors topped with syrup, etc., etc.
c) the concoction was a favorite family dessert of Billy Sunday, who published the recipe and lent it his name

23. The term "soda jerk" comes from the fact that

a) fountain workers typically wore a type of apron called a jerkin
b) servers had to jerk the soda machine's lever to dispense the soda
c) "jerk" was a rude but common term for a waiter in the 1920s, and the source of the still rude and common term for a jerk
d) the movements of the hardworking servers were rapid and jerky

24. Soda-jerk lingo was, during its heyday in the 1930s, a specialized vocabulary that served as a shortcut in communications as well as an insider's code. See if you can match the lingo (1–10) with the realities (a–j):

1. Chicago
2. burn one all the way
3. in the hay
4. houseboat
5. black bottom
6. white cow
7. Hoboken special
8. black stick
9. mode mode
10. black & white

a) chocolate soda, vanilla ice cream
b) pineapple sundae or soda
c) banana split
d) vanilla milkshake
e) chocolate sundae, chocolate syrup
f) chocolate ice cream cone
g) pineapple soda, chocolate ice cream
h) strawberry milkshake
i) chocolate shake with chocolate ice cream
j) pie or cake with two ice cream scoops

MEASURE FOR MEASURE

By Barbara Glasgow

Steve LaRue was ready to open his singing act in a small New Jersey lounge when he learned to his horror that his accompanist had lost all the sheet music and could only remember the first few measures of each song. Thinking fast, LaRue told the audience he was doing something different that night. He would sing only a couple measures from some famous pop songs, then let the crowd guess the name of each tune. The audience loved it, management hated it, and LaRue was fired that night. See if you can name each tune from the bits of music and lyrics that LaRue sang. *Answers, page 185*

SLEUTHS IN SHADOW

By Cilla Whett

Nine famous detectives from films and television are shown below. Since they're all on undercover work, we have disguised them so that only their outlines are visible. Can you deduce the identity of each detective from his or her silhouette and the surrounding scene? When you've done this, see how many of the actors portraying these characters you can name—we guess a lot of them will leave *you* in the dark! Answer, page 186

1

2

3

4

5

6

7

8

9

SORRY, WRONG NUMBER

By Lou Kesten

All the objects below may look real, but you'll see at second glance that some of them are fake. For example, the gold bar (#1) is clearly phony; pure gold is 24 karats, so a 28K gold bar would be impossible. Likewise, the numbers on many of the other objects identify them as impostors. Can you pick out the fakes from the bona-fide items and explain why?

Answers, page 186

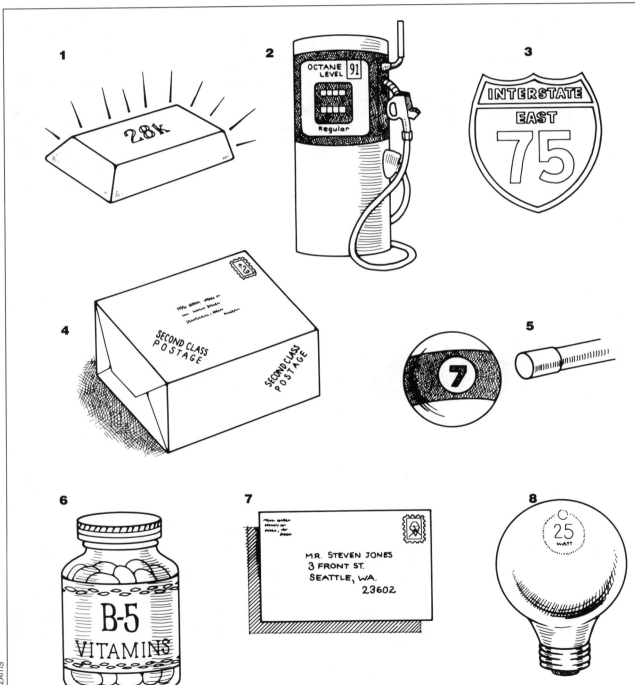

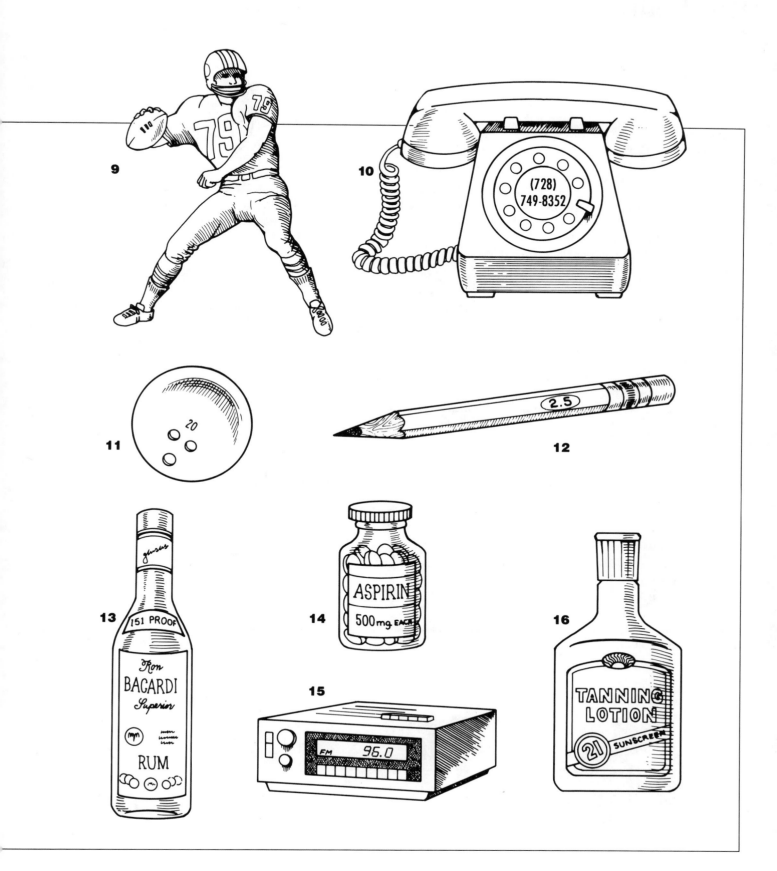

WHATCHAMACALLITS

By Curtis Slepian

Thingamabob, gizmo, doodad. These names won't help you score in this quiz. Nor will dingus or widget. No … you're going to have to come up with the *actual* names of some everyday objects. Choose each doohickey's correct name from the three choices offered between its picture and description.

Answers, page 186

1. The frames in which the glass panes of a window are set

a) mullians
b) muntins
c) borks

2. The open-sided box a book is kept in

a) biblios
b) mini-house
c) forel

3. What a phone's headset (the thing you pick up and talk into) rests on

a) cradle
b) nest
c) telecouch

4. The part of the stairway you step on

a) tread
b) riser
c) footstep

5. The magazine subscription cards that always fall on the floor when you open the magazine

a) blow-ins
b) cardiacs
c) drop-cards

6. The loop on the front part of a belt, which secures the tip of the belt

a) blatz
b) tongue biter
c) keeper

7. The little metal band around a pencil, right below the eraser

a) ferrule
b) squeezer
c) circumflex

8. The very beginning of a roll of film that feeds first into the sprockets

a) follower
b) leader
c) grabber

9. The plastic or metal tip of a shoelace

a) aglet
b) agular
c) aginwit

10. The part of the eyeglass frame on the side of the head, extending from the front to the endpiece

a) rail
b) skull temple
c) side bar

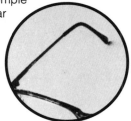

11. The front of an office desk that extends down toward the floor

a) modesty panel
b) knee blind
c) anti-peeper

12. The short, flexible part of a power cord that's closest to the appliance

a) safety pull
b) strain relief
c) yank piece

13. A charred, partly consumed candlewick

a) sniff
b) snuff
c) snurf

14. The two slots on either side of the front of a clothes iron

a) cuff sash
b) button nook
c) collar cut

15. The top pocket on a man's suit jacket with two pockets on one side

a) conductor's pocket
b) change pocket
c) ticket pocket

16. In a piercing-type can opener, the little metal flange than extends from the handle to below the triangular puncher

a) can nib
b) lance-form
c) fulcrum

17. The small, curved end on a suit hanger than forms a letter "C"

a) turnback
b) switchback
c) peacock's eye

18. The leather fringes at the end of the shoelace on a tasseled loafer

a) kiltie
b) surry
c) prepsy

19. The pointy, curved end of the handle of a chef's knife

a) tang
b) slub
c) neb

20. The rounded, top portion of a key

a) tooth
b) gum
c) bow

21. On a matchbook, the abrasive surface a match is struck on

a) drag strip
b) igniter
c) friction strip

SPORTS ABBREVIATED

By Lou Kesten

Sports statisticians have a language all their own, but even if you aren't a sports maniac, you'll probably recognize most of the games being played here. Or will you? Below are excerpts from 15 sports scores torn from the pages of the newspaper. Most of the sports are common, although a few are off the beaten path. How many of them can you identify?

Answers, page 186

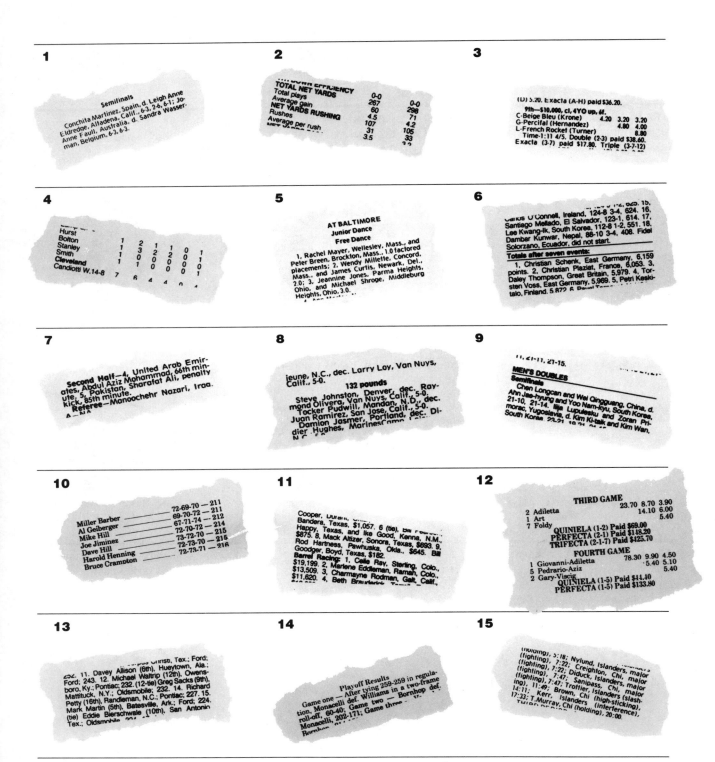

1

Semifinals
Conchita Martinez, Spain, d. Leigh Anne Eldredge, Altadena, Calif., 6-3, 2-6, 6-1; Jo-Anne Faull, Australia, d. Sandra Wasserman, Belgium, 6-3, 6-3.

2

...DOWN EFFICIENCY
TOTAL NET YARDS
Total plays 0-0 0-0
Average gain 267 298
NET YARDS RUSHING 60 71
Rushes .... 4.5 .... 4.2
Average per rush 107 105
                        31 33
                        3.5 .... 3.2

3

(D) 5.20. Exacta (A-H) paid $36.20.

9th—$10,000, cl, 4YO up, 6f.
C-Beige Bleu (Krone) 4.20 3.20 3.20
G-Percifal (Hernandez) 4.80 4.00
L-French Rocket (Turner) 8.80
   Time-1:11 4/5. Double (2-3) paid $38.60.
Exacta (3-7) paid $17.80. Triple (3-7-12)

4

Hurst
Bolton
Stanley
Smith
Cleveland
Candiotti W.14-8

(scattered box score digits)

5

AT BALTIMORE
Junior Dance
Free Dance
1, Rachel Mayer, Wellesley, Mass., and Peter Breen, Brockton, Mass., 1.0 factored placements; 2, Wendy Millette, Concord, Mass., and James Curtis, Newark, Del., 2.0; 3, Jeannine Jones, Parma Heights, Ohio, and Michael Shroge, Middleburg Heights, Ohio, 3.0.

6

Carlos O'Connell, Ireland, 124-8 3-4, 624. 16, Santiago Mellado, El Salvador, 123-1, 614. 17, Lee Kwang-Ik, South Korea, 112-8 1-2, 551. 18, Dambar Kunwar, Nepal, 88-10 3-4, 408. Fidel Solorzano, Ecuador, did not start.
Totals after seven events:
1, Christian Schenk, East Germany, 6,159 points. 2, Christian Plaziat, France, 6,053. 3, Daley Thompson, Great Britain, 5,979. 4, Torsten Voss, East Germany, 5,969. 5, Petri Keskitalo, Finland, 5,872 ...

7

Second Half—4, United Arab Emirates, Abdul Aziz Mohammad, 66th minute. 5, Pakistan, Sharafat Ali, penalty kick, 85th minute.
Referee—Manoochehr Nazari, Iraq.

8

...jeune, N.C., dec. Larry Loy, Van Nuys, Calif., 5-0.
132 pounds
Steve Johnston, Denver, dec. Raymond Olivera, Van Nuys, Calif., 5-0. Tocker Pudwill, Mandan, N.D., dec. Juan Ramirez, San Jose, Calif., 5-0. Damion Jasmer, Portland, dec. Didier Hughes, MarinesComp., N.C. ...

9

11, 21-11, 21-15.
MEN'S DOUBLES
Semifinals
Chen Longcan and Wei Qingguang, China, d. Ahn Jae-hyung and Yoo Nam-kyu, South Korea, 21-10, 21-14. Ilija Lupulesku and Zoran Primorac, Yugoslavia, d. Kim Ki-taik and Kim Wan, South Korea, 23-21, 19-21 ...

10

Miller Barber .... 72-69-70 — 211
Al Geiberger .... 69-70-72 — 211
Mike Hill .... 67-71-74 — 212
Joe Jiminez .... 72-70-72 — 214
Dave Hill .... 73-72-70 — 215
Harold Henning .... 72-73-70 — 215
Bruce Crampton .... 72-73-71 — 216

11

Cooper, Durant, ... Bandera, Texas, $1,057. 6 (tie), Bill ... Happy, Texas, and Ike Good, Kenna, N.M., $875. 8, Mack Altizer, Sonora, Texas, $693. 9, Rod Hartness, Pawhuska, Okla., $645. Bill Goodger, Boyd, Texas, $182.
Barrel Racing: 1, Calie Ray, Sterling, Colo., $19,199. 2, Marlene Eddleman, Ramah, Colo., $13,509. 3, Charmayne Rodman, Galt, Calif., $11,620. 4, Beth Bru... Texas ...

12

THIRD GAME
2 Adiletta 23.70 8.70 3.90
1 Art 14.10 6.00
7 Foldy 5.40
QUINIELA (1-2) Paid $69.00
PERFECTA (2-1) Paid $118.20
TRIFECTA (2-1-7) Paid $425.70
FOURTH GAME
1 Giovanni-Adiletta ... 78.30 9.90 4.50
5 Pedrario-Aziz 5.40 5.10
2 Gary-Viscig 5.40
QUINIELA (1-5) Paid $44.40
PERFECTA (1-5) Paid $133.80

13

252. 11, Davey Allison (6th), Hueytown, Ala.; Ford; 243. 12, Michael Waltrip (12th), Owensboro, Ky.; Pontiac; 232. (12-tie) Greg Sacks (9th), Mattituck, N.Y.; Oldsmobile; 232. 14, Richard Petty (16th), Randleman, N.C.; Pontiac; 227. 15, Mark Martin (5th), Batesville, Ark.; Ford; 224. (tie) Eddie Bierschwale (10th), San Antonio Tex.; Oldsmobile, 204 ...

14

Playoff Results
Game one — After tying 259-259 in regulation, Monacelli def. Williams in a two-frame roll-off, 60-40; Game two — Bornhop def. Monacelli, 202-171; Game three — Bornhop ...

15

(holding), 5:18; Nylund, Islanders, major (fighting), 7:22; Creighton, Chi, major (fighting), 7:22; Diduck, Islanders, major (fighting), 7:47; Sanipass, Chi, major (fighting), 7:47; Trottier, Islanders (slashing), 11:49; Brown, Chi (high-sticking) 14:11; Kerr, Islanders (slashing) 17:33; T.Murray, Chi (holding), 20:00.

NUMBER, PLEASE!

By Mary Ellen Slate

Simple arithmetic—and a little knowledge of trivia—are all it takes to solve this numerical puzzle. Each clue is in the form of a two-part equation. When you know the answers to both parts, perform the calculation indicated by the arithmetic symbol (addition, subtraction, multiplication, or division) and write the result in the box corresponding to the letter of the clue. When all the boxes have been correctly filled in, each horizontal and vertical row and both corner-to-corner diagonals will total the same key number. Note: Once you've determined the key number by completing one row, you'll have an additional clue to finishing the others. Some numbers appear more than once in the puzzle.

Answer, page 186

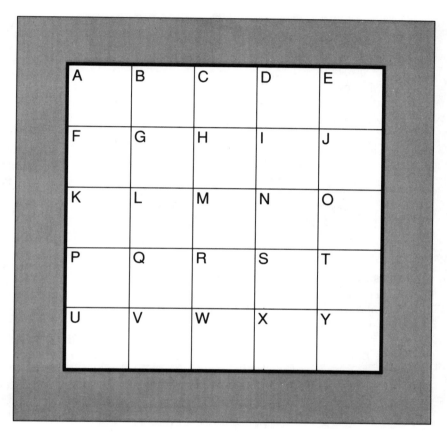

CLUES

A. Legs on a spider x Legs on a stool

B. Days in a fortnight – Deadly Sins

C. Members of the Supreme Court + Members of the Supremes

D. RPM of a "single" ÷ The ___ Stooges

E. ___ *Minutes* ÷ *Years Before the Mast*

F. Karats in pure gold – Hills of Rome

G. Cards in a pinochle deck – Contiguous U.S. states

H. Kellogg's Product ___ + VHF channels

I. Innings in a baseball game – ___ *Easy Pieces*

J. Points on a Star of David x Points for a touchdown

K. Ali Baba's Thieves – ___ *Candles*

L. Hats of Bartholomew Cubbins ÷ U.S. Senators

M. Heinz varieties ÷ Men in a tub

N. Lives of a cat x Mittenless kittens

O. Disney's dalmatians – Piano keys

P. King Henrys of England + Nixon's "Crises"

Q. *Route* ___ – Winks in a nap

R. Days in June ÷ Blind mice

S. Baskin-Robbins flavors + Feet in a fathom

T. Olympic rings – The ___ Seasons

U. "Kings of Orient Are" x ___-Mile Island

V. "Little Indians" x "Little Peppers"

W. Beethoven's symphonies + Stars in the Big Dipper

X. Dimes in a dollar ÷ Lights "if by sea"

Y. Beatles' "When I'm ___" ÷ Beatles' "___ Days a Week"

THINKING PHYSICS

By Lewis C. Epstein and Paul G. Hewitt

You could call it painless physics. There's nary a theory nor an equation in these 11 illustrated questions—just some practical problems that test your intuition of how and why things work the way they do. Warning: Some of the answers may surprise you. Think of them as mental push-ups, and be prepared for a workout.   *Answers, page 186*

1. MAGNET CAR Will hanging a magnet in front of an iron car, as shown, make the car go?

   a) yes, it will go
   b) it will move if there is no friction
   c) it will not go

2. COLD BATH This is a bathtub brim full of ice-water with an iceberg floating in it. When the iceberg melts, the water in the tub will …

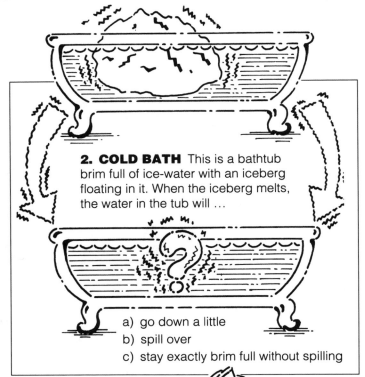

   a) go down a little
   b) spill over
   c) stay exactly brim full without spilling

3. RUBBER BULLET A rubber bullet and aluminum bullet both have the same size, speed, and weight. They are fired at a block of wood. Which is more likely to knock the block over?

   a) the rubber bullet
   b) the aluminum bullet
   c) both the same

4. GOING DOWN You suspend a boulder weighing 50 pounds and lower it beneath the surface of the water. When the boulder is fully submerged, you find you have to support less than 50 pounds. As the boulder is submerged still farther, the force needed to hold the boulder is …

   a) less
   b) the same
   c) more

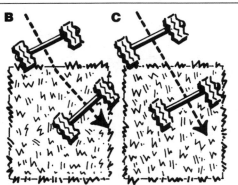

5. TURNING CART WHEELS
Suppose a pair of toy cart wheels connected by an axle is rolled along a smooth sidewalk and onto a grass lawn. Due to the interaction of the wheels with the grass, they roll slower there than on the smooth sidewalk. When the wheels are rolled at an angle onto the lawn, which of the paths at right will they take?

ELLIOT KRELOFF

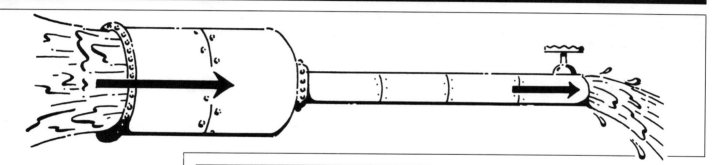

6. BOTTLENECK Ten gallons of water per minute is flowing through this pipe. Which of the following is correct? The water goes ...

a) fastest in the wide part of the pipe

b) fastest in the narrow part

c) at the same speed in both parts

7. TOUGH NUT A nut is very tight on a screw. Which of the following is most likely to free it?

a) cooling it

b) heating it

c) either

d) neither

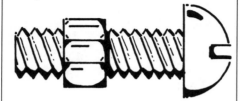
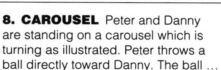

8. CAROUSEL Peter and Danny are standing on a carousel which is turning as illustrated. Peter throws a ball directly toward Danny. The ball ...

a) gets to Danny

b) from Peter's standpoint goes to the right of Danny

c) from Peter's standpoint goes to the left of Danny

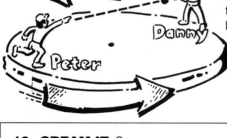

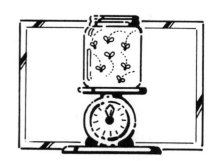

9. JAR OF FLIES A bunch of flies are in a capped jar. You place the jar on a scale. The scale will register the most weight when the flies are ...

a) sitting on the bottom of the jar

b) flying around inside the jar

c) neither; the weight of the jar is exactly the same in both cases

10. CREAM IT Suppose you are served coffee at a restaurant and want it to be hot when you are ready to drink it a few minutes later. You should add the room-temperature cream to it ...

a) right away

b) when you're ready to drink it

c) either—the effect will be the same

11. TORQUE Harry is finding it difficult to muster enough torque to twist the stubborn bolt with a wrench, and he wishes he had a length of pipe to place over the wrench handle to increase his leverage. He has no pipe, but he does have some rope. Will torque be increased if he pulls just as hard on a length of rope tied to the wrench handle?

a) yes

b) no

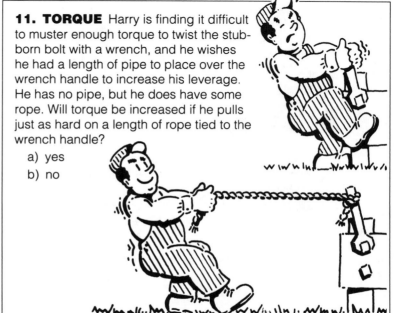

WOODSTOCK RE-GENERATION

By Barry Simon

In August 1969, thousands of people flocked to upstate New York to attend a rock concert. What they wound up witnessing was nothing less than a cultural phenomenon. The Woodstock Music and Arts Fair was a symbol of the Sixties, the high point of hippiedom, three days of peace and love that shook the world. Even if you're not a member of the Woodstock Generation, join us on this groovy trip back in time and see if you know these far-out facts.

Answers, page 186

1. The festival was originally planned for a site in Walkill, NY. It eventually took place at:

a) White Lake, NY
b) Woodstock, NY
c) Middletown, NY

2. Why was the festival called Woodstock?

a) To pay for a children's hospital in Woodstock
b) To pay for replenishing of the forests in the Catskill mountains
c) To pay for a recording studio/retreat for musicians in Woodstock

3. Which was the official logo used for the festival?

4. The promoters initially expected 40,000 people to show up. Approximately how many people attended the event?

a) 100,000   c) 800,000
b) 400,000

5. Attendees had a choice of buying tickets for one, two, or three days. How much was the ticket for all three days?

a) $ 10
b) $ 18
c) $ 30

6. The festival took place on more than 600 acres of land, which were rented from a farmer for $50,000. What was his name?

a) Country Joe MacDonald
b) Moon Dog
c) Max Yasgur

7. For three days, the concert site was the third most populous city in New York. To serve its sanitation needs, how many "Port-O-Sans" were installed at the festival?

a) 500
b) 2,000
c) 10,000

8. The late Yippie leader Abbie Hoffman demanded $50,000 from the promoters. If he didn't get it, what did he threaten would happen?

a) The Yippies would put LSD in the water supply
b) He would fire bomb the stage
c) He would organize a strike by the performers
d) The Yippies would "streak" throughout the concert

9. A group of hippies from New Mexico flew to New York to act as organizers and spiritual advisers. What did they call themselves?

a) Hog Farm
b) The Merry Pranksters
c) Students for a Democratic Society

10. The leader of the group in question 9 acted as, among other things, stage announcer. Name him.

a) Tom Hayden
b) Wavy Gravy
c) Chip Monck

11. The opening act walked on stage and said, "Thank you. I hope it was worth the wait." Who was it?

a) Richie Havens
b) Joan Baez
c) John Sebastian

12. The festival began on a high note. Which of the following announcements came on the first day of the event?

a) "The Vietnam war is over!"
b) "The Mets have won the World Series!"
c) "The promoters of this concert have declared this a free festival!"

13. What group refused to go on unless it was paid $7,500 in cash?

a) The Grateful Dead
b) Sly & the Family Stone
c) Canned Heat

BARON WOLMAN

14. The most any act was paid was $18,000. Who was it?

a) The Who
b) Jimi Hendrix
c) Blood, Sweat & Tears

15. Two children were born at the festival. How many people died and how?

a) Two; one was run over by a tractor; the other died of a drug overdose.
b) Three died from food poisoning.
c) Four were killed in a fight.

16. When The Beatles were asked to perform at the concert, what was John Lennon's response?

a) Only if the money went to charity
b) Only for $1 million
c) Only if the Plastic Ono Band could play

17. A total of 31 acts performed at Woodstock. Which two of the following groups or performers did *not* appear at the festival?

a) Bob Dylan
b) Quill
c) Iron Butterfly
d) Creedence Clearwater Revival
e) Janis Joplin

18. Match the acts (a–f) to the songs they performed (1-6).

a) Jimi Hendrix
b) Joe Cocker
c) Joan Baez
d) Crosby, Stills, Nash & Young
e) Mountain
f) Canned Heat

1) "Marrakesh Express"
2) "Theme for an Imaginary Western"
3) "Izabella"
4) "Sweet Sir Galahad"
5) "Woodstock Boogie"
6) "With a Little Help From My Friends"

19. Match the performers (a–e) to their quotes (1–5).

a) Melanie
b) Arlo Guthrie
c) Graham Nash
d) Jimi Hendrix
e) Grace Slick

1) "Everybody's vibrating."
2) "New York State Thruway is closed, man!"
3) "We'd like to do a medley of our hit."
4) "I'm beautiful, wet people too."
5) "Maybe the new day might give us a chance, blah-blah, woof-woof."

20. What was the major medical problem at the concert?

a) drug overdoses
b) cut feet
c) snake bites
d) poison ivy

21. The albums of the concert sold over 5 million copies. Which group's recording was so bad that it had to be redubbed in the studio?

a) Crosby, Stills, Nash & Young
b) The Who
c) Jefferson Airplane
d) The Grateful Dead

22. The concert ended Monday morning with the playing of an unorthodox version of the "Star Spangled Banner" to a ragged crowd of 25,000 people. Who played the anthem?

a) The Who
b) Crosby, Stills, Nash & Young
c) Jimi Hendrix

23. On the last day of the festival, the headline of the Sunday New York *Daily News* read:

a) Hippies Mired in Sea of Mud
b) Three Days of Sex and Violence
c) Festival Locals Say "Get Out!"

24. In three days, the audience produced lots of good vibes. It also produced plenty of garbage. Approximately how much?

a) 5 tons
b) 100 tons
c) 500 tons

25. In the late Sixties, music festivals were all the rage. Put these festivals in the proper chronological sequence.

a) Altamont
b) Woodstock
c) Monterey Pop
d) Watkins Glen

IDENTIFYING THE ISSUES

By Robert Leighton

When 200 magazines compete for your attention on the newsstand, a distinctive logo is an important asset. *Esquire* and *People*, for example, are immediately recognizable because of the unique appearance of their titles.

For the 15 magazine titles on these pages, we've blurred the issues a bit by rendering each in another magazine's lettering. For instance, *Rolling Stone* is lettered in the style normally used by *National Lampoon*, while *National Lampoon* is rendered in the style of another magazine, etc. Can you match each magazine with its proper logo style? You may have the *Time* of your *Life* trying—if the puzzle doesn't drive you *Mad*.

Answers, page 186

TYPOGRAPHY BY DAVID HERBICK

ROLLING STONE

The New Yorker

Playboy

GAMES

TIME

OMNI

ESQUIRE

GOURMET

National Lampoon

ScientificAmerican

MAD

READER'S DIGEST

PEOPLE

Mademoiselle

CAN YOU ANSWER THIS?

By Henry Hook

You don't need to be a walking encyclopedia to do well on this quiz ... but it wouldn't hurt. Here are twenty questions on the extraordinary, the arcane, and the just plain trivial. This quiz is a toughie, but when you're done (and we mean after you've checked the answers), we're pretty sure you'll have added to your storehouse of interesting but useless knowledge.   *Answers, page 187*

1. In 1894, a man named Fred Ott made history when he sneezed. Explain.

2. Per acre, which was our better bargain: Alaska, or the Louisiana Territory?

3. Statues of heroes on horseback sometimes show the horses rearing. What is the significance, if any, of the horse's position?

4. Sheepdogs are trained to herd and guard sheep. Sled dogs are trained to pull Eskimo sleds. What are firedogs useful for?

5. What fruit has its seeds on the outside?

6. Why was it necessary for Admiral Byrd's Antarctic expedition to take along a refrigerator?

7. Among Michelangelo's many masterpieces, why is his Pièta unique?

8. Why did Orville—and not Wilbur—Wright make that first flight at Kitty Hawk?

9. French artist Claude Monet became financially independent at the age of 50. How? (No, not by selling his paintings.)

10. Before Iran was known as Persia, what was it called?

11. What creature can outrun a horse and roar like a lion but, unlike most other creatures of its type, can't fly?

12. What must happen to you before you can join the Caterpillar Club?

13. At 7:30 A.M. on January 22, 1943, the temperature in Spearfish, South Dakota was -4° F. So what?

14. In 1978, what book achieved the dubious distinction of being the book most frequently stolen from the public libraries in England?

15. The girl from Ipanema, the two gentlemen of Verona, or the little Dutch boy—who'd be most likely to stand up if an orchestra played "The Battle Hymn of the Republic"?

16. In 1925, a large crowd filled a hall in New York City's Hotel Roosevelt and watched Yale defeat Harvard in the finals of the first intercollegiate ... what?

17. Why is Beethoven's Fifth Symphony sometimes called the "Victory Symphony"?

18. In 1974, Seabee Leon L. Louie made naval history by being the first person court-martialed for hitting a commanding officer with a ___.

19. The traditional hangover cure in Hungary is to sip a jigger of vodka through a slice of something not usually found at a bar. What?

20. What's the commonest breed of canine housepet in Reykjavik, Iceland?

ACROSS, DOWN, AND ALL AROUND: CROSSWORDS WITH A TWIST

PATHFINDER

By Scott Marley

You'll need some straight thinking to work your way through this twisty crossword. Every answer makes one or more right-angle turns through the grid, beginning at the appropriately numbered square and proceeding in a path for you to determine. The letter after the clue number indicates the answer's starting direction—north, south, east, or west. The number in parentheses after the clue indicates the length of the answer. It will help you to know that each letter in the completed grid will appear in exactly two words—no more, no less. The first answer has been filled in as an example.

Answer, page 187

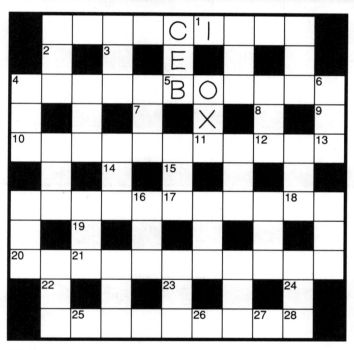

CLUES

1W Old-fashioned cooler (6)
1E South Sea locations (5)
2N Group of stores (5)
3N Because (5)
4E Coffee-chocolate blend (5)
5W *Outrageous Fortune* costar (5,6)
6S Chopping, as a tree (5)
7N Yankees' co-hometown club (4)
7S Noisy, acquisitive bird (6)
8N Gretel's brother (6)
9N Kubla Khan's home (6)
10N Far, far away (6)
11N Book after Genesis (6)
12W Promenading dance (8)
13W Yardstick marking (4)

14S Twerp (9)
15N Swampy spot (8)
16S Walk impatiently (4)
17E Like adhesive (6)
18E The "A" in Chester A. Arthur (4)
19S Forecast for Noah? (4)
20N Kind of day or hockey (5)
21W 1966 Michael Caine role (5)
22S Strict precision (5)
23N Speak from memory (6)
24N Suez or Panama (5)
25W "Material ___" (Madonna hit) (4)
26W Lake of Hollywood (8)
27W Vacillate (5)
28W Swing back and forth (4)
28N Scamp (8)

HELTER-SKELTER

By Mike Shenk

Helter-Skelter is a crossword variation in which the answers interlock in eight different directions. To solve, write the answer to each clue beginning in the grid square corresponding to the clue number and proceeding in a straight line toward—and, if necessary beyond—the next consecutive number. The first two answers—BEELINE and EL PASO—have been entered in Helter-Skelter 1 as examples. When each puzzle is completed, every square in the grid will be filled.

Answers, page 187

HELTER-SKELTER 1

¹B	²E	⁵E	L	¹²I	N	E	¹¹
		19	¹⁷L	18			
			4	³P			
⁶			27	⁷A			
13	9			S			10
5		20		24		23	O
		16	25				26
14	8	15		21		22	

HELTER-SKELTER 2

⁷	1				6	2
		4	22	21	25	24
8				18		9
		11	26		12	
	20					
	19	3		10	27	5	23
	16			17		
15					13	14

CLUES

1 Direct course
2 Texas city: 2 wds.
3 Patriot pamphleteer Thomas
4 *M*A*S*H* star
5 "Slowly" or "surely," e.g.
6 Stamp, as a parking lot ticket
7 Turn aside
8 Performance by Mr. Bojangles: 2 wds.
9 Muslim whirler
10 Puts on the burner
11 In one's dotage
12 Homer classic
13 Surrealist Salvador
14 Suffering from poison ivy
15 Per ___ income
16 TV reception aid
17 Inclined
18 Sprite
19 Used an emery board
20 Hudson's frequent costar
21 Hindu exercise system
22 Uncut diamond or ruby
23 Light motorbike
24 Salary
25 Geometry class calculation
26 In the thick of
27 Oxford VIPs

CLUES

1 Jack Webb's series
2 Found, as a missing person
3 Phone user
4 Feat for Houdini
5 South Dakota's capital
6 Fencer's cry: 2 wds.
7 Flow forth from a source
8 Players in a "best players" game
9 Quest
10 Kingdom
11 Cupid, for one
12 Favorite place to hang out
13 Mao ___-tung
14 Sites of stolen loot
15 Motorcycle attachment
16 Fragrant smoke source
17 Build
18 Journey
19 Played the stripper
20 Sunrise site
21 Driver's aid?
22 The Protestant work ___
23 Woman's undergarment
24 Once, in olden days
25 Feature of a skunk's back
26 Find another purpose for
27 Fancy coffee dispenser

PENCIL POINTERS

By Karen Hodge

In this crossword the clues appear in the grid itself. Enter the answers in the direction of the pointers.

Answer, page 187

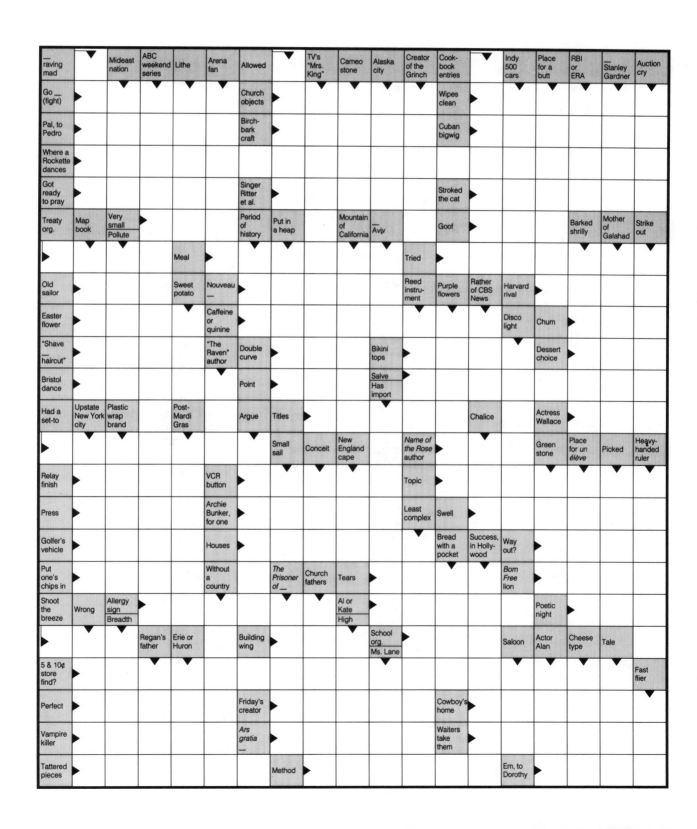

A MATTER OF MINUTES

A CROSSWORD MYSTERY

By Scott Marley

The missing words in this story will solve the puzzle, and vice versa—solving the puzzle will decipher the story. (A = Across; D = Down)

I was too excited to remain late in bed last Wednesday morning. The previous day's mail had brought me a whole batch of one **49A** stamps from a friend stationed near Milan— his return address was an **50D** (abbr.) number in Tampa, **48A** (abbr.)—and I had risen early, eager to begin pasting them in my album.

So I was understandably annoyed when Alex Knight phoned me and said he needed my help at once. Still, when the great detective sends out an **36D**, there's always a good reason for it. I reluctantly closed the album and **45D** uphill the seven blocks to his apartment.

I discovered him squinting at his fried eggs through the **73A** of his magnifying glass. "I shall have to instruct Georgina once more on the **41A** and don'ts of what the Romans called '**35D** fricta,'" he sighed. "And this melon isn't **3D** at all." He sprinkled oregano and **8D** on his eggs and began to eat.

"So what's going on?" I asked, as I **70A** on the mantelpiece. "Why is Lieutenant Igglesby here?"

"Don't be obtuse. It's the Mankos case," said Alex, pouring me a cup of undrinkably strong **29A**. "Surely you've heard about it?"

"I read the **39A** (abbr.) report in the morning paper," I replied. "Joshua Mankos, the music critic, was murdered late last night."

"Mankos was writing in bed when someone came in and shot him five times," said Lieutenant Igglesby. "He stumbled out of bed just before

he died. There was more **1A** than in a low-budget horror movie."

"I'm all **64A**," said Alex eagerly. "Describe the scene of the crime to me."

"It's a large bedroom," said Igglesby, "and looks even larger because of the **21A** that covers the entire south wall from floor to ceiling. The bed is against the north wall. On the left of the bed is a **57A**; on the right stood a **32D**. The woman next door saw the scene just moments after the shooting. Perhaps you'd like to come to the station and have a **14D**-à-**14D** with her yourself."

Fifteen minutes later we were listening to Millicent Featherdown describe the events of the previous night. "It was a clear, **9D** night," she began. "I was watching **72A** (2 wds.) reruns on the television when suddenly I heard shots from next door. I ran over at once to **24D** if Mr. Mankos was all right. The door was locked, but the bedroom curtains weren't quite **9A**. I looked through the **57A** and there was Mr. Mankos lying on the floor next to the bed. He was **74A**, and all the blood everywhere made me feel **22D**. I couldn't **52A** a sound. I was so horrified that I **46A** fainted." Mrs. Featherdown wiped away a **38D**. "He had **54A** the **32D** next to the bed, and everything on it had tumbled to the floor."

"What was on the floor?" asked Alex.

"I remember a clock, and a picture in an **2D** frame. I only got a quick glimpse of the room, because at **37A** moment someone—the killer, no doubt—came up behind me and hit me on the head, knocking me out. I don't remember anything else until the police found me lying in the **56D**."

"Do you know what time you were knocked out?" asked Alex.

"It was **4D 29D** exactly. I know because of the clock on the floor."

After Igglesby had taken Mrs. Featherdown into the next room, we talked.

"What kind of **13A 1D** in one's **56A** (abbr.) makes one capable of such a grisly crime?" I said.

"More likely it's cash, not chromosomes," said Alex, writing in his notebook. "Had Mankos an **10D**?" he asked Igglesby.

"Three of them, and we're pretty sure one of them did it. There were no signs of a break-in. Mankos always **5A** the key to his house under the **47D** so his children could **65A** at any time. Since only his children knew about the key, it has to be one of them. **17A** one of them stands to inherit a bundle. I've had them **53D** since last night, but so far none of them has done anything suspicious. The big problem is, each one has an ironclad **28D**. I've got the **30A** right here," he said, picking up a sheet of paper.

As Igglesby spoke I watched Alex draw a round clock face in his notebook. Then he **61D** the paper out of the book, turned it over, and held it up to the light. His actions mystified me.

"The eldest child is named **58D**," Igglesby continued. "Three years ago he became a devout orthodox Jew, and since then has criticized his father for having neglected his heritage and not knowing any of the Jewish **68A**. Last night he had a late class a few blocks from Mankos's house, and witnesses say he didn't leave until **4D 29D** precisely. Even driving his **51A**, he'd need a minute or two to get to his father's house."

"What sort of class?" I asked.

"He was learning the **14A**. Funny thing, though: He doesn't know how to read or **24A** in Hebrew, so he's memorizing it by **69A**."

"The second child is named **40A**, and she's a famous operatic soprano starring in **18A** here in town."

"Not the divine Rigatoni?" I gasped. Only Friday I had heard her sing the beautiful **62D** "O patria mia." She had a **67D** that made her look truly Egyptian, although she had certainly acquired it on the Riviera. Her backless, floor-length costume had shown off the **16A** of her neck, and as she walked I had glimpsed now and then a delicate **20D**. "But isn't she Italian?"

"No, she's **40A** Rigatoni **66D** Mankos, all right. She was on her way to a nearby cast party after the opera last night, and witnesses say she showed up precisely at **4D 29D**. Even in a taxi, it would have taken her a minute or two to get there from her father's house."

"Any motive besides the money?"

"Mankos was as tyrannical as a Russian **12D** with her. There's been a **26D** between them for years. He was writing a review of her latest role when he was murdered. Have a look."

We read the paper Igglesby handed us. It was handwritten, and began: "Last night, Ms. Rigatoni may have been trying to **19A** opera to new heights, but instead she sank it down a mine **31D** of unfathomable depths. May I be **26A**? Sensitive ears were **42D** by each harsh note, and her entire performance was enough to **27D** all who truly **5D** music. Every time she raises her voice, she **34A** our morale. Though it is now too late to **11D** the harm she did last night, perhaps there is still time to ask the governor for a **25D**."

"If she shot him, I can't say I blame her," laughed Alex. "Who's number three?"

"The youngest child is named **43A**. He's a ne'er-do-well, and as slippery as an **33A**. He's spent the last five summers bumming around Europe, traveling **7D** and wide, from the south of Greece to old **71A** in the north. He's been constantly in **44A**; when he was home he was always asking his father to **63D** him a few **15A** or twenties, which he spent in various **60D** of iniquity. At **4D 29D** he was making a connection at the airport 15 miles from here. He arrived on a flight five minutes **6D** the crime, and five minutes after it he was on another flight heading due **23A** (abbr.) out of town."

Alex closed his eyes and spoke. "So we have one suspect whose **28D** ends precisely at **4D 29D**, another whose **28D** *starts* at **4D 29D**, and a third who has no **28D** for **4D 29D** exactly, but who couldn't have killed Mankos unless he could travel 30 miles in a matter of minutes."

"Exactly," replied Igglesby. "So can you figure this out?"

"A trivial case for a detective of my abilities," said Alex.

"Your head's starting to **55D**," I warned him. "Surely you can't have solved the case already?"

"I think I'm getting **57D**," smiled Alex, scribbling a few words on a piece of paper. "Give this **59D** to Mrs. Featherdown, and ask her to answer the question I've written on it." Igglesby took the paper out of the room and returned a few moments later.

"She says it was **60A**," said Igglesby.

"Just as I suspected," chuckled Alex. "And now I know who killed Joshua Mankos."

What question did Alex ask Mrs. Featherdown?

Who killed Joshua Mankos?

Answer, page 187

MARCHING BANDS

By Mike Shenk

The words in this puzzle march around the grid in two ways. In one formation ("Rows"), words march across—two words for each numbered line, reading consecutively from left to right. The dividing point between these answers is for you to determine, except in row 7, where the words are separated by a black square. In the second formation ("Bands"), words march around each of the six shaded and unshaded bands, starting at the lettered squares (A, B, C, D, E, and F) and proceeding in a clockwise direction, one word after another. For example, Band "A," when filled, will contain six consecutive words (a through f) starting in square "A" and reading around the perimeter of the grid. Band "B" will contain a similar series of six words starting in square "B." Again, the dividing point between these answers is for you to determine. All clues are given in order. When the puzzle is completed, each square in the grid will have been used once in a Row word and once in a Band word.

Answer, page 187

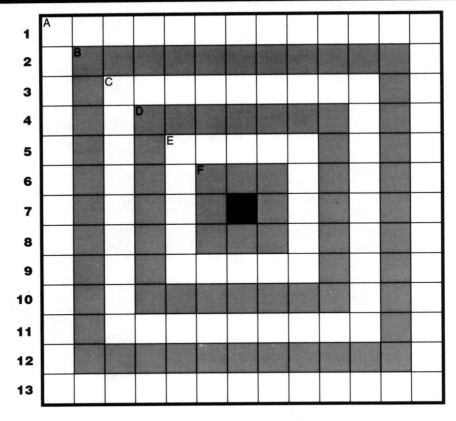

ROWS

1 a Stole stuff?
  b Temperature adjuster
2 a Diving unit
  b Grave engraving
3 a Shriner's topper
  b Occurring by chance
4 a "Lonely Boy" singer
  b Hidden from sight
5 a Prepared the beef
  b Business gain
6 a Take to one's heels
  b Coast
7 a Prepare porkers for the fair
  b Goes like a bat out of hell
8 a Crackers
  b Zigzag
9 a Ruffles feature
  b Poke fun at
10 a Skillful
  b Poison for Christie
11 a Impertinent
  b Outdoor
12 a Go by
  b Like lamas
13 a Supplies with a crew
  b Gland output

BANDS

A a Remotest
  b Olympics participants
  c Check out the enemy territory
  d Piper rival
  e Arizona city
  f Dregs of society
B a Occurring in the house (hyph.)
  b Heart sound
  c Tactless
  d Takes the bait
  e *Have Gun Will Travel* hero
  f Independently
C a Whitish metal
  b Pointed out
  c Indy winner Al
  d Criticize harshly
  e Part of Miss Muffet's meal
  f Shipbuilding wood
D a Is for you?
  b Sympathy card sentiments
  c 10:1, for example
  d Peter's watch
E a TV tycoon Turner
  b Not C.O.D.
  c Singer Cara et al.
F a Riders

SIAMESE TWINS

By Mike Shenk

This puzzle gives you two grids for the price of one. And two sets of clues to go with them, so you can work both crosswords at the same time. What's the catch? Each clue number is followed by two different clues to two different answers. The puzzle is to figure out which answer goes in which grid. The answers to 1-Across have been filled in for you. *Answers, page 188*

ACROSS

1 Noted circus founder ... ... and his partner
7 Clergyman
  Fact
12 Shows up
  Pseudonyms
14 Last Greek letter
  Make amends
15 Butte's state
  Most hip
16 Unhip ones
  Hat trick trio
17 Science magazine
  Elmer's antagonizer
18 Part of a disguise, often
  ___-tac-toe
20 What Oliver Twist wanted
  Actor Kristofferson
21 Thumbs-down vote
  Altar vow: 2 wds.

22 Folk hero ___ Bill
  Portions out
24 "Golly!"
  Butterfly catcher
25 Wine stewards' needs
  Like the best cabins on the liner
27 Like many newspapers
  Porterhouse, e.g.
29 Breakfast bread
  Castle surrounders
30 Went crazy: 2 wds.
  Bedtime farewells: 2 wds.
32 Rowboat propeller
  Needless bother
33 Queen ___ lace (wildflower)
  Valentine, for one
34 Once around the track
  On the "pro" side
37 Tubs
  Coal boat

39 Nipper was its mascot
  Talk, talk, talk
40 Building toy brand
  Cassette contents
41 Site of England's Derby
  Old TV parts
43 Two-continent land mass
  Persuaded: 2 wds.
45 Inventor Howe
  France's longest river
46 Flying high
  Project's beginning
47 Velocity
  Pool table triangles
48 Convulsions
  Double sawbuck

DOWN

1 BLT ingredient
  Thumper's friend
2 Spoken
  Scent
3 Fab Four drummer
  Sarcastic writing style
4 Turner and "King" Cole
  1953 Leslie Caron movie
5 Genesis name
  "Born in the ___"
6 Road repair sign: 2 wds.
  Days gone by
7 Panel truck
  Astro or Pluto
8 News article
  Run ___ (go wild)
9 Riot control aid: 2 wds.
  Small crown
10 Julie of *Victor/Victoria*
  Least attractive

11 Lumps of matter
  Fixes a fast clock
13 Goes yachting
  Gum helping
19 Yuri Gagarin and comrades
  Be fired: 3 wds.
22 First Family of 1845
  Singer Ross
23 Highlanders
  Tonto's horse
25 G-man
  Spy's org.
26 ___ Vegas
  Scoundrel
27 Blood Count?
  Fizzy drink: 2 wds.
28 1982 Dustin Hoffman film
  Like some exercises
30 "Old Folks at Home" composer
  Judges' bangers
31 Chops into cubes
  Chews
34 Avoids eating
  Deathtrap author Ira
35 Morphine source
  Actor's rep
36 Bess's beau
  Harvests
38 Tender
  Needing Charles Atlas's course
40 Scarlett's home
  Folk tales
42 Old draft org.
  Pre-___ (doc-to-be's major)
44 Slangy denial
  Run-DMC's music

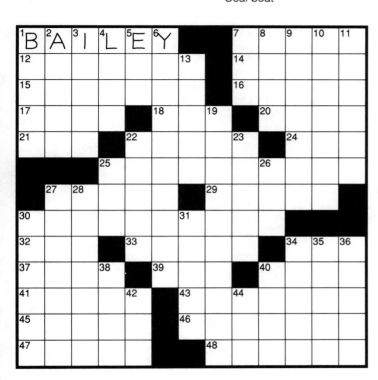

TRICKSTER CROSSWORD

By David Shulman

This is GAMES's only crossword puzzle in which the answers were decided by a vote of the magazine's editors. It's also the only crossword to have provoked fights in the office. The reason is that each clue in the puzzle suggests two arguably correct answers. Is 1-Across, for example, MESH or MESS? The answers reveal our choices, based on logic, word use, and general appropriateness, as decided by the majority vote of the editors when presented with the two words. Our reasons—and the votes—are given, too, so you can compare your thinking with ours.

Answers, page 188

ACROSS

1 Sometimes you get this when you try to mix two different things.

5 ___ about a person can annoy him if he's sensitive.

6 The faulty casting of this might get one off on the wrong foot.

8 It doesn't pay to be ___ when you are questioned by the police.

9 After a Halloween party, the host may find several ___ of apple cider left unfinished.

11 An experienced cowboy can identify a ___ of cattle as his own, even from a distance.

13 It takes a steady pilot to ___ an airplane through a rough storm.

14 If he is ___, a job hunter might have an improved chance of being hired.

15 People should be careful when handling one that is fragile.

DOWN

1 Getting a good ___ may stimulate a patient.

2 At the right time, a ___ may alert one to impending danger.

3 Our beach day was disappointing because we didn't have any ___.

4 The ___ hardly covers the starlet's famous legs.

7 Many political candidates ___ their campaign promises.

10 In the middle of the ___, some soldiers undoubtedly think about deserting.

11 Its value is reduced when it has leaks.

12 A gambler may have started on the road to ruin with this.

STEPQUOTE

By Eugene T. Maleska

The "Stepquote" is a crossword featuring a quotation running in stairstep-fashion down the grid. The invention of Eugene T. Maleska, now the crossword editor for the *New York Times*, the puzzle made its controversial debut in the *Times* back in July 1964. Many solvers then couldn't make heads or tails of the puzzle gimmick, and the paper was deluged with complaints. Today, however, the Stepquote is one of crossword puzzling's standards. The puzzle on this page is based on a favorite quotation of Maleska's. Can you solve the crossword to discover it?   *Answer, page 188*

ACROSS

1 Stepquote
5 I.R.A., for one
9 Author of the Stepquote
14 Wing-shaped
15 Whom Moslems praise
16 Sight at New Orleans
17 "Vive ___!" (old French cry)
18 Tropical climber
19 Coeur d'___, Idaho
20 The sun
22 Persephone's mother
24 Bedouin
26 "Runaway" singer Shannon
27 Cobbler's equipment
30 TV character from Melmac
33 Studio time
35 Embezzler's target
37 Below, in poesy
39 *Amadeus* setting
40 *Brigadoon* costume designer's choice
42 Spent
44 Pickpocket
45 Still kicking
46 Shepherd's home
48 The Holy Grail, e.g.
49 Digression
51 Robot's creator
55 Fabric first made in 1941
57 Like a tumbler
58 Battle of Britain VIPs
61 Near-sighted cartoon character
64 Pony Express method
65 Minos's mother
67 Two-dimensional
69 Old-fashioned teaching method
70 Pays a short visit
72 Hall-of-Famer Williams
73 Word above WALK
74 Tortoise's snapper
76 Get the wash ready
77 Necessities for hay fever season
80 Mary Hart of *Entertainment Tonight*, e.g.
84 Jim Croce's "I Got ___"
86 Miss USA prop
88 First all-electronic computer
90 Source of the Stepquote, March 15, 1963
91 Plume source
92 Scout leader?
93 Express checkout units
94 Aptly named English poet

DOWN

1 Sidekick
2 Butter substitute
3 Viscount's superior
4 Walked on
5 Noted retiree of 1979
6 Habilimented
7 Thrashed
8 Henley Regatta site
9 Motorist's headache
10 Flack's issuance
11 Break a watch, perhaps
12 Hundredth of a Brunei dollar
13 Pipe joint
15 Pacified
21 Algerian port
23 Soccer squad
25 Ham's father?
28 Anderson of *WKRP* fame
29 Quick pic
30 How some stocks are sold
31 Charles de Gaulle's birthplace
32 Show one's inability to swim
34 Liqueur-brandy cocktail
36 Boiling over
38 Left in a hurry
41 Leaves in a hurry
43 Miami-to-NYC heading
47 Tavern order
49 Pitcher's "soupbone"
50 All, for one
52 Series starter, often
53 Delight
54 Entered, as computer data
56 Metropolitan business weekly
58 Funnyman Foxx
59 Gold: Prefix
60 Land abutting the street
62 Klutzes
63 Sandlot game
66 Best
68 River that gave Iberia its name
71 Like German words after "das"
75 Stocking shade
78 Pictures
79 Pulitzer poet Teasdale
81 ___ about (roughly)
82 ___-Soviet relations
83 Words from an Exeter exiter
84 Bird: Prefix
85 "The Road ___ Taken" (poem by 9-Across)
87 Cherry, e.g.
89 Barracks feature

LOVE LETTERS

By Trip Payne

In honor of lovers everywhere, this novel crossword puzzle appears in the shape of a heart. Each answer is to be entered across or down in the grid starting in the appropriately numbered square. In rows and columns containing two or more words, consecutive words will "embrace" each other—that is, overlap by one or more letters.

Answer, page 188

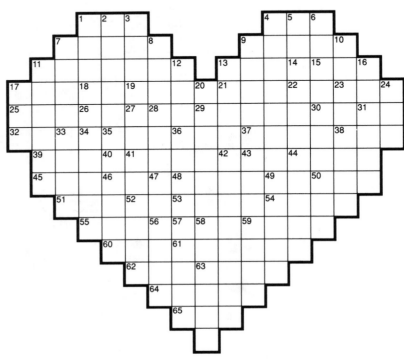

ACROSS

1 *Love of Life*'s network (1951-80)
4 Robust energy
7 Small stream
9 Trite
11 Place for a date, perhaps
13 Leia's love, Han ___
14 Buckeye's state
17 What to "let me call you"
21 ___ *Romances* ('60s comic book)
22 Twangy
25 At love-all, in tennis
26 "That's Amore" singer Martin
27 ___ Boleyn (one of Henry VIII's loves)
29 Breadwinner
30 Heart ___ (EKG reading)
32 Remove a fastener from
34 Inherent
36 "Perfect" beauties
37 Tracked prey
39 Like Keebler's bakers?
40 Passionate
43 Actress Brennan
45 Hearts, for one
46 "Toodle-oo!"
48 Greek goddess of wisdom
49 Identified

51 Sing "shooby-dooby-do"
52 Use a keyboard
53 Became cheerful: 2 wds.
55 "___ go bragh!"
56 And not
58 Took a break
60 Richard Lovelace, for one
61 Henry VIII and kin
62 Basketball great Archibald
63 Ernie Kovac's love, ___ Adams
64 James Dean character
65 "Love Touch" singer Stewart

DOWN

1 Statement of belief
2 Vanquished
3 Son of Adam and Eve
4 February card
5 Hole-___ (golfer's ace)
6 ___-jongg
7 Chick's sound
8 Peachy
9 Afrikaaners
10 Actress Bonet
11 Strings
12 Carry on
13 Laurel and Musial
14 *Love Story* star
15 Cotton Club setting

16 Horse's morsel
17 Character actor Erwin
18 Massive building
19 Barbera's cartooning partner
20 Come into again
23 Japanese drink
24 Was a forerunner
28 Smartly dressed
31 Take care of, with "to"
33 Asset
35 Bug larva
36 Tempest's place, perhaps
37 Searches for
38 1981 #1 hit "___ on Loving You"
41 Land
42 Followed Oliver North's example?
44 Loads cargo
46 Waterproofed canvas
47 *Cagney and Lacey*'s Daly
50 Kid's pie filling
54 Raison d'___
56 Close to
57 Playful mammal
58 Be sorry for
59 Earth
63 Black

THREE-WAY

By Brian Greer

You'll have to think in three directions at once to solve this hexagonal crossword puzzle. Words run across, down to the left, and down to the right. Every hexagon is used in at least two words.

Answer, page 188

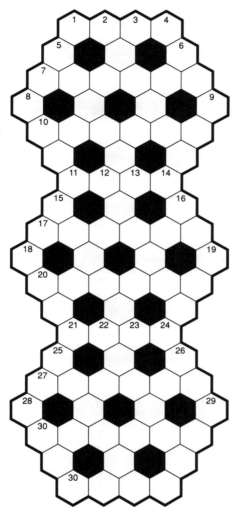

ACROSS

1 Once, long ago
7 Botch royally
10 Like waltz time
11 Short-term secretary
17 *The Count of Monte ___*
20 Baltimore flyer
21 Collector's goals
27 Bird related to the carp?
30 You can depend on it
31 Hippocrates wrote one

DOWN LEFT

1 Poet Lazarus
3 Lady of Spain
6 Go by
9 Hard to fathom
11 Diplomat's need
13 ___ d'
16 Ineffective
19 They're said to be attention-getting
21 Droops
23 Boy Scout units
26 Spain, to the Spaniards
29 Stocking material

DOWN RIGHT

2 Entertain superbly
4 Prepared to drive
5 Communism, Beijing-style
8 Rat-___ (machine gun sound)
12 Hands down
14 Christopher's bear
15 He makes a scene
18 Stocking stuffers?
22 Spews lava
24 Appear
25 "___ thee!" ("Begone!")
28 Not so hot

FOLD THIS PAGE

THE WORLD'S MOST ORNERY CROSSWORD

By Merl Reagle

The crossword on this and the next two pages has two independent sets of clues: "Hard" and "Easy." First, fold this page back on the dashed line so the clues below face the solving grid on page 145. If you use only the Hard Clues (appearing below and continuing under the grid), you'll find the puzzle uncommonly challenging. If you want help, or prefer a less severe challenge, open to the Easy Clues (tucked in beneath your fold on page 144).

Answer, page 189

HARD CLUES

ACROSS

1 Fills all vacancies
11 Fixes greens, perhaps
15 Washer-dryer?
24 Confirmed
25 Kind of bonds or dollars
26 Drop the ___ (make an awaited revelation)
27 Anagrams
28 Olympic fighter?
29 *From the Earth to the Moon* traveler
30 Greek salad ingredient
31 1980 Olympic mascot
33 One for the road?
34 French political division
35 Cato's "with"
38 "Ain't That Peculiar" singer
40 Steinbeck's ___ *Down*
43 Nirvana attainer
46 Weak-looking
48 Be convinced, eventually
51 "Thy ___ warm": *Romeo and Juliet*
53 Eppie's guardian of fiction
54 Stephen Scheuer reference book
55 Little Leticia
56 M.P.H.
57 Weighs ___ (is massive)
58 Glass of Bordeaux?
59 Scalp ointment
61 Robt. E. Lee title
62 Clothes-beating clubs
64 Escaping the sheriff, perhaps
67 Uranologist
68 Fled safely
69 Letter openers?
70 Job-hunter's edges
71 Friends in fraud
72 Like a perfect game
75 "Kisser"
78 Became, in British suffixes
80 Furnaceman
81 Words of emphasis
83 RMN's '68 opponent
84 Top student's org.
85 Hammock cords
86 Federal watchdog, for short
87 Hwy.
88 Mexican city or state
91 Like TV's Jessica Fletcher
92 Capital of *Österreich*
93 Acquiescent
94 Dog in an Inge title
95 Anyone
97 Actor Bannen
98 "Sweet as Apple Cider" girl
100 Basque region
102 Balance-beam queen of 1972
107 Arabian, e.g.
109 Popular candidates
110 Piccadilly Circus statue
111 Domestic-affairs course
112 Papal museum
113 Facility
114 Pickpocket, in slang
115 Agents, for short
116 Aspen and others
119 Piece of gossip
120 Silent's length, perhaps
122 Walkman's bulky relative
123 *Ghosts* writer and family
124 Inverted V
125 Means to an end
127 Application form abbr.
129 Actress Ruby
130 "Boy, ___ dummy!"
132 Atlanta's Turner
133 Empties a pool
136 Russian poet Mandelstam
138 Penguins' realm
141 Where Anna Owens taught
142 Stoogean statement
147 Careless comments
148 River through the Fens
149 Justice of the peace

THE WORLD'S MOST ORNERY CROSSWORD *(Continued)*

Don't Peek Until You Read Page 143!

EASY CLUES

ACROSS

1 Sells every seat: 2 wds.
11 Puts in new turf
15 "His" or "hers" item: 2 wds.
24 Settled in habit
25 Continental prefix
26 Drop the ___ (end the suspense): 2 wds.
27 Shuffles
28 Greek war god
29 Jules Verne moongoer (CARIBBEAN anag.)
30 Greek cheese (FATE anag.)
31 Actor Auer (CHAIM'S anag.)
33 Mustang or Pinto
34 *Coup d'___*
35 *Summa ___ laude*
38 Singer Marvin
40 ___ *Blue* (controversial movie of 1953): 3 wds.
43 Monk who has attained nirvana (A HART anag.)
46 Short of hemoglobin
48 Wake up: 2 wds.
51 "Our ___ Sealed," Go-Gos hit: 2 wds.
53 Eliot's ___ *Marner*
54 Best-selling film guide: 3 wds.
55 "Oh, ___-tosh!"
56 Speed: Abbr.
57 Hit like ___ of bricks: 2 wds.
58 Window: Fr. (REEF NET anag.)
59 Perfumed ointment (APEDOM anag.)
61 Military commander: Abbr.
62 Badminton-like rackets (DEBTOR'S TALE anag.)
64 Leaving on horseback: 2 wds.
67 Copernicus was one
68 Escaped when seconds counted: 4 wds.
69 *20/20*'s network
70 ___ and outs
71 Heist helpers
72 Like a perfectly pitched game
75 ___ *in Boots*
78 Past-tense ending, in England
80 Ore refinery
81 "There's no doubt in my mind ...": 2 wds.
83 LBJ's veep
84 School honor group: Abbr.
85 Fastening cords
86 Govt. drug agency: Abbr.
87 Road: Abbr.
88 Mexican state (AGROUND anag.)
91 Having lost a husband
92 Vienna, to a native
93 "Blessed are the ___ ...": 2 wds.
94 Solomon's Queen of ___
95 Unspecified person
97 Author Fleming
98 Actress Lupino
100 French-Spanish mountain range: 2 wds.
102 Popular 1972 gymnast: 2 wds.
107 Arab or Israeli, e.g.: 2 wds.
109 Successful politicians
110 God of love
111 School cooking course: 2 wds.
112 Roman museum (A RENTAL anag.)
113 Leisure
114 Ice cream scoop
115 Congressmen, for short
116 Stowe and Vail: 2 wds.
119 Vague rumor (I DON'T anag.)
120 Movie-short length: 2 wds.
122 Sound system type: 2 wds.
123 Playwright Henrik and family
124 Insertion mark
125 Advantageous
127 867-5309, e.g.: 2 wds., abbr.
129 Ruby or Sandra
130 Mudfish genus (in MACADAMIAS)
132 TV's Koppel
133 Tub outlets
136 Poet Mandelstam (IPSO anag.)
138 Of the South Pole
141 Thailand, once
142 Comment from Curly: 4 wds.
147 Irresponsible gossip: 2 wds.
148 English river (in MOUSETRAP)
149 Police-court judge
150 Campers' meccas: 2 wds.
151 Japanese apricots (MUSE anag.)
152 Rose-flowered European herb: 2 wds.

DOWN

1 Indian town (RIB anag.)
2 Dollar bill
3 Laboratory eggs
4 Notch made by a saw (in BEAKERFUL)
5 River of New York: 2 wds.
6 Washington state airport (A CASTE anag.)
7 Yea ___: 2 wds.
8 Fall behind
9 Article
10 Mr. Arnaz
11 *The ___* (1955 John Wayne movie): 2 wds.
12 Term for Dudley Do-Right: 2 wds.
13 "You're kidding yourself!": 2 wds.
14 "Help!"
15 Comedians ___ Ray: 2 wds.
16 Popular video game company
17 By way of: Abbr.
18 Heracles' wife (in THE BEATLES)
19 Three-chambered tomb (HIT TRAP anag.)
20 Annual film awards
21 Cry of discovery: 4 wds.
22 Geologic period
23 Singer Peggy
32 Navigates
33 Makes complex
35 Winter melon
36 Quarterback Johnny
37 New York Giants slugger of the '30s: 2 wds.
39 Cost cuts
41 Came up with better strategies
42 Inserted: 2 wds.
44 Sports hall
45 Actor Savalas
47 Krishna verses (TRANS AM anag.)
49 End ___ (tumbling): 2 wds.
50 Bishops' caps (REMITS anag.)
52 ___ *a Letter to My Love*, '81 film: 2 wds.
54 "The Devil made ___ it!": 2 wds.
55 Piglike jungle animal
58 Swordfighting sport
60 Engine
61 Physicist George ___ (GO MAW anag.)
63 Lofting tennis shot
64 Intermediary
65 Artists' studios (EARLIEST anag.)
66 Cotton machines
68 Final words from Pac-Man: 2 wds.
73 "It must've been something ___": 2 wds.
74 TV's *Star ___*
75 Univ. degrees, for short
76 "Nope!": 2 wds.
77 Con artist: 2 wds.
79 The Broadway crowd: 2 wds.
80 Able to look from side to side, as some turtles
82 Erich von ___, *Chariots of the Gods!* author
85 Resistant to wear
86 Hand's end
89 Lie-___ (late risers)
90 Former soccer league: Abbr.
91 Not as well
92 ___ Mondale: 2 wds.
93 Weasellike carnivores (STAR MEN anag.)
96 *Outland* director Peter (AM SHY anag.)
97 Steep odds: 3 wds.
99 Period
101 Girlish giggle
103 Turkish officials (SAGA anag.)
104 Like an abacus
105 Pertaining to bears
106 Sleeping sickness fly
107 Type of French wine (CODE M anag.)
108 Women's chess figure Levitina (IN AIR anag.)
109 Biblical queen of Persia (VA. HITS anag.)
112 Star of TV's *Life With Father*: 2 wds.
115 Calls it quits
117 Metallic element
118 Clear the cassette again
119 Woodwind players
121 Put a new disguise on
122 Small spots
123 Not take "no" for an answer
126 Scrabble 8-pointer: 2 wds.
128 Funnyman Morris
131 Play's start: 2 wds.
134 ___ de plume (pen names)
135 Playwright George Bernard
137 Lima's country
138 European peak
139 Free of taboo, in Tahiti (ONA anag.)
140 Rat-a-___
141 Not care a ___
143 Mature
144 Helium, for one
145 Actress Hagen
146 Longing

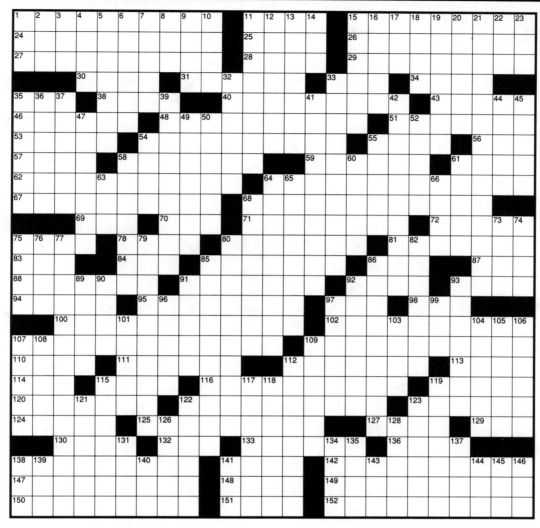

HARD CLUES (CONTINUED)

150 The Badlands and the Everglades, e.g.
151 Japanese ornamental trees
152 Flybane plant

DOWN

1 Hyderabad district
2 Countdown penultimate
3 Eggs
4 Sawyer's notch
5 Northern New York falls
6 Seahawks' airport
7 "Yea" follower
8 Trail
9 Object of gossip
10 Lucie's dad
11 WWII Wayne actioner, 1955 (with *The*)
12 "When we last left him, ___ …"

13 1973 Aerosmith hit
14 Sinking signal
15 ___ *Carol and Ted and Alice*
16 Video game pioneer
17 Via: Abbr.
18 Cupbearer to the gods
19 Tomb with three chambers
20 13½-inch statuettes
21 "Well, now!"
22 Long, long time
23 Antietam loser
32 Takes the wheel
33 Coils
35 Muskmelon's cousin
36 Super Bowl III quarterback
37 He hit 36 homers in '38

39 Alan Greenspan's worries
41 Bested, schemingly
42 Hid, in a way
44 Bowl
45 English "box"
47 Veda hymns
49 End ___ (spinning)
50 Holy hats
52 "___ a letter to my love"
54 "Love ___," Beatles hit
55 Rhino cousin
58 Selling stolen goods
60 Drive a roadster
61 Nuclear physicist George
63 Toss, as a grenade
64 L.P. Hartley novel (with *The*)

65 Couturiers' digs
66 Rummy finales
68 Arcade sign-off
73 "… ___ the whole thing"
74 Take a hike
75 Some doctorates
76 Lazy denial
77 Shark
79 Performers
80 Like some turtles
82 Author Erich von ___
85 Proven, in a way
86 Printing place?
89 Lie-___ (lazy ones)
90 The League of the Cosmos
91 Sicker
92 Fritz, as in Mondale
93 Weasel's cousins

96 *2010* director Peter
97 Long shot
99 "i" piece
101 Snicker sound
103 High Turks
104 Covered with drops
105 Bearlike
106 Dread fly
107 Bordeaux variety
108 Actress Demick
109 Biblical queen
112 Judy Garland's father in *Meet Me in St. Louis*
115 Hits the hay
117 Pen point metal
118 Clear the board again
119 Violist's neighbors
121 Cover up anew
122 Motes
123 Be adamant

126 High value Scrabble piece
128 Mandel of *St. Elsewhere*
131 Broadway opening?
134 Mark Twain and Lewis Carroll
135 *St. Joan* author
137 Cuzco's country
138 Gran Paradiso, e.g.
139 Profane, to a Maori
140 Make lace
141 Old French coin
143 Vital statistic
144 Laughing, e.g.
145 Iguana-like lizard
146 Dough for rice cakes?

PETAL PUSHERS

By Will Shortz

This magic flower blooms only when you recite the mystical incantation of 32 seven-letter answers. You can discover these special words with the help of the flower petals and the two sets of clues. Answer the clues and enter the words inward from the tips of the petals to the heart of the blossom (one letter in each space). Half the words proceed clockwise from the numbers; the other half counterclockwise. When you are done, take off your shoes, chant the words three times under a full moon, and all the magic properties of the flower will be yours.

Answer, page 189

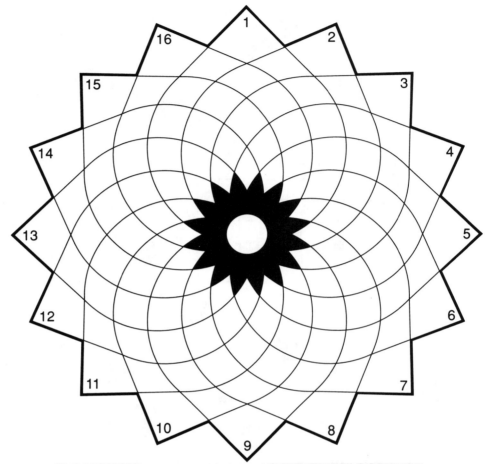

CLOCKWISE

1 Singer named after a Dickens character
2 Sculpted plant garden
3 Hostage takers
4 Ice cream in a glass
5 Solicit votes
6 In the black
7 Responsible for
8 Drives recklessly
9 Christ, in the Douay Bible
10 Port on the Gibraltar strait
11 Shells
12 Surrounded
13 Sellers' *Pink* ____
14 Biceps and others
15 Causing pain
16 Branding tool

COUNTERCLOCKWISE

1 Commits arson
2 Whispered gossip
3 Pine tree
4 Dead Sea Scroll material
5 Congressional hill
6 Leading 19th-century engraver
7 Follow the crowd
8 Crucifixion site
9 Bad: Fr.
10 Most succinct
11 Art emulsions
12 Say "yes"
13 Ominous engine sound
14 Actress Wallace and others
15 Bettors' intuitions
16 Con artist, of a sort

AMAZEMENT

By Mike Shenk

This puzzle is both a crossword and a maze. To solve, first complete the crossword in the usual manner. Then, starting in the first square of 1-Across, wind your way one square at a time (left, right, up, or down, but not diagonally) to the last square of 126-Across, traveling only through squares containing one of the letters in the answer at 69-Across. Watch for twists, turns, and dead ends, and don't get lost.

Answer, page 189

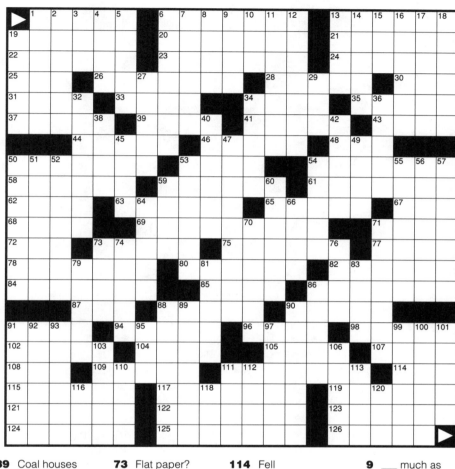

ACROSS

1 Hikers' route
6 Elections
13 Give one ___ (surprise)
19 Fender of Nashville
20 Magnetite, e.g.
21 Well-drilling tool
22 Elopement aid
23 Knesset home
24 Yom Kippur song
25 Past
26 Corn fodder, chopped sorghum, etc.
28 Plutonium or uranium
30 Ingmar's favorite actress
31 Turner of tunes
33 Sweatered songman
34 Needle source
35 Variety, to life
37 Bloodhound's track
39 Coal houses
41 Sicilian peak: Var.
43 Ultimate
44 Marcus Aurelius's doc
46 Bide one's time
48 "Life ___ jest": John Gay
50 Oblique
53 Hardens
54 Raising the spirits
58 Armpit
59 Like our numerals
61 Bulldozer
62 Bowling or passing, e.g.
63 Blueprint
65 Parenthetical comment
67 Mauna ___
68 He played Mingo in *Daniel Boone*
69 SEE INSTRUCTIONS
71 Fictional rafter
72 Massive
73 Flat paper?
75 Strengthen
77 Mil. school
78 Doodle's position
80 Tail
82 At the construction lot
84 Daytime TV, in part
85 Hand or foot
86 Harness racer
87 Nabokov novel
88 Take a shot
90 Opposite of *solo*
91 Zeus's disguise for Leda
94 O. Henry specialty
96 Disposition
98 Set foot in
102 Helmsman
104 Formicary residents
105 Originating in
107 Storm wind
108 Moreover
109 Gandhi's tongue
111 Like Oreos
114 Fell
115 Takes potshots
117 Satellite
119 Grammatical case
121 Hastings, to Poirot
122 ___ stone unturned
123 Played it up
124 Where the Windel winds
125 They lead sumwhere
126 Duke's ex

DOWN

1 Like *Hamlet* or *King Lear*, e.g.
2 Made over
3 Affix
4 Historical Senate date
5 Hart's contribution to Rodgers
6 A, C, or E
7 Mt. Hood's home
8 Painted tinware
9 ___ much as
10 Veterans' mo.
11 Filthier
12 Sexagenarian's goal
13 Geometer's calculation
14 Hawks
15 Randy's rinkmate
16 Aviatrix Putnam
17 Keepsakes
18 Tureen stand
19 Motoring delays
27 Like the brain or the ear
29 King topper, in pinochle
32 Part of L.A.
34 Bombay worshipper
36 Catcher's "home"
38 Exaggerated
40 Sultry
42 Was under the weather
45 Grazing greens
47 Calgary natives
49 Except
50 House owner, in Judaism
51 Give the once-over
52 Pickling need
53 Diving birds
54 Root of old politics
55 Not authorized
56 Infant
57 More stately
59 Cries of insight
60 "I ___ tell a lie"
64 Tobacco pipes
66 Haricot, e.g.
70 Result of overuse of salt
71 Quick weight-loss plan
73 Cargo
74 Chou ___
76 Left at sea
79 Nero's instrument
81 Sen. Long et al.
83 Jot down
86 Henry VIII's house
88 Blimp cabin
89 Peppy
90 *Corrida* heroes
91 Convulsions
92 Sift
93 Italic type style
95 Bled
97 Ruffle one's feathers
99 Gauguin setting
100 Lucky roll at craps
101 Emulate Zsa Zsa
103 Motif
106 Jason's helpful sorceress
110 "The doctor ___"
111 Take a bride
112 Akhenaten's god
113 Obstructs
116 Steno's need
118 Misbehaving
120 Kindergartner

HEX SIGNS

By Mike Shenk

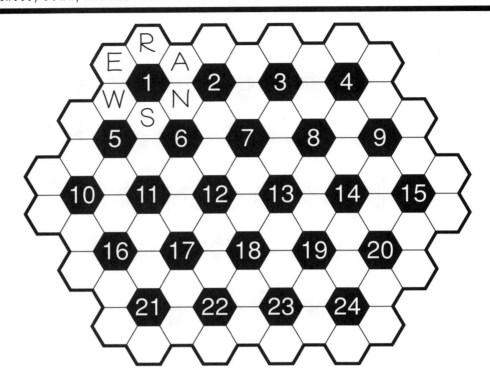

Each answer in this puzzle is six letters long. These six letters are to be entered into the six hexagons surrounding the appropriate number in the grid, reading clockwise or counter-clockwise. The direction, as well as the starting place, are for you to determine. Each clue consists of a sentence from which the consecutive letters of the answer have been removed and replaced with a star. The object is to reinstate the missing letters (supplying spacing as needed) to complete a sensible sentence. For example, the answer to #1 is ANSWER, which completes the sentence "The techniciANS WERe working with a salt water solution." As a bonus hint, each clue also contains a synonym or short definition of the answer (like "solution" in the example) somewhere within it.
Answer, page 189

1. The technici★e working with a salt water solution.
2. The spoiled child held the bowls and silverw★tily refusing to share.
3. On my movie scale, *Gandhi* is the k★te a four-star film.
4. In the desert stood a lone sagu★er a circling vulture.
5. Zack's unusu★pirits were a result of his failing to get any college grants.
6. The company chemist★ough indigo to make blue dye.
7. I didn't have to wait long for the razor bla★quested at the drugstore.
8. Overwork make★rict attorney become a cruel fellow.
9. Whenever I hear *Que S★a*, it eliminates my sorrows.
10. After riding a fa★er coaster, it may seem great just to walk.
11. That loafer's cousin is a nice guy, wart★l.
12. The self-ma★erived his income from his mail-order business.
13. The king's subjects sang the national an★pecially loud on his birthday.
14. The combo included two saxop★hree trombones, and an upright piano.
15. A host who is of good character will serve soup i★en.
16. Some health s★t their patrons' agility with pogo sticks.
17. For a dinner that's truly romanti★ritif is just the thing to whet the appetite.
18. The youngest Brownie be★ttled when she was separated from the troop.
19. A fellow for w★athing is difficult should see a doctor.
20. You'd be crazy to bet the far★lor at roulette where so much gambling is done.
21. To tell the truth, I prefer to for★ling bees if possible.
22. The police broad★d to the arrest of the man who tried to rook me.
23. The toy animals were made of bron★s, and tin.
24. Wh★oys get dolls, they're more likely to bury them than play with them.

LETTER DROPS

By Henry Hook

Once you've completed this crossword puzzle, drop the letters from the two shaded spaces in each column of the grid, in order, into the squares beneath that column. The result, reading from left to right, will spell a quotation and its source. *Answer, page 189*

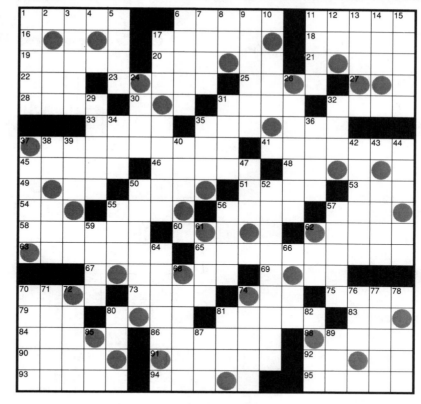

ACROSS

1 Yemen, in biblical times
6 "___ Theme," from *Doctor Zhivago*
11 Jeopardizes
16 *Battlestar Galactica* villain
17 Lapis follower
18 ___ form (at one's peak)
19 Fortification
20 Outfielder's cry
21 Nest egg
22 Radar dir.
23 Provide incentive
25 Advantage
27 Colorless
28 Near, in a kids' game
30 Oohs' mates
31 ___ about (roughly)
32 Lane co-worker
33 Be tangent to
35 "___ fool according to his folly": Proverbs
37 Tungstenlike element
41 Least unkempt
45 Steeds with spirit
46 On a streak?
48 Inlay alloy
49 Houston campus
50 Lines of fashion?
51 Acquired character
53 ___ *amis*
54 Nonsense
55 Word on a lunar map
56 Lesage hero Gil
57 Motions of agreement
58 1963 Lionel Bart musical
60 Snow obstacle
62 Depend (on)
63 "... before, and ___ it again"
65 Sans gifts?
67 Being a killjoy
69 Blent
70 Big name in cosmetics
73 Unescorted

74 Beachgoer's goal
75 Give audience to
79 Purpose
80 Vidal hero(ine)
81 It comes from the heart
83 Half of CIV
84 Former South African president
86 Michigan Indian
88 Babes in the woods
90 Comic strip county
91 Evolve on screen
92 Reputation
93 Gossipmonger
94 "The Road Not Taken" poet
95 More sprightly

DOWN

1 Cheat, none too nicely
2 Laughing one

3 Respected one
4 Accessory for Madame
5 Morrow or Murray
6 Nigerian capital
7 Radio-controlled bomb
8 The same old thing
9 1986 film sequel
10 Kind of strike or meal
11 Approach flood stage
12 Acct. addn.
13 Vermont resort
14 Islam Bible
15 Exhausted
17 Coffee additive
24 Trinket
26 ___ grass
29 Unsure reply
31 "This one's ___"
32 Allie's ally
34 Hardly the big shot?
35 Arctic divers

36 Minsky's event
37 Core
38 Memorial Stadium player
39 Milky
40 Undid the anonymity
42 Long Island city
43 TV's ___ *Hammer!*
44 Made the salad
47 Dutch earthenware
50 With enduring strength
52 Twin-hulled craft
55 Maître d's handout
56 Bob's *Road* pal
57 Beethoven's "Choral" symphony
59 Be inconstant
61 Mysterious letter
62 Hoodoo
64 Switch position
66 Pocket filler?
68 Where Eleanor Rigby kept her face
70 Mouseketeer on drums
71 "___ Mio"
72 Wyoming range
74 Namely
76 Bronco QB John
77 Danny of the NBA
78 Stair part
80 Crib cry
81 Fortas and Vigoda
82 Not care ___
85 Stolen
87 Veiled comment?
89 Docs' grp.

TRIBUTE TO ARTHUR WYNNE

By Mike Shenk

A few days before Christmas 1913, Arthur Wynne gave the world–and the readers of the *New York World*– a present bigger than he'd expected: the world's first crossword puzzle. Appearing in the newspaper's Sunday "Fun" section, his original Word-Cross (reprinted at right) was an immediate hit. Much to Wynne's surprise, the public demanded more—and crosswords have been with us ever since.

To mark the birthday of the crossword's creator, we wrapped a special present in the grid on the opposite page: Wynne's original puzzle. We took the grid from his Word-Cross (the shaded section of the grid) and built a modern crossword around it, incorporating the old words into the new puzzle. To join in our tribute, just add some words of your own in the blanks.

Answer, page 190

ACROSS

1 Hound
7 Delicately charming
13 '70s police show
17 Made an exit
21 ___ *Dying* (Faulkner novel)
22 Maestro Toscanini
23 Movie editor's technique
24 Plot unit
25 Wish for the Word-Cross
27 Starless casts
29 *Greystoke* extra
30 Indefinitely
31 No longer a minor
33 Dough distender
34 Tab, e.g.
35 Typesetting spaces
36 Saucer riders
37 Sleekly graceful
38 Tower town
41 Negligent
43 Join in Dungeons & Dragons
46 Gangster's gun
47 "Jawbone of ___" (Samson weapon)
49 Courtroom oath
50 $100-a-plate dinner, e.g.
52 Wedding ring setting

FUN'S *Word-Cross Puzzle.*

FILL in the small squares with words which agree with the following definitions:

2-3. What bargain hunters enjoy.
4-5. A written acknowledgement.
6-7. Such and nothing more.
10-11. A bird.
14-15. Opposed to less.
18-19. What this puzzle is.
22-23. An animal of prey.
26-27. The close of a day.
28-29. To elude.
30-31. The plural of is.
8-9. To cultivate.
12-13. A bar of wood or iron.
16-17. What artists learn to do.
20-21. Fastened.
24-25. Found on the seashore.

10-18. The fibre of the gomuti palm.
6-22. What we all should be.
4-26. A day dream.
2-11. A talon.
19-28. A pigeon.
F-7. Part of your head.
23-30. A river in Russia.
1-32. To govern.
33-34. An aromatic plant.
N-8. A fist.
24-31. To agree with.
3-12. Part of a ship.
20-29. One.
5-27. Exchanging.
9-25. Sunk in mud.
13-21. A boy.

Arthur Wynne's first crossword puzzle appeared on December 21, 1913. Although other crossword-like puzzles had appeared before 1913, Wynne was the first to include the all-important pattern of squares to be filled in.

54 With 61-Across, a refund requirement
55 Court divider
56 Comfort
60 Use the OR
61 See 54-Across
63 Discard
65 Par-birdie difference
66 Just
67 Stable position?
69 Cloud over

70 Northern auk
72 Racetrack fence
74 Goober's cousin
75 Prosciutto, e.g.
78 Subject of a Dean Martin hit
79 Speak Southerner
81 In-office phone no.
82 Perfect
84 Knotty
86 Like hippie T-shirts

88 Lifted, as hot coals
90 Androcles's friend
92 Bunker fill
93 More fastidious
97 Required
99 Sundown
101 Now
102 Light type
103 Goofball
105 Steer clear of
106 Gets up late
107 Frightened
110 Charlotte's home
111 Bing Crosby's label
112 '65 Ursula Andress role
115 Chills
116 Shows senility
118 Comic Mort
119 Craving
121 Ran into
122 Spell-off
123 Tooth part
125 Hymn accompanier
126 Poisons
128 Ace, e.g.
130 Gen. Lee's side
133 Carpal
135 Puzzle directions
138 Filly feature
139 Refuge
140 Pinch pennies
141 Start eating
142 Cyclone centers
143 Waiting aid
144 Napped leathers
145 Showy

DOWN

1 Punchline response
2 Without delay, in memos
3 Auspicious
4 The Matterhorn, for one
5 Authority
6 Prophetesses
7 Defy
8 Erté's forte
9 Cartesian premise
10 Some Picassos
11 Singing syllable
12 Jerk
13 Mister Rogers's trademark
14 Up to ten feet, for a condor
15 Bishop's seat setting
16 PGA peg
17 Care instruction site
18 Bakery treat
19 The Raisin Capital
20 Checked out
26 Queued up
28 Words of disbelief
32 Crystalline mineral
34 Fidel and family
37 Eschewed food
38 ___ Verdes (California hills)
39 Bumbling
40 Morley of *60 Minutes*
42 Ring up

43 Occupy the throne
44 "___ by land ..."
45 Stretched the truth
48 "Move it!"
50 Mug
51 Camera-ready type
53 George Peppard series, with *The*
54 Dried up
57 "___ no questions ..."
58 Heat-resistant glass
59 Wield
61 Walter Mitty specialty
62 Wall Street business
64 Like a good scout
66 Fable's finish
68 Bogged down
71 Play-___ (child's "clay")
73 Young buck
75 Proposition, in a way
76 Pueblo home
77 Edison's Park
80 Word-Cross's creator
83 Geriatrics focus
85 Cooing site
86 Polynesian nature god
87 With the most humidity
89 Broncos' home
91 Of a birthmark

92 Flank
94 Cavaradossi's lover
95 Author Segal
96 Kidney-related
98 "I Got You Babe," e.g.
100 European matgrass
101 '88 Winter Olympics site
104 Devil's island?
106 Play room?
108 Mole, perhaps
109 Vista view
110 "Alas!"
112 Missourian's challenge
113 "Yippee!"
114 Locomotive
116 Lacking
117 "___ be a major motion picture"
120 Xenon and radon
122 Ballet practice rail
124 Burger and fries to go, perhaps
126 Sow suitor
127 Cheek
129 Nile reptiles
130 Julius Dithers's wife
131 Houlihan's portrayer
132 George I's predecessor
134 Diner sandwich
136 Heart ward: Abbr.
137 *Night Court* DA

THE SPIRAL

By Will Shortz

This puzzle turns in two directions. The spiral's Inward clues yield a sequence of words to be entered counterclockwise in the spaces from 1 to 100. The Outward clues yield a different set of words to be entered clockwise from 100 back to 1. Fill in the answers, one letter per space, according to the numbers beside the clues. Work from both directions to complete the puzzle, and have many happy returns.   *Answer, page 190*

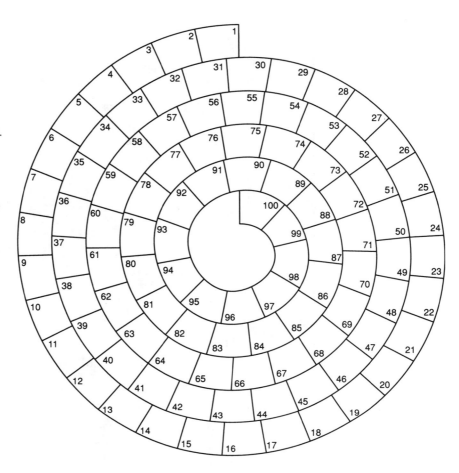

INWARD

1-4	Moniker
5-12	___ on rye
13-18	___ acid (oak bark extract)
19-26	Cigarette substance
27-33	Obvious, as a mistake
34-40	Choir voice
41-46	Mentally doddering
47-51	Dirt
52-60	Neighbor of Mexico
61-66	___ and feathered
67-73	Archenemy
74-77	Kind of express or tail
78-82	*Love Story* author
83-90	Reading ability
91-95	Small, deadly snake
96-100	Wicked forces

OUTWARD

100-93	Split off, as wood
92-86	___ center (mothers' aid)
85-79	Farming
78-71	Story summary
70-66	Change
65-60	Mistakes
59-56	Rather poor, as an excuse
55-50	Instructed
49-42	Source of vital assistance
41-37	Submarine equipment
36-28	After birth
27-22	___ Mussolini
21-12	Home of the Bengals and Reds
11-7	Shopping centers
6-1	Tarzan, for one

GAMES, MAGIC, AND THINGS TO DO

8

PLATFORM DIVING

By Charles Banasky

Place pencil on platform 1. Close eyes. Draw a line into the pool below. Open eyes. If dive successfully lands in pool, climb to platform 2, close eyes, and repeat. Continue until a dive is unsuccessful. *Score:* Number of the highest platform from which you successfully dove. Have a friend take the test, and compare scores.

10
9
8
7
6
5
4
3
2
1

STACKING THE DECK

By Dick Cavett

Many magicians can read minds across great distances. I can't. But I can read *cards* across great distances—yes, even ordinary playing cards. Get yourself a deck and I'll prove it to you.

Shuffle the cards well. Holding them face down, turn over the top card and place it face up on the table. Imagine that its face value represents the number of cards in a stack, and deal face up on top of it as many more cards as needed to make a stack of 10. For instance, if it's a 3, deal seven cards on top of it; if it's a 5, deal five cards. Face cards count as 10, so no more cards are needed. An ace counts as 1 and needs nine more cards.

Continue making 10-stacks as above, keeping the stacks separate, until the deck is exhausted. If there are not enough cards to complete a final stack, keep that incomplete stack in your hand.

Now choose, at random, any three stacks that contain at least four cards each and turn these stacks face down. Gather all the remaining cards in any order and keep them in your hand. Pick any two of the three face-down stacks on the table, turn up the top card on each of them, and add their values together. Discard that many cards from those in your hand, then discard 19 additional cards.

Count the number of cards remaining in your hand. Now turn up the top card on the third stack. Don't tell me what its value is, because I already know it. In fact, I've written it down in the … *Answer, page 190*

What A Card!

SCORE FIVE

A PENCIL-AND-PAPER STRATEGY GAME FOR TWO PLAYERS

By Sid Sackson

All you need to play are a sheet of paper, two pencils, and at least one player who can add. The game is played on a 6 x 6 grid like the bottom one in the box at right (which you can use for your first game). After reading the rules below, warm up with the puzzle at right to get acquainted with the strategy.

The Setup One player randomly fills in the squares of a 6 x 6 grid with the numbers 1 to 9, using each number four times. Earned scores are tallied in two columns on one side of the grid, and a running total is kept on the other side, as explained below.

The Play Determine the first player by flipping a coin *after* the grid is set up.

The first player chooses one of the four corner squares and circles the number in it. This number starts the running total. The second player chooses a square next to the corner—horizontally, vertically, or diagonally—and circles the number in it. This number is added to the running total. Each player in turn circles an unused number next to the last one circled. If there is no unused number next to the last one circled, the player may choose any unused number in the grid.

Scoring Each time a player circles a number that brings the running total to a multiple of five (ending in either 5 or 0), he writes that total in his scoring column, adding each new score to his previous total. The game ends when the running total (not a player's score) reaches or passes 170. (As a check, the remaining unused numbers should bring the total to 180.)

Puzzle Your opponent leads by a 5-point margin, and the game is entering the home stretch. It's your move from the 4 in the dotted-circle. The right sequence of moves will win the game, but a wrong first choice will almost certainly lead to defeat. What's your move? *Answer, page 190*

Opening Game We've drawn the grid and filled in the numbers for you. All you need to start play is an opponent.

Example

The first nine plays of a game are shown in the example at left. There was no unused number next to the 9, so player A has chosen the circled 7. The column to the right is the running total, with scoring totals circled.

Winning The winner is the player with the highest score when the running total reaches or passes 170.

NAMYSTICS

By GAMES Editors and Readers

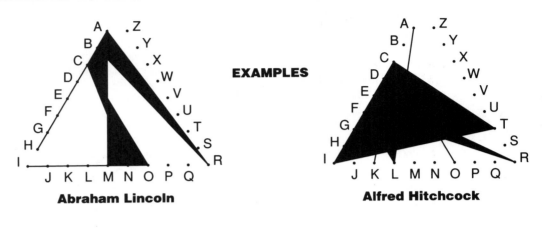

EXAMPLES

Abraham Lincoln

Alfred Hitchcock

Namystics. A revolutionary tool of science? A source of mystic revelations? Or simply an entertaining way to interpret a name? All of the above were claimed for Namystics by *French Humor*, a weekly magazine in which this game first appeared in the 1920s.

Namystics (pronounced nay-MISS-tix) can be played with your own name or the name of any other person, place, or thing. All you need are a pencil, ruler, and blank Namystics triangle (see bottom of next page). Start with the first letter of the selected name, draw a straight line to the second letter, then to the third, and so on. (Doubled letters are treated as if they were a single letter, since you can't draw a straight line from a letter to itself.) When you're done, blacken in any enclosed areas. Nearly every name forms a unique visual pattern.

As a science, Namystics ranks somewhere below phrenology, but it does create some striking designs. At top right are two examples of Namystic art with the names they illustrate. Below them and on the next page are 10 more examples, but with the names omitted. Can you figure out who or what they are?

The blank Namystics triangles on the next page are provided for you to draw your own name or any other name. For more copies, just photocopy the page. *Answers, page 190*

CAN YOU SOLVE THESE?

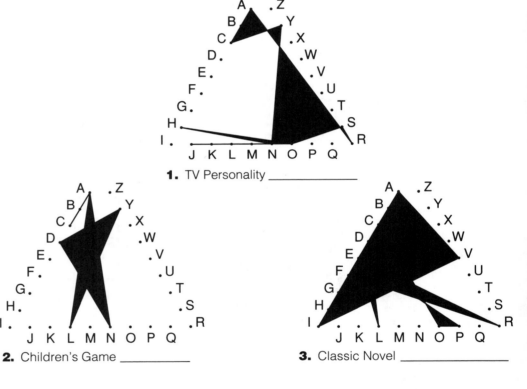

1. TV Personality _____

2. Children's Game _____

3. Classic Novel _____

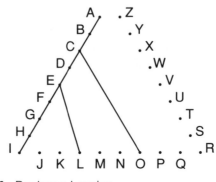

4. Business Leader _____

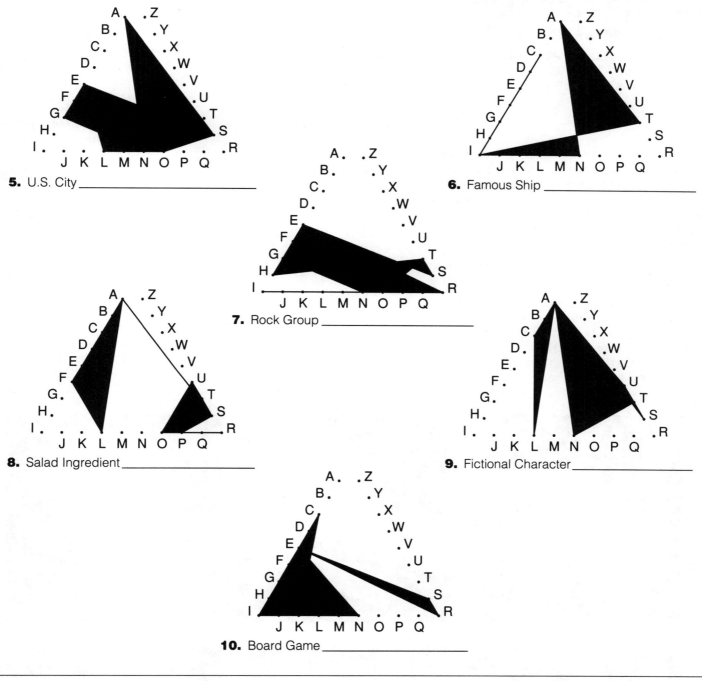

5. U.S. City _____

6. Famous Ship _____

7. Rock Group _____

8. Salad Ingredient _____

9. Fictional Character _____

10. Board Game _____

MAKE YOUR OWN

CREASED LIGHTNING

SIX PAPER-FOLDING PUZZLES

By Steven Caney

The six paper sculptures pictured here are folding puzzles, and the challenge is to re-create them. This won't require such intricate folding as origami (although a few straight cuts will be needed). And the folding instructions shouldn't be too confusing—because we won't *give* you any folding instructions.

What we will give you are a few ground rules and an example.

Each sculpture is folded from one quarter of a sheet of standard typing paper ($4\frac{1}{4}$ by $5\frac{1}{2}$ inches) and requires up to three *straight cuts* (but no part of the paper is ever cut *off*). Each cut originates from either an edge or another cut. The number of cuts required is given for each sculpture.

There are no folds, cuts, or facets hidden from view in the photos, and no glue, tape, or staples are used. Now a quick example: Re-create the sculpture shown at right, using one straight cut.

How it's done

1. *It's useful to know what unfolding the folds will do, so drawing the "flattened" version is a big help. (Dotted lines indicate folds.)*

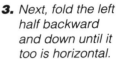

2. *To begin, make the cut along the solid line shown, and hold the paper vertically, cut edge up. Then fold the right half forward and down at a right angle to the rest of the paper.*

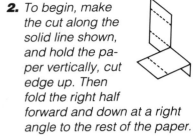

3. *Next, fold the left half backward and down until it too is horizontal.*

4. *Finally, fold the two end flaps downward until they are both vertical. Voilà!*

Now try your hand at the six sculptures below. If all else fails, you can always fold back the pages to the Answers, page 190.

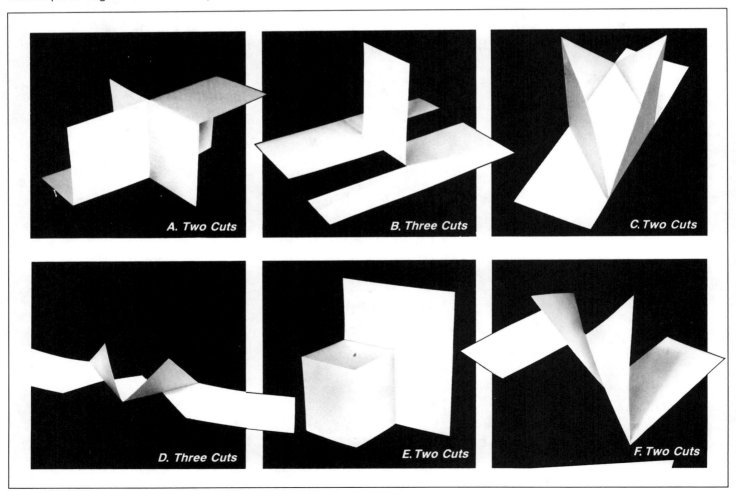

A. Two Cuts

B. Three Cuts

C. Two Cuts

D. Three Cuts

E. Two Cuts

F. Two Cuts

THE BEADLESS ABACUS

By Mel Stover

You may have heard claims that an abacus, used properly, can enable you to perform lengthy arithmetic computations as quickly as with a calculator. With the "beadless abacus" shown here, you can impress your friends without resorting to a computing device of any kind.

Show a friend this diagram, in which each hexagon-shaped cell contains an arithmetic operation. Now, perform the following feats:

1. Ask your friend to designate, by laying a matchstick across them, any *three* touching cells that lie in a straight line. (Each cell must touch the next along an entire edge, not just at a corner point.) Tell your friend in advance that you will perform the operations in each of the three designated cells and add together the three results, giving the total out loud almost immediately after the matchstick is placed.

2. Next, ask your friend to designate any *four* touching cells in any line. This time, you will perform the operations and add up the results even faster than in the first trick.

3. For your grand finale, have your friend choose a cluster of *seven* cells—any cell not on an edge, plus the six surrounding cells—by covering them with a shot glass. You will then glance through the shot glass, look away, and a moment later give the sum of the results of all seven operations.

Ponder these feats awhile if you will, but to learn how to do them, turn to

Answers, page 190

JON VALK

DIPLOMATS

A BLOODLESS BATTLE FOR TWO PLAYERS

By R. Wayne Schmittberger

If chess is an abstraction of war, how differently might the game have evolved in a world where war was unknown? Perhaps a strategy game like this one is played on some peaceful planet, where a nation can conquer its neighbor not by war but by infiltrating its citizenry with enough key people to gain political control.

EQUIPMENT

Players will need the board shown and two contrasting sets of pieces, each consisting of seven "emigrants" and four "diplomats." Each set of diplomats consists of two "consuls," one "negotiator," and one "ambassador." Coins may be used as pieces, one player showing "heads," the other "tails," with the pennies as emigrants, nickels as consuls, dimes as negotiators, and quarters as ambassadors. Or pieces may be improvised from chess sets, paper, or cut-up photocopies of the pieces shown on the board.

SETUP

The pieces are placed on the board as shown (each piece is represented by its initial). The players move alternately; either side may move first.

OBJECT

The first player to move all seven of his emigrants into the embassy on the opponent's side of the board is the winner. A player also wins if none of his emigrants is able to move (such a position is extremely rare).

PLAY

1. Each player moves one of his pieces per turn.

2. An emigrant may move onto any adjacent unoccupied square. Here, as well as everywhere else in these rules, "adjacent" is defined as one square away in any direction—horizontally, vertically, or diagonally.

3. A diplomat may move any number of squares in a straight line in any direction (horizontally, vertically, or diagonally), onto an unoccupied square, provided that *all* the squares that it passes over are completely *unoccupied* or completely *occupied* by other pieces. In the latter case, the pieces jumped over may belong to either or both players. However, a piece may never jump over the opposing ambassador.

4. Unlike other pieces, an ambassador—in addition to having the same movement abilities as any other diplomat—may move onto an occupied square if he began his move adjacent to that square. The previous occupant of that square is pushed to the next square along the same line that the ambassador moved. If the next square is also occupied, its occupant too is pushed one square in the same direction, and so on. An ambassador may push pieces belonging to either or both players.

   There are two restrictions: An ambassador may not push (or cause to be pushed) the opposing ambassador; and an ambassador may not push any piece off the board. There is one important exception: An emigrant that has advanced to the last row may be pushed into the embassy.

5. Consuls and negotiators improve the mobility of their own emigrants to which they are adjacent, as follows:

   (i) An emigrant adjacent to one of its consuls may move either one *or two* squares in a straight line in any direction; an emigrant next to *both* of its consuls may move up to *four* squares in a straight line in any direction. In either case, the emigrant may not land on or pass over any occupied squares.

   (ii) An emigrant adjacent to its negotiator may move any number of squares in a straight line in any direction and onto an unoccupied square, so long as all squares passed over are *occupied*. The pieces jumped over may belong to either or both players—but an emigrant may not jump over the opposing ambassador.

6. Diplomats may not enter the embassies or otherwise leave the playing area.

7. No piece may ever capture another.

ENTERING THE EMBASSY

An emigrant enters the embassy on the far side of the board by moving beyond the last rank of squares. An emigrant may enter the embassy with a normal one-square move, or as the result of a push by any ambassador, or by making a special move with the help of its negotiator or one or both consuls. An emigrant may not move off a corner of the board diagonally away from the center.

VARIATIONS

Players may experiment by adding or substituting additional kinds of diplomats of their own invention or some of the following types:

Delegate—switches places with one of its own emigrants, provided that both are on the same line (horizontal, vertical, or diagonal) and that none of the intervening squares are occupied.

Peacekeeper—eliminates all special powers of any opposing diplomats to which it is adjacent (including the ambassador's ability to push and its immunity from being pushed or jumped over), unless the peacekeeper itself is adjacent to an opposing peacekeeper.

Courier—attracts or repels any one piece belonging to either player, any number of unoccupied squares along a straight line on which both the courier and the affected piece are located.

Plenipotentiary—rearranges any or all adjacent pieces onto any or all adjacent squares; affected pieces may belong to either or both players, but only one emigrant may be so moved in a turn. The opposing ambassador may not be moved.

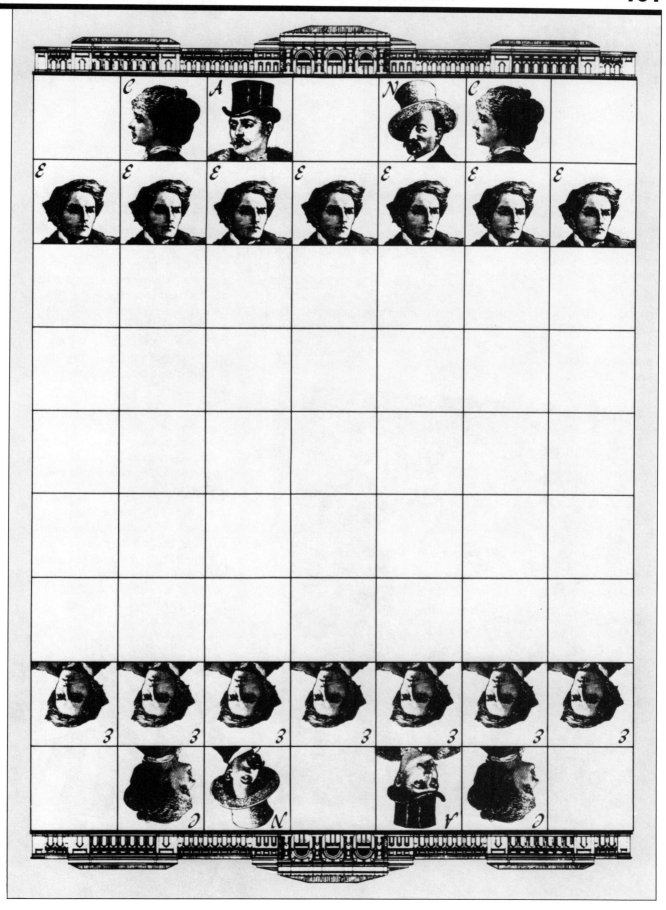

LUCKY LADY

By Max Maven

Most everyone will agree that 7 is a lucky number. But what's the luckiest card in a deck of cards? There's no doubt in my mind that it's the queen of diamonds. If you're willing to participate in a little experiment, we can prove it together.

From a standard deck of cards remove the queen of diamonds and a black ace, 2, 3, 4, 5, and 6. These are the only cards we'll need. Put the queen aside for the moment, and arrange the six black cards in numerical order, either from 1 through 6 or 6 through 1.

Hold the stack of six cards face down. Deal the top card face down to the table, then the next card on top of the first, then the third card on top of the first two. Place the remaining three-card stack face down next to the cards just dealt.

Now place either three-card stack on top of the other. Pick up the six cards and cut the stack—that is, transfer as many cards as you like from the top to the bottom. If you wish, cut the cards a second time in the same manner.

Pick up the queen, insert it in the stack anywhere you like, and again cut the cards once or twice. Now deal all seven cards into two stacks, alternating stacks with each card dealt. Pick up either stack and put it on top of the other. Cut the cards once or twice more, if you like.

Now look at the faces of the cards, keeping them all in order. If the queen is on either end of the stack, cut the stack once more so that the queen will be somewhere in the middle.

You'll agree you've been given a lot of latitude to make choices, and yet I can confidently predict that the queen is now located between two cards whose sum (counting an ace as 1, if necessary) will be found in Answers, page 190.

EXTRA-TOUGH PUZZLES FOR EXTRA-SHARP SOLVERS

9

HEADCRACKER

By Will Shortz

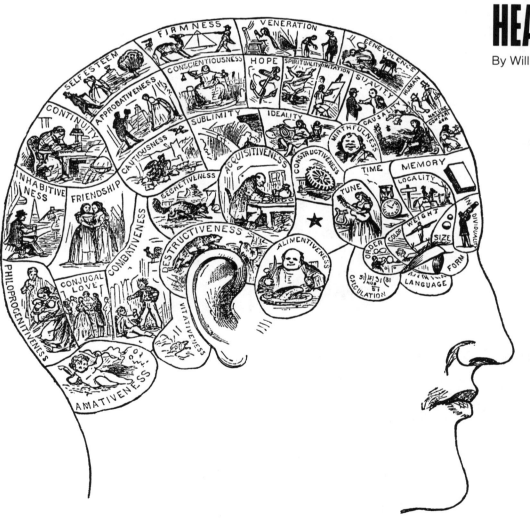

At left is a picture of the head as carefully mapped for *The American Phrenological Journal* in 1868. We were wondering, as we studied this remarkable drawing: How many of the 43 areas shown can be colored so that no two colored areas touch along a border? (Touching at corners is okay.) For purposes of the puzzle, the eye, eyelid, and ear don't count as areas, but the starred section does. *Answer, page 190*

LOGIQUIZ

By Jules Roth

The nine quizzes here are of progressively increasing difficulty, and though separate, all have something in common. The challenge is to determine the logical basis of each puzzle, whether synonyms, rhymes, homophones, related phrases, or some other form of wordplay. In each case the solution will consist of single letters that go in the appropriate boxes of the vertical grids between words. In the first few quizzes, blanks are provided as an aid to solving; after that, it's sink or swim. The puzzles get pretty tricky around #5.

Answers, page 191

1

__OURNFUL		__OROSE
__NNATE		__NHERENT
__NCIENT		__RCHAIC
__EAN		__ALICIOUS
__NFURIATED		__RATE

2

SHOR__		__ALL
__GLY		BEA__TIFUL
EAR__Y		__ATE
FA__T		__LOW
PL__IN		F__NCY

3

C ST		T SSED
CLAI		BLA E
W IST		P STE
LOAT E		CLOT E
B LD		C LLED

4

WEIGH		WAI
TAT		TAGHT
HASTE		HASED
LEAT		LEAED
RWED		RAD
EW		GU

5

MDEOR		WE
NDAK		NDU
SDREH		LYI
CYRZ		IENNS
AADFI		SACDE
SNNIY		LNA

6

OGL		EGGRI
SRBS		KSTC
ANMTUIP		DEOBN
MUMUNIA		OFI
DLE		OLNBOL
RVLEI		OPNO

7

EJMS		DIMNOS
DEEHOOR		EELOORSV
ADILMR		EFILMOR
HRRY		MNRTU
ADERW		ACJKOS
CEEHRS		AHRRU
DLNOR		AEGNR

8

EFHLTW		GHIN
DHIT		DLOW
EEHINNNTT		HLO
EEHSTV		AEEHV
FFHI		ADEEMMNN
FHRTU		DEIIMNNS
CDEOS		ADH

9

CEFH		AADL
ABKRS		DNOZ
BMNSSU		DHILOY
ACEEHRS		EP
ACCEHRS		IMT
BEMPRSU		EEHPR
ADELRS		CCHIO

KNIGHT MOVES

By Ulrich Koch

Sometimes it's a good thing to jump to conclusions. Take this chess maze, for example. How can the knight in the lower left corner square move in a series of jumps to the chessboard in the middle? Each jump must be a regular knight's move—two squares hori- zontally and one vertically, or two vertically and one horizontally— and must end on a black or white square. The knight may jump over the wavy lines, but he cannot land on them. The first two jumps are shown to get you started.

Answer, page 191

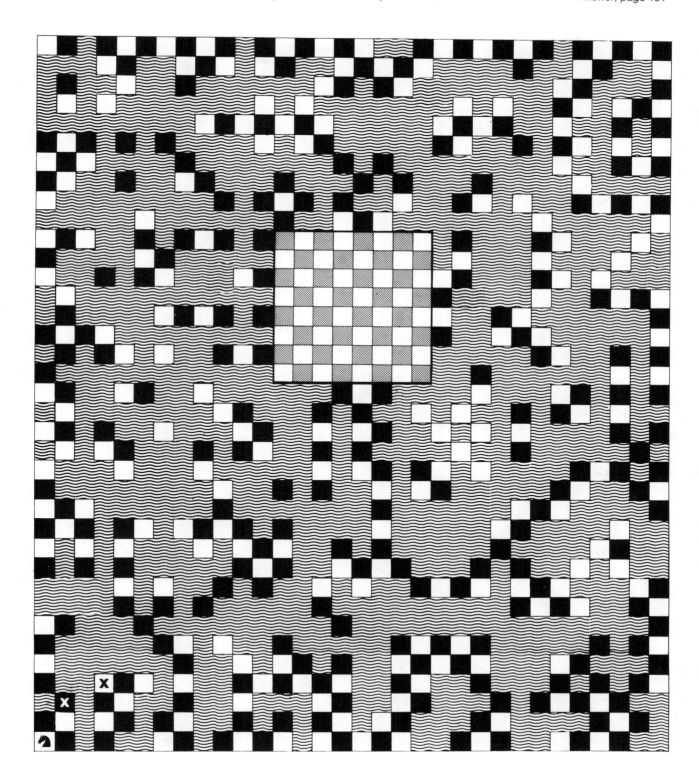

MEASURING UP TO MENSA

ON THIS TEST, IT'S THE THOUGHT THAT COUNTS

By Abbie Salny

We've never put much stock in intelligence tests. So far as we can tell, they don't indicate anything very useful—like who's most likely to win the office football pool or whether you can get your tomatoes to ripen in July.

Still, every so often people like to measure their gray matter against some standard. Whenever that urge strikes us, we call some friends at Mensa and ask them to make us a test.

Mensa is a social organization in which people who meet certain intellectual standards (as determined by tests like this one) gather and correspond to exchange ideas and match wits. The test presented here is typical of actual Mensa admissions tests, and was created by Dr. Abbie Salny, advisory psychologist for both American and International Mensa. To take the test, get a pencil and paper to record your answers, and follow the instructions below.

Answers, page 191

HOW DO YOU RATE?

Scoring is based on the number of questions that you've answered correctly and the time it took you to complete the test. Before you start, set a stopwatch or note the time, and when you're finished, record the elapsed time. Score 1 point for each correct answer, and add or subtract points according to the following table. Then compare your final score with the evaluation chart below to find out how well you've done.

Elapsed time

20 minutes of less: Add 3 bonus points
25 minutes: Add 2 bonus points.
30 minutes: Add 1 bonus point.
31–44 minutes: No bonus points
45 minutes or longer: Subtract 3 points

Evaluation

27–36 points: Bravo! Mensa would be proud to have you as a member.

19–26: Very good potential for passing the Mensa admissions test.

12–18: Good but not outstanding by Mensa standards; you should get a respectable score on an actual Mensa test.

11 or less: Probably not Mensa material. But you're in good company—neither is 98 percent of the U.S. population.

1. Some collywobbles are genuines.
   All genuines have six legs.
   Therefore, which of the following must be true?
   a) All collywobbles have six legs.
   b) All genuines are collywobbles.
   c) Some collywobbles have six legs.
   d) It cannot be determined whether any of the above are true.

2. Insert the same four-letter word in both sets of blanks to make two words.
   D O __ __ __ __   __ __ __ __ T A I N

3. Complete the series in the top row of figures with one of the lettered diagrams in the bottom row.

4. Pick the numbers that most reasonably come next in the following series:
   2 8 3 7 5 6 8 5 __ __
   a) 8 6   b) 11 4   c) 12 4   d) 12 6

5. Find a word that in one sense means the same as the phrase on the left and in another means the same as the word on the right.
   RUN AWAY _____ FASTENING

6. In this analogy,

7. Meg is younger than Beth.
   Amy is older than Meg.
   Jo is older than Amy.
   Therefore (choose one):
   a) Amy is older than Beth.
   b) Beth is older than Amy.
   c) Meg is older than Jo.
   d) Jo is older than Meg.

8. Star is to constellation as petal is to
   __ __ __ __ __ __ m.

9. Which of the figures below can be obtained by rotating the figure at far right?

10. What number, multiplied by 3, is three-fourths of 120?

11. Insert the same three-letter word in both sets of blanks below to make two sets of two new words each. (Example: Inserting the word ACT in F __ __ __ RESS and in TR __ __ __ UAL makes FACT, ACTRESS, TRACT, and ACTUAL.)
    P L __ __ __ L E R   G R __ __ __ I Q U E

12. Alarming is to marginal as enraged is to
    a) angered   b) caustic
    c) dormant   d) belligerent

13. In this analogy,

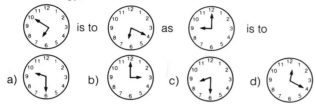

14. If I III V = SAT, and IV III VI = RAY, and VI III II = YAM, then what is I II III IV V?

15. Jim has as many sisters as he has brothers, but his sister Sally has twice as many brothers as she has sisters. How many boys and how many girls are there in the family?

16. All winkles are franchies.
All franchies are light blue.
Some franchies are hornswoggles.
Therefore (choose one):
    a) All winkles are light blue.
    b) All hornswoggles are winkles.
    c) Neither a) nor b) is true.
    d) Both a) and b) are true.

17. The numbers in the square at left, below, have been placed following a certain mathematical rule. If the numbers in the square at right were placed following the same rule, what is the missing number?

18. In this analogy,

 is to as   is to   a) □   b) ▷   c) ◁

19. Think of a wooden cube measuring three inches on each side. Imagine painting it red all over—on the six exposed surfaces. If you now cut the cube into one-inch cubelets (there will be 27 of them), how many will have paint on exactly two faces?

20. Capitalism is to entrepreneur as feudalism is to:
    a) horse   b) serf
    c) lord   d) fief

21. Which set of letters logically comes next in the following series?
    Z Y X U V W T S R ___ ___ ___
    a) O P Q   b) P O Q
    c) O Q N   d) N O Q

22. There are four houses in a row along a dead-end street. The Wilsons live next to the Joneses but not next to the Ronsons. The Browns do not live next to the Ronsons. Who are the Ronsons' next-door neighbors?
    a) the Wilsons
    b) the Joneses
    c) the Wilsons and the Joneses
    d) It cannot be determined from the information given.

23. Sally types 50 characters in 10 seconds. Jane can type only 40 in the same time. Working together, how long will it take them to type 360 characters?

24. Below are three views of the same cube. Which of the four lettered patterns is opposite the blank white face of the third cube?

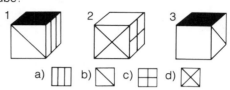

a) ▥   b) ◺   c) ▦   d) ⊠

25. The number of dresses owned by Susan is the same number owned by Tess divided by the number owned by Jane. Tess has 42 dresses and would own 8 times as many as Jane if Tess had 14 more. How many dresses does Susan have?

26. In this analogy,

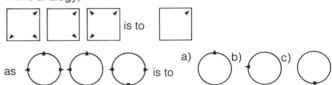

27. You buy an elephant for $5,500. A traveling circus buys it from you for $5,500. After the season, they sell it back to you for $5,000 and you sell it to a zoo for $6,000. How much money have you made or lost on this series of transactions?

28. What is the price of the last item below?
Leather	$3.00
Linen	$9.00
Sateen	$10.00
Worsted	$ ____

29. If A + B = 18, and A x B = 72, then $A^2 + B^2 =$
    a) 144   b) 160   c) 180   d) 252

30. Below are four views of the same alphabet block, which has a different letter on each of its six faces. What is the missing letter in view d?

31. "You can't tell a book by its cover" is closest in meaning to which of the following?
    a) People who live in glass houses shouldn't throw stones.
    b) Beauty is in the eye of the beholder.
    c) Where there's smoke, there's fire.
    d) All that glitters is not gold.

32. A man bets $30 and wins back his original wager plus $60. He spends one-third his new total on a present for his wife, $10 for taxi fare home, and 10 percent of what's left to tip the driver. How much does he have when he gets home?

33. Which of the figures below can be obtained by reversing and rotating the figure at right?

STAR HOPPING

By Thomas Hirsch

There's more to this star than meets the naked eye. Place a coin or other token on each circle below, leaving one circle empty. Then try to remove all the coins but one in as few moves as possible.

A move consists of jumping a coin over an adjacent coin in a straight line, landing in the empty circle beyond it. The coin that is jumped over is removed. (For example, with coins on circle 1 and 3, with circle 6 empty, you may jump 1 to 6 and remove the coin on 3.) A series of consecutive jumps with the same coin counts as a single move (such as 4 to 11 to 13, removing 8 and 12.)

No matter which circle is empty at the start, it's possible—though tricky—to remove all but one of the coins from the star. But for Sirius solvers the challenge is to complete the puzzle in only nine moves. To do so, you'll have to plan ahead to make use of multiple jumps. If you succeed, consider yourself a star of the first magnitude.   *Answer, page 191*

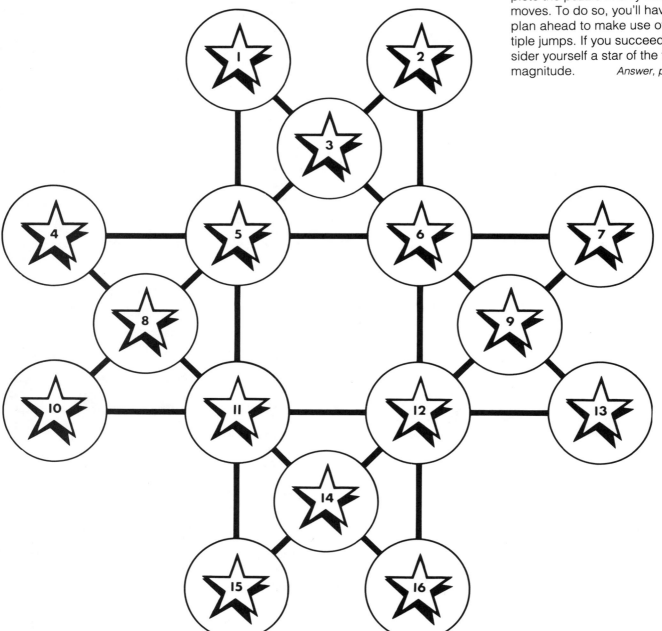

ABC CRYPTIC

By Emily Cox and Henry Rathvon

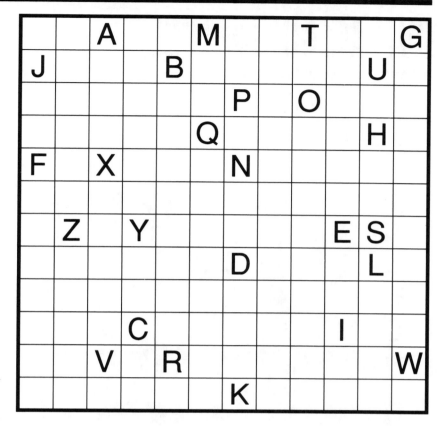

The 26 letters of the alphabet have been planted in an otherwise blank diagram. These letters may serve as guides for locating answers to the clues (numbered 1–40 for convenience only), each of which reads as usual from left to right or top to bottom. Some clue answers may not cross any of the 26 planted letters; but in the completed diagram, of course, each of the 26 will be used in at least one answer. (Hint: If you add heavy bars to separate words, the completed diagram will be symmetrical about the center point—that is, it will look the same if turned upside-down.)   *Answer, page 191*

CLUES

1 Part of Near Eastern region (4)

2 Audibly manipulate some evergreen shrubs (4)

3 Bringer of bad luck makes first of jokes in *Times* (4)

4 Topless fur fit (4)

5 English navy hasn't a vice (4)

6 Greek with two aces holding jack and ten (4)

7 Lie around with Hawaiian garlands in the sound (4)

8 Seer translated Gaelic (4)

9 Article which in Rome is greenish-blue (4)

10 Killed host (4)

11 Streak of light atop synthetic material (5)

12 Peculiar way of expressing "left in hurry" (5)

13 Dotty or Len is a solitary sort (5)

14 Football coach was tagged in the midsection (5)

15 Northern plot of land yields pearly stuff (5)

16 U.S. President in fog speech-ified (5)

17 Recoils from fermented juices with carbon added (6)

18 Mann also keeps records (6)

19 Insure dancing of bears (6)

20 French novelist in terrible stupor (6),

21 Shiny ornament for use in exotically clothing queen (6)

22 Walk in street, then go by car (6)

23 New store stocking excellent hi-fi equipment (6)

24 A severe rear (6)

25 Sticks kilo in drainage pipes (7)

26 State laboratory kept by a doctors' group (7)

27 Vast abuse of cocaine (7)

28 Car entered, carrying final character—a Russian ruler's wife (7)

29 The woman's supporting great American oil wells (7)

30 Yonder's a name for a woman (7)

31 Before sex comes up, Boleyn forms an attachment (7)

32 Slippery eel isn't capable of stretching (7)

33 Rock in one RV's surroundings (8)

34 Fight in front of one half of Quebec's store (8)

35 Bloom has nothing left for disciple (8)

36 Garbage overturned amidst merry escapes (4,4)

37 Send old bum last of brandy as though in a drunken state (8)

38 Dog discovered holding ox by end of leash (8)

39 Bugs prophet outside of Ecuador's capital (10)

40 Intoxicated doctor interrupts joke bit (5-5)

OUTRAGEOUS FORTUNE

A TAROT CARD LOGIC PUZZLE

By Scott Marley

I felt goosebumps. Could she have read my most secret thoughts about Mother and Prunella, my lovely but domineering fiancée?

She must have seen my discomfort. "Madame Opal is right? But of course. Madame Opal is always right."

I trembled as she pointed at the square. "Let us look at the rows," she continued. "In one row, all three cards are from the minor arcana. This means you will be offered a job underground.

"In another row, the left card contains a J, the middle card contains an A, and the right card contains an M. You will be caught in heavy traffic.

"In the remaining row, a card showing a sword separates two cards showing animals. One of the animals is black; the other is a sea creature. You will be in a dogfight over the Black Sea."

"A dogfight!" I gasped. For a hardware clerk who had never traveled farther than the county line, this was exciting news indeed. "But how will it come out?"

"You want to know much," chuckled Madame Opal. "For that we must check the columns. In one column, all three cards show seated persons. This prophesies a period of rest.

"In another column, the top card shows water, the middle card shows a cup, and the bottom card shows a large coin with a star on it. You will lose money in a soda machine.

"In the remaining column, a card showing the moon separates two cards showing crowns. You will have two teeth capped at night. The reading is over. Next, please?"

As I stumbled out of the tiny, dark tent and returned to the sunlight of the crowded traveling carnival, I thought about the gypsy's predictions. To my surprise, I couldn't remember how the cards had lain on the table.

The cards are shown above left, but not in their correct order. Using the information above, can you discover how they were arranged in the square Madame Opal dealt? *Answer, page 191*

"So you want to know your future?" purred the gypsy woman as she pocketed my fiver. "Madame Opal, she will tell you all."

Madame Opal then turned up nine tarot cards to form a square on the velvet-covered table. Four of the cards were from the major arcana: the Magician, the High Priestess, Justice, and the Moon. Five were from the minor arcana: the Ace of Swords, the Queen of Wands, the Knight of Pentacles, the Page of Cups, and the Two of Swords.

"The two most important women in this square," whispered Madame Opal, "are the High Priestess and the Queen. They both occupy corners. You feel cornered by the women in your life, no?"

500 RUMMY

A CARDS-AND-WORDS PUZZLE

By Jules Roth

	A	2	3	4	5	6	7	8	9	10	J	Q	K	
♠	H	A	N	G	L	I	S	T	A	C	O	R	U	♠
♥	I	S	H	E	T	T	W	E	Y	S	Q	U	E	♥
♦	S	B	C	A	R	D	Y	N	T	H	E	A	R	♦
♣	U	N	U	S	E	F	K	H	S	M	U	L	B	♣
	A	2	3	4	5	6	7	8	9	10	J	Q	K	

Can you score 500 or more points in Word Rummy hands from the card spread at right?

How to Play

Find as many common seven-letter words as you can whose cards form Word Rummy hands. A Word Rummy hand is a seven-letter word whose letters appear on cards that make up one *set* (three or four cards of a kind, like 7 7 7 or K K K K) and one *sequence* (three or four cards of the same suit in numerical order, like ♠ A 2 3 or ♣ 9 10 J Q). Either the *set* or the *sequence* may come first. The letters of a *set* may be used in any order; the letters of a *sequence* must be used in the left-to-right order given in the grid. The same card cannot be used twice in one hand. Sets and sequences may be used over and over in different words to form other words. Proper names, foreign words, and variant spellings of other answers are not allowed, but plurals are fine.

Scoring

Each card in a Word Rummy hand scores its face value. A 6 scores 6 points, for example. Aces are low and count 1 point each. Jacks, queens, and kings count 10 points each.

Example

In the puzzle at right the word ANGUISH forms a Word Rummy hand. The ♠ 2 3 4 are a sequence with the letters A-N-G; the ♣ A ♥ A ♦ A ♠ A are a set with the letters U-I-S-H. The cards used have values 2 3 4 1 1 1 1, for a total of 13 points.

Ratings

Knock: 350 points (good game)
Gin: 500 points (winning game)
Gin-off: 923 points (our best score)

Answers, page 191

CARDS & WORDS	POINTS	CARDS & WORDS	POINTS
A N G U I S H 2 3 4 A A A A	13		

COLUMN 2 TOTAL

COLUMN 1 TOTAL

COLUMN 1 TOTAL

TOTAL SCORE

HEREWITH THE ANSWERS

7 NO LEFT TURN

The route is shown below:

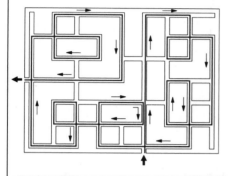

8 LIMBERICKS

1. Swift, miffed, needed, pleaded, drift
2. Time, crime, faulty, salty, rhyme
3. Fought, distraught, disagreed, concede, thought

9 CAN IT!

1. Tennis balls
2. Ham
3. House paint
4. Hershey's Cocoa
5. Lubricating oil
6. Coffee
7. Tomato paste
8. Sardines
9. Pepper or other spice
10. Sucrets cough drops
11. Shoe polish
12. Band-Aids

10 EXCLAMATIONS!

1 - h ("Duck!")
2 - e ("Hail!")
3 - i ("Check!")
4 - b ("Pop!")
5 - c ("Match!")
6 - a ("Present!")
7 - g ("Hut!")
8 - f ("Fire!")
9 - j ("Ring!")
10 - d ("Safe!")

13 PICTURE IMPERFECT

Pictures with something added:
1B (cat's whiskers)
1D (clothespin)
2C (drop from the hose)

Pictures with something deleted:
1A (mailbox hooks)
3B (puddle)
3D (baseball stitching)

Pictures with something moved:
2A (car window divider)
2B (washcloth)
3C (bucket handle)

Pictures with no changes:
1C
2D
3A

14 CRIME AND TREASON

1. Tooth and nail
2. Pork and beans
3. Law and order
4. Nuts and bolts
5. Stars and stripes
6. Black and blue
7. Hide and seek
8. Pencil and paper
9. Ham and eggs
10. High and mighty
11. Show and tell
12. Fun and games
13. Cops and robbers
14. Rank and file
15. Song and dance
16. Fine and dandy

14 THE SIGHS OF IT

1. Siren
2. Saigon
3. Simon
4. Cyclone
5. Cider
6. *Psycho*
7. Siam
8. Citation
9. Siberia
10. Scientist
11. Sinai
12. Cyclops
13. Cyanide
14. Scythe

15 MISTAKEN IDENTITIES

By combining logic and pictures, one can see that G is the only face that fits the facts of the puzzle. The thief had a pencil mustache, dark hair, bushy eyebrows, a scar on his left cheek, no glasses, and no scarf.

16 SCRAMBLED COMICS

BEAUTY AND THE BUST: B, D, F, C, G, E, A
TOTALED RECALL: C, A, E, D, G, B, F
CHECKING OUT: F, E, B, D, A, G, C

18 LEFT AND RIGHT

12 WANDERFUL

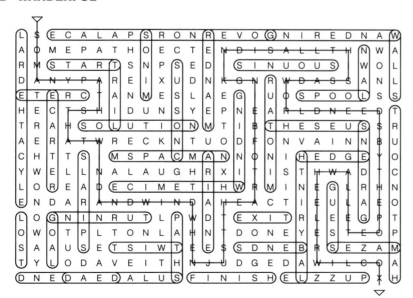

19 PLAYER PIANOS

The answer is D (which has been rotated 90° clockwise).

20 CONNECT-THE-DOTS

A. Scissors

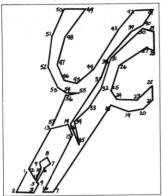

B. Umbrella

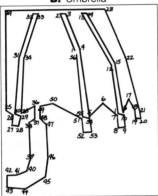

C. Telephone

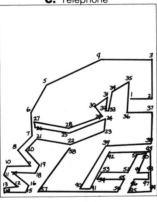

D. Turntable

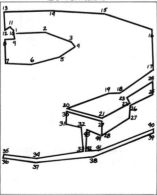

21 CAMERA SHY

Sheldon's route is shown in gray:

22 CIRCULAR REASONING

1. The total in each circle is 16.

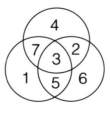

2. Starting with point A (see grid at right), mark each intersection in the grid with the number of ways it's possible to get there by moving clockwise or inward. For example, the points on the outer ring are all numbered 1, since you can reach them in only one way. The points on the second ring are numbered 1, 1, 2, 2, 3, 3, 3, and 4; each is the same number as the one before it on the same ring or the one on the next outer ring, or the sum of the two if connected to both. Continuing to add numbers on the inner rings in the same way, we find the total number of routes from A to the middle is 143.

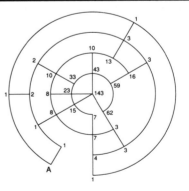

3. The solution depends on the fact that if there are three rings that interlock in the manner shown on the next page, then one of them must be flexible if they are all to lie flat. Note that, proceeding clockwise, each ring goes over each successive ring. Three rings with this property are called Borromean rings, after the Italian family that used them as their heraldic emblem. In this puzzle, C is over D, which is over E, which is over C, so one of

(*Answer continued on next page*)

these rings must be flexible. Similarly, one of D, B, and C is rubber, and so is one of A, B, and C. The only common ring is C, which is therefore the rubber ring.

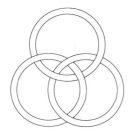

4. A penny.

5. The numbers passed in order are 1, 50, 25, 20, 20, and 20.

6.

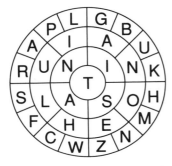

7. Dudeney's answer was to space the cottages 1, 1, 4, 4, 3, and 14 miles apart respectively around the circular road. Other answers are also possible.

WOTWOTWOTWOTWOTWTOTWOTWOTWOTWOTWOT

25 TYPE CAST

The 20 face-up letters are identified below. The six face-down letters, when unjumbled, form the word JUMBLE.

24 PRODUCT RECALL

The actual logos are shown here. The area where each has been changed is indicated by a loop.

26 HANDIWORK

1. Holding a baseball bat (or an oar)
2. Playing golf
3. Holding a bow and arrow
4. Playing a violin
5. Unscrewing a jar lid
6. Shooting a marble
7. Threading a needle
8. Playing pool or billiards
9. Lighting a cigarette
10. Opening a pop-top can
11. Playing a piano
12. Holding a steering wheel

27 BIT PARTS

Before reading the answers to any photos you couldn't identify, you might try viewing the pictures from several feet away for better resolution.

1. *King Kong* (original version; Kong on Empire State Building)
2. *Casablanca* (Humphrey Bogart)
3. *The Birds* (Tippi Hedren in jungle-gym scene)
4. *Close Encounters of the Third Kind* (Devil's Tower)
5. *Star Wars* (the robot C-3PO)
6. *Gone With the Wind* (Clark Gable and Vivien Leigh)

To create these pictures, the Armstrongs freeze a frame of a videotaped movie. That image is then fed to a digitizer, which "reads" the picture's areas of contrast and converts the image to a binary code. The code is fed to a computer, which displays it as pixels, or dots, which are reproduced by the printer.

28 RANGEFINDER

The hidden images are found according to the key below:

1. jackrabbit; 2. coyote; 3. arrow; 4. spur; 5. Conestoga wagon; 6. Bowie knife; 7. wagon wheel; 8. derringer; 9. hangman's noose; 10. Indian headdress; 11. cactus; 12. sheriff's star; 13. Texas; 14. canoe; 15. guitar; 16. bow; 17. vulture; 18. boot; 19. tepee; 20. six-gun; 21. tomahawk; 22. totem pole; 23. horseshoe; 24. bullet; 25. peace pipe; 26. rifle; 27. buffalo.

30 ICING ON THE CAKE

31 PURTLE'S PLIGHT

To find the fifth April Fools, hold the page back at arm's length. You should see the words APRIL FOOLS in large letters formed by elements in the art.

32 LEFTY AND RIGHTY

1. Rosalinda. The knife was held in the right hand, since traces of butter remain on the left side of the blade.
2. Lavinia. The head of the pin was held in the left hand and the point pushed toward the right.
3. Lavinia. The dice rest against the right side of the backgammon board, as a lefty would have thrown them.
4. Rosalinda. Rosalinda poured the iced tea into the glass by holding the heavy pitcher in her right hand. Note the position of the pitcher's handle.
5. Rosalinda. Rosalinda held the bottle in her left hand (and the spoon in her right, or steadier hand), since syrup is dripping down the right side of the bottle.
6. Lavinia. Lavinia used salt, not pepper, on her french fries, and replaced the shaker to the side nearer her hand.

33 YOU ARE WHAT YOU ATE

1-i, 2-c, 3-a, 4-e, 5-h, 6-b, 7-j, 8-g, 9-d, 10-f

34 MIME'S THE WORD

1. Serving a tennis ball
2. Blowing up a balloon
3. Addressing, sealing, and stamping an envelope
4. Pulling a rabbit out of a hat
5. Walking a tightrope
6. Painting a canvas
7. Placing a call on a pay telephone
8. Playing tug-of-war

36 UFO'S

The objects seen in the photos—not spacecraft, alas—are:
1. an automobile hubcap
2. a bicycle wheel
3. a typewriter element
4. a trashcan lid
5. a car's rearview mirror
6. a colander
7. a wok
8. a water tower

38 GONE BUT NOT FORGOTTEN

1. Gas pump: no trigger to pump gas
2. Ladder: no side hinge to keep ladder from opening too far
3. Can opener: no lip for can lid
4. Envelope: no hole for clasp
5. Baseball mitt: no webbing
6. Doorway: no hinges
7. Tape measure: no end hook/catch
8. Stapler: no indentation to guide staple
9. Flag and flagpole: no rope (halyard) to raise and lower flag
10. Belt: no loop for belt end
11. Hypodermic needle: no finger flange
12. Parking meter: no turn handle

39 ROUND TRIP MAZE

40 SHADOW PLAY

1. Swan 2. Goat 3. Pig

4. Squirrel 5. Elephant 6. Bull

7. Hare 8. Camel

REETHREETHREETHREETHR

41 TRAIL-BLAZING

Booze, daze, doze, dozen, fez, gaze, glaze, kazoo, laze, ooze, zag, zeal, zone, zoo, zoom; adz(e)

42 SKETCHWORDS

Names of contributors appear in parentheses following their answers.
1. HALLOWEEN (M.L. Pearce, North Bay, Ontario)
2. CAMEL (Michael St. Martin, Grimsby, Ontario)
3. FIREMAN (Jenna Rosenberg, Oradell, NJ)
4. OPERATOR (Christine Sudol, Brookhaven, PA)
5. DEVIL (Colin North, Washington, MO)
6. HARVEST (Robert Riggs, St. John's, Newfoundland)
7. SAILBOAT (Ann Judkins, North Mankato, MN)
8. COMMUNIST (Jack Anderson, Hillsdale, NJ)
9. BIRTHDAY (Chris Mohan, Butler, PA)
10. HOLLYWOOD (Tedde Klingenhöfer, Alpine, CA)
11. BABY (Marsha Torsberg, Hickory Hills, IL)
12. CUPID (Craig Hamilton, Mountain View, CA)
13. PAINTER (Richard Sun, San Francisco, CA)
14. CHRISTMAS (P.J. Tanaka, Gardena, CA)
15. QUIXOTE (Richard Sun, San Francisco, CA)
16. THUNDERSTORM (Mayank Keshaviah, Plymouth, MN)

43 BUILDING BLOCKS

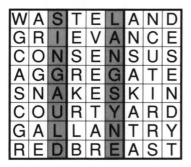

43 VCR WORDS

1. Vicar
2. Vociferous
3. Victoria
4. Voucher
5. Overcharge
6. Viceroy
7. Vehicular
8. Avuncular
9. Vector
10. Lovecraft
11. Vocabulary
12. Vernacular
13. Overcrowd
14. Viscera

44 CRYPTO-MATES

1. Bugle bulge
2. Pirates traipse
3. Crooner coroner
4. Throw worth ($100, of course)
5. Host shot
6. Cobbler clobber
7. Squatter quartets
8. Large regal lager

46 BLANKETY-BLANK

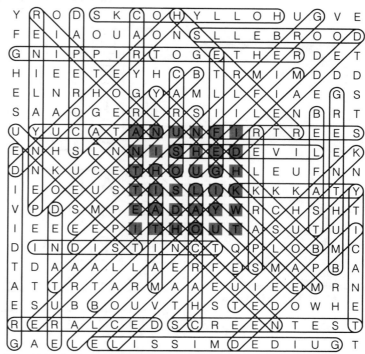

Quip: "An unfinished thought is like a day without…"

47 MISSING LINKS

```
M A T R I M O N Y
U N R U L Y     E
S T A R K   C   S
H   M A   C A R T
I   P L I E S   E
N I L   N E A R
E   E     T   D
S A D D L E   A
S   O   R E L Y
```

```
  S E A M
B A T H R O B E S
L   R   C U E   Y
O R E S   S T E M
W I T H   E     B
E S C O R T   G O
R E H E A R S A L
S   E   M A T S
  C R I S P Y
```

48 COMMON ELEMENTS

1. Sweden, Denmark (Scandinavian countries)
2. Opal, topaz (gemstones)
3. Superior, Erie (Great Lakes)
4. Seven, eleven (numbers)
5. Shad, haddock (fishes)
6. Scorpio, Capricorn (zodiac signs)
7. Ounce, pound (units of weight)
8. Bronze, iron (metals)
9. Salem, Raleigh (state capitals)
10. Venus, Uranus (planets)
11. Chess, checkers (board games)
12. Giants, Indians (baseball teams)
13. Peach, pear (fruits)
14. Carter, Arthur (U.S. presidents)

48   PRESTO CHANGO

1. Apple, lemon, orange
2. Square, oval, ellipse
3. Perch, herring, tuna
4. Crocus, peony, daisy
5. Bridge, whist, hearts
6. Carrot, parsley, radish
7. Copper, iron, uranium
8. Scotch, gin, whiskey
9. Ankle, knee, wrist
10. Tackle, center, fullback
11. Tango, hustle, jitterbug
12. Colon, dash, bracket

49   MIX WELL

HOSE—SHOE
LAMP—PALM
SOUP—OPUS
POTS—SPOT (on dog)
SINK—SKIN
DIAL—DALI
PEARS—SPEAR
BEARD—BREAD
SCALE—LACES
BRUSH—SHRUB
EARTH—HEART
MELON—LEMON
DRAPES—SPREAD (oleo)
FINGER—FRINGE
PETALS—PLATES
BASTER—BREAST (turkey)
CLOVER—VELCRO
DRAWER—REWARD
PICTURES—PIECRUST

50   INGENIOUS INVENTIONS

1. Hot doghouse
2. Candy bar graph
3. Tickertape measure
4. Flapjackhammer
5. Rolling pincushion
6. Handcufflinks
7. Horseshoehorn
8. Scarecrowbars
9. Trash can-opener
10. Teakettledrum
11. Goalpost office
12. Slot machine gun

52   TOPS OFF

1. Jumbo jet
2. Case closed
3. Easter egg
4. Good grief
5. Self serve
6. India ink
7. Happy hour
8. West wind
9. After all
10. Paper plates
11. Fast food
12. Top ten
13. Olive oil
14. Catch cold
15. Love letter
16. Fruit fly

52   LETTER LOGIC

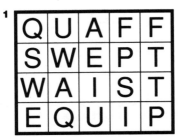

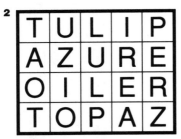

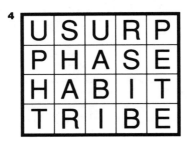

53   SPLIT DECISIONS

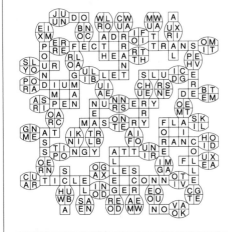

54   ALTERED EGOS

1. Bob Hope (bib, pope)
2. Bert Parks (beet, Paris)
3. Cary Grant (card, giant)
4. Dick Tracy (duck, track)
5. Hank Aaron (hawk, apron)
6. Marco Polo (March, pole)

55   CONSTELLATIONS

1. *The French Connection*
2. *Raiders of the Lost Ark*
3. *Sophie's Choice*

55   SHORT CHANGES

1. Plump, slender
2. Violent, calm
3. Float, sink
4. Ebony, white
5. Married, single
6. Rapid, slow
7. Kind, mean
8. Stable, shaky
9. Ornate, plain
10. Scold, praise
11. Complete, lacking
12. Moron, genius
13. Placid, stormy
14. Tacit, stated
15. Bungler, expert
16. Uninformed, learned

56   HINKY-PINKIES

1. Stupid cupid
2. Lazy daisy
3. Sloppy copy
4. Cricket picket
5. Baronet's clarinets
6. Barber harbor
7. Frightening lightning
8. Miner diner
9. Colonel's journals
10. Leaf thief (*or* book crook)
11. Creature teacher
12. Sailor tailor

58 FRACTURED PHRASES

1. Ignorance is bliss
2. *The Scarlet Letter*
3. Low man on the totem pole
4. One potato, two potato
5. Full speed ahead
6. A big fish in a little pond
7. "Call Me Irresponsible"
8. *Raiders of the Lost Ark*
9. Two's company, three's a crowd
10. *E pluribus unum*
11. "Rock-a-bye baby on the tree top"
12. As a matter of fact
13. No charge for alterations
14. *The Picture of Dorian Gray*
15. Fourscore and seven years ago
16. Eight ball in the side pocket
17. The Greatest Show on Earth
18. All dressed up and no place to go
19. "Hickory Dickory Dock"
20. I pledge allegiance to the flag
21. Just in the nick of time
22. "A Bicycle Built for Two"
23. Speak softly and carry a big stick
24. Snap, crackle, and pop
25. Dead men tell no tales

59 BULL'S-EYE 20 QUESTIONS

1. Sates (here'S A TESt)
2. Bass
3. Taxes (Texas)
4. Hanky
5. Conking (*King Kong*)
6. Plague (plaque)
7. Horseshoer
8. Lonely (Tylenol)
9. Bravest (bra, vest)
10. Coroner (colonel)
11. Supersede (spree)
12. Stench (scent)
13. Conserve (converse)
14. Forestall (forced all)
15. Raze (raise)
16. Reminiscent (minis, recent)
17. Everything (very thin)
18. Festival (Fe-S-Ti-V-Al)
19. Cobra (Freud)
20. Edges

"Horse racing is animated roulette."—Roger Kahn

60 AROUND THE WORLD

1. INITIALLY
2. AIRPLANE
3. SPEARMINT
4. VAGABOND
5. FRAGRANCE
6. PERFUME
7. ORCHARD
8. MAGNOLIA
9. INCUBATE
10. CLAUSTROPHOBIA
11. PYROMANIAC
12. CHINCHILLA
13. VINDICATE
14. DISGRACEFUL

60 MENTAL BLOCKS

61 CRYPTO-FUNNIES

Panel 1: Have you ever stolen from an employer? *Applicant:* Yes.
Panel 2: Ever sold secrets to a competitor? *Applicant:* Lots of times!
Panel 3: I've just given the new guy our lie-detector test. *Boss:* How'd he do?
Panel 4: Good news. He's completely honest.

62 CARTOON REBUSES

Readers are credited in parentheses following their prize-winning entries:
1. *Psychology Today* (SIGH-COLLEGE-E-TWO-DAY) (Dominick Rampa, Tarrytown, NY)
2. *The Great Gatsby* (THE-GRATE-GATS-B) (Rick Zimmerman, South Euclid, OH)
3. Walter Cronkite (WALL-TURK-RON-KITE) (T. and C. Dick, Corvallis, OR)
4. Chesapeake (CHESS-UP-EEK) (Clare Grundman, South Salem, NY)
5. Frankie Valli (FRANK-EVE-ALLEY) (David LaRochelle, Coon Rapids, MN)
6. Fidel Castro (FEED-L-CAST-ROW) (Lisa Goodwin, Memphis, TN)
7. Aphrodite (AFRO-DYE-TEE) (Jennifer Jones, Justice, IL)
8. San Diego Zoo (SAND-E-A-GOES-OOO) (Marilyn Brongo, Tucson, AZ)
9. Trapper John (TRAP-URGE-ON) (Nancy Gordon, Elgin, IL)
10. New Delhi (NUDE-EL-E) (Jon Kalos, New York, NY)
11. *Tora! Tora! Tora!* (TORAH-TORAH-TORAH) (Craig Hamilton, Mountain View, CA)
12. Perry Como (PAIR-REEK-OH-MOW) (Gabriel Miller, Clearwater, FL)

64 SEASONAL DOUBLE CROSS

A. DYLAN THOMAS
B. IN THEE TONIGHT
C. CHIMNEY
D. KERCHIEF
E. ELEVENTH
F. NUTMEG
G. SHANGRI-LA
H. AWAY IN A MANGER
I. CITY
J. HO HO HO
K. RUFFED
L. IN THE EAST
M. SNOWPLOW
N. THOMAS NAST
O. MISTLETOE
P. APPARITION
Q. STUFFED GOOSE
R. CLEMENT MOORE
S. ABATE
T. RINK
U. OVENBIRD
V. LEEWAY

I have always thought of Christmastime … as a good time; a kind, forgiving, charitable, pleasant time; the only time I know of, in the long calendar of the year, when men and women seem by one consent to open their shut-up hearts freely. — (Charles) Dickens, *A Christmas Carol*

OURFOURFOURFOURFOUR

65 IT'S A PIP!

The path is shown below:

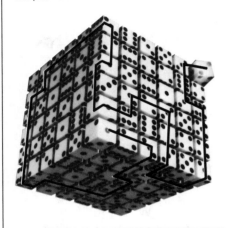

66 WHICH IS WHICH?

1.	Left: Hardy	Right:	Laurel
2.	Left: MacNeil	Right:	Lehrer
3.	Left: Cagney	Right:	Lacey
4.	Left: Japanese	Right:	Chinese
5.	Top: Crocodile	Bottom:	Alligator
6.	Left: Siskel	Right:	Ebert
7.	Left: Janet	Right:	Vivien
8.	Left: Ernie	Right:	Bert
9.	Left: Whopper	Right:	Big Mac
10.	Left: Manet	Right:	Monet
11.	Left: Vermont	Right:	N. Hampshire
12.	Left: Abbott	Right:	Costello
13.	Left: Eva	Right:	Zsa Zsa
14.	Left: Hutch	Right:	Starsky

Photo credits MacNeil/Lehrer Productions (2); © New York Zoological Society (5); Buena Vista Television (6); Children's Television Workshop, Ernie photo by Anita and Steve Shevett, Bert photo by Richard Termine (8); Whopper ® photo by Gamma (Chicago), Big Mac photo property of McDonald's (9); © Rosenthal Art Slides, courtesy of Metropolitan Museum of Art (10)

68 MIRROR LAKE

The reflections in the lake differ from the real world in the following ways (roughly left to right):

Deciduous trees have replaced the evergreens.
The shape of the tent opening is round.
The campfire and smoke have disappeared.
A raccoon has replaced the beaver.
The fisherman's shirt is checked instead of plaid.
The fisherman's belt buckle has become two belt loops.
The tops of the fishing rod and line have disappeared.
The duck's neck band has disappeared.
Pine trees have replaced the hikers atop the mountain.
The woman with the camera has shorter hair.
Her companion's clothes have switched colors.
The dog's stick is reversed.
The reflections of the two mountains in the background are switched.
An airplane has replaced the bird.
Cirrus clouds have replaced the cumulus clouds.

The low central mountain has disappeared.
Some of the bushes (to the left of the cabin) have no reflection.
The chimney and smoke have vanished.
A pine tree is reflected where there is none.
A board roof has replaced the cabin's shingle roof.
The cabin's window has disappeared.
The canoeist's direction is reversed.
The paddle has no reflection.
The 9 in the canoe's registration number is not flipped.
The woman's jacket has become long-sleeved.
The backpacker's sunglasses have disappeared.
His sleeping bag has changed from red to yellow.
The rocks by his feet have disappeared.
The squirrel's orientation has changed.
A doe has replaced the buck.

80 PHOTO FINISH

The pictures suggest the letters of the alphabet, as listed at right; the letter A, in the photo at far right, completes the set.

1.	V	**6.**	Q	**11.**	O	**16.**	B	**21.**	R
2.	J	**7.**	Z	**12.**	I	**17.**	C	**22.**	G
3.	P	**8.**	D	**13.**	K	**18.**	F	**23.**	S
4.	Y	**9.**	H	**14.**	W	**19.**	U	**24.**	M
5.	T	**10.**	N	**15.**	X	**20.**	E	**25.**	L

70 NUMBERS, PLEASE

1. Personal check
2. Clock
3. Hopscotch area
4. Thermostat
5. Ingredients list (percentage of USDA recommended allowances)
6. Thermometer
7. Suntan lotion
8. Radio dial
9. Social Security card
10. McDonald's "burgers sold" sign
11. Measuring cup
12. One-dollar bill
13. Heinz ketchup
14. Golf club (an 8-iron)
15. Battery
16. License plate (NJ)
17. Music staff
18. Postage stamp (with postmark)
19. UPC (Universal Product Code) symbol
20. Typewriter

72 POP PARTY

The rock stars present are listed below, as they appear from top to bottom within each area.

Far left: The Doors, America, The Four Aces.

Middle left: The Cars, The Beatles, The Police, Prince, The Dixie Cups, The Platters, Bread, The Monkees, The Crickets.

Center left: The Animals, Chubby Checker, Queen, Air Supply, Styx.

Center right: Wild Cherry, The Beach Boys, The Bee Gees.

Middle right: Three Dog Night, The Byrds, The Carpenters, Men at Work, Madonna, Earth, Wind & Fire, The Mamas & the Papas, The Four Tops.

Far right: The Rolling Stones, The Eagles, Chicago, Strawberry Alarm Clock.

Other answers are possible.

74 FAMILY FOOD

The correct sequence is: A, I, L, E, B, F, H, J, K, G, D, C. Photo **A** was taken before breakfast, and photo **I** after (fewer muffins, less milk, orange juice, and butter). Photo **L** was taken while lunch was being made (salami, bacon, and Coke missing, fewer eggs and tomatoes). Photo **E** was after lunch (some salami is gone, lettuce is cut in half, bacon package opened, Coke, mustard, and mayonnaise have been used). Photo **B** was taken after a between-meals snack of fruit, a banana, and cheese; in photo **F** only a can of 7-Up is missing. Some new groceries have been added in photo **H** (chicken, donuts, broccoli, and wine). During photo **J**, dinner was being prepared, largely with the products just purchased (the chicken and wine are missing, as is part of the broccoli). Photo **K** was taken during dinner, with the same items missing as in photo J, along with the 7-Up and the butter. After dinner, photo **G** shows the cooked chicken returned to the refrigerator, as well as a shorter butter stick. Photo **D** was taken during a healthful after-dinner snack of bananas and fruit, while photo **C** shows a not-quite-so-healthful late-night snack of milk and donuts.

78 THE I'S HAVE IT

The "I" objects are (from top to bottom within each area):
Far left: Billy Idol, inverted Jenny airmail stamp, Israeli flag, industry, Ivory Snow, Indian, internal combustion engine, Instamatic camera, icing, insect, iron.
Center left: income tax, inning, infield, indigo bunting, iris, ice cream, index finger, illustrator (and illustration), Chevy Impala, Indianapolis, Indiana, Ike, initials.
Center right: *I Love Lucy,* interstate, Illinois, IBM, incandescent bulb, Holiday Inn, Jeremy Irons, indoor pool, infant, inches, integers, John Irving, Chrysler Imperial, index, Julio Iglesias, *It Happened One Night.*
Far right: ink, Independence Hall, I-beam, interchange, *I Dream of Jeannie,* inner tube, *It,* instant coffee, International Harvester, Irish setter, Lee Iacocca, Jill Ireland.

This puzzle was adapted from *Arlene Alda's ABC Book and Poster* (Celestial Arts, Berkeley, CA); © 1981 by Arlene Alda. Besides being a successful photographer, Ms. Alda is the wife of actor Alan Alda.

76 THE SAGA OF SUBWAY SAM

Sam went to stay with his girl-friend, who lived in Jackson Heights, Queens (on the "F" line). Starting at South Ferry, Manhattan, on the "1" train, his route (marked on the map, at right) was as follows:

"1" north to 96th St.
"2" north, passing into the Bronx, continues east to 149th St.
"5" south back into Manhattan to Grand Central
"7" west to 42nd St.
"RR" south, east into Brooklyn and south to 36th St.
"B" southeast to Coney Island
"F" northwest to Hoyt St.
"A" northeast to Broadway
"J" west to Myrtle Ave.
"M" northeast to Wyckoff Ave.
"LL" west to Lorimer St.
"GG" north into Queens to Queens Plaza
"N" west to Queensboro Plaza
"7" east to Elmhurst Ave.
"F" west to Jackson Heights

A more direct route would have been:
"1" north to Times Square
"7" east to Elmhurst Ave. in Queens
"F" west to Jackson Heights

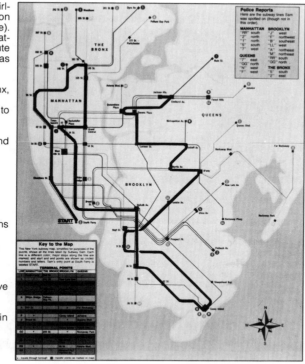

82 FOOD, GLORIOUS FOOD

1. c
2. a–whole-wheat bread, b–coleslaw, c–rice pudding
3. b
4. a–4, b–5, c–1, d–2, e–3
5. a–Wendy's Single, b–McDonald's Big Mac, c–White Castle, d–Burger King Whopper
6. Nouvelle cuisine–a, cuisine minceur–b, grazing–b
7. e (tomato), b (Iceberg lettuce), h (cucumbers), f (bacon bits), g (fresh fruit), d (hard-boiled eggs), c (coleslaw), a (raw green beans)
8. d
9. a–4, b–1, c–2, d–3, e–6, f–5
10. a–8, b–5, c–7, d–1, e–9, f–6, g–2, h–4, i–3, j–10
11. a
12. a–4, b–5, c–2, d–1, e–3
13. d
14. c
15. b (The avocado is 75% fat, devil's-food cake is 40%–50%, flank steak 30%–40%, pancakes 20%–30%, buttermilk less than 20%.)
16. c
17. a–al dente (Tender pasta contains more water, thus has fewer calories per unit volume.)
   b–yolk (A cup of yolks has 846 calories, a cup of egg whites has 396.)
   c–they're the same (You shouldn't eat the pits.)
18. d (In 1977, the reported price in Hong Kong for an ounce of wild ginseng from China's Chan Pak Mountains was $23,000. By comparison, First Choice Black Perigord truffles sell for $13.20 per .44 ounce.)
19. b
20. c (Since 1912, about 100 billion Oreos have been sold.)
21. a (Technically, a peanut is a legume, and Brazil nuts and almonds are seeds.)

84 TIME OUT

Break Time
There are four pieces, adding up to 18, 19, 20, and 21, as shown.

Flibberty-Digits
The clock is upside down.

Double Trouble
It's 3:15. The correct time can be determined by adding the two clocks' times together (and, if necessary, subtracting 12 from the total), since the time lost by the backward-running clock will offset the time gained by the double-speed clock. Thus, 8:45 plus 6:30 equals 14:75, which would be 15:15 on the clock. This reduces to 3:15.

A Sticky Situation
The numbers were placed as shown.

Minute Mystery
The butler did it. The numbers on the clocks are set to 5:14, 7:12, 9:19, 8:13, and 1:14. Using the code A=1, B=2, etc., down to Z=26, the clocks spell out ENGLISHMAN. None of the lord's guests was British, and the maid was a woman.

86 AH, WILDERNESS!

The "journeys," from macro to micro, are as follows:
A-G-O-P (Cascade Canyon, Grand Teton National Park, Wyoming)
B-I-K-R (Phantom Ship, Crater Lake National Park, Oregon)
C-F-M-T (Turk Mountain, Shenandoah National Park, Virginia)
D-J-N-Q (Bass Harbor Head Lighthouse, Acadia National Park, Maine)
E-H-L-S (Long House, Mesa Verde National Park, Colorado)

Maps A, B, D, H, and O are from *National Geographic Atlas of the World* (1966); F, G, J, and N, *Rand McNally National Park Guide* (1984); I, Rand McNally road map of Washington and Oregon; E, *The Times Atlas of the World* (1981); L, *The Sierra Club Guide to the National Parks: Desert Southwest* (1984). Photos Q, S, and T, Image Bank; P, Bruce Coleman; R, Photo Researchers.

88 BEMUSEMENT PARK

Upper left:
One stuffed doll has three (yellow) feet; one of the panels on the awning has square edges; a flag in the foreground goes behind the ride in the background; one of the bottom cars on the Ferris wheel is different from the others; the man in sunglasses is wearing them upside-down, and his shirt collar is crooked.

Lower left:
The boy in green is dressed in winter clothes; one milk bottle is upside-down, one bottle is transparent, and one is missing; the sign says "3 Balls $1,000"; the boy's cotton candy has blue spots, the color patterns of his sleeves do not match, and he has one short pants leg and one long one; one baseball on the counter is an egg; the man is throwing an apple instead of a baseball, he is wearing a football shirt with the name of a baseball team (Mets), his belt disappears into his pants, and he has only four fingers on his right hand; his girlfriend's doll is frowning; a girl is eating an apple instead of a baseball; one horse on the carousel is facing the wrong way, and the pole on that horse is uneven.

Upper right:
There is a dog on the ride; one of the boats is a pink elephant; the red flag is blowing in the wrong direction; there is no bell on the bell-ringer; the boy next to it is using a baseball bat instead of a sledgehammer, and the bell-ringer is a glass; one balloon is upside-down and another is missing a string; one stripe on the tent is orange instead of green.

Lower right:
A boy is wearing high heels; a girl's socks are two different colors; the shirt on the boy with the gun reads "USC Bruins" (USC's team is the Trojans); one gun is not connected to a hose, and the second boy is holding a handgun instead of a watergun.

90 DRAWN AND QUARTERED

1. A case of do or die (Duer dye)
2. Throwing a little light on the subject (Lite beer)
3. Talking a blue streak
4. Call of the wild
5. Ready, willing and able (red E, Will Ling, and Abel)
6. Ducking the issue
7. Kiss and tell (rock group Kiss and William Tell)
8. Out on a limb
9. Looking at the world through rose-colored glasses
10. Fishing for compliments (complements: the bat and the ball, etc.)
11. Stealing his thunder
12. Sign on the dotted line (dotted lion)
13. Passing the buck

Puzzles by George Gipe, Robert Leighton, Peter de Sève, Mary Ellen Slate, and Stephanie Spadaccini, and based on an idea by George Gipe.

94 SELL MATES

(Where applicable, the name of the character appears after the product.)
1. Pillsbury Poppin Fresh Dough (Pillsbury Dough Boy)
2. Mr. Salty pretzels
3. Rice Krispies (Snap & Crackle)
4. Campbell's Soup (Campbell's Soup Kid)
5. Uncle Ben's Rice
6. Keebler Cookies (elf)
7. 9 Lives Cat Food (Morris)
8. Pampers disposable diapers
9. Hamburger Helper
10. Starkist Tuna (Charlie the Tuna)
11. Charmin toilet paper
12. Peter Pan Peanut Butter
13. Trix cereal (the Trix rabbit)
14. Kool-Aid
15. Orville Redenbacher popcorn
16. Little Debbie Snack Cakes
17. 3 Musketeers candy bar
18. Swiss Miss cocoa mix

96 COLOR CROSSWORD

O	R	G	A	N	I	S	M		D	
U		G		C		A	Q	U	A	
F	R	I	E	D	E	G	G		C	
A		N		S	L	I	N	K	Y	
S	L	E	D	S		O		E		E
I		R	A	I	N	B	O	W		L
Z	G		X		E	D	S	E	L	
E	L	O	P	E	S		D		V	
	I		O	R	I	G	I	N	A	L
J	A	W	S		G		T		D	
R		H	O	N	E	Y	B	E	E	

"Colour Crossword" is a trademark of Wellingtons Ltd.

92 MISSION: IMPROBABLE

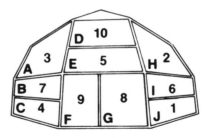

Working through the night, Chuck was finally able to put the photos in the correct chronological order.

J: The gauge that points to "Full" can be traced to the fuel line (labeled in section E and again in section A). The vacuum tubes in the radio are lit. (Chuck figures Cragg is listening to that Martian country-and-western station again.)

H: Engine 2 is overheating, which is what you'd expect on a spaceship with four million light-years on its odometer.

A: The cooling system for engine 2 is on. The oxygen tank is full and the whiskey bottle unopened. (Cragg rarely has his first drink before leaving the solar system.)

C: The radio fuse is blowing.

E: Cragg has donned the oxygen tank, which still reads full, and is leaving the *Doberman* for the hostile green atmosphere of Verdanta.

I: The gauge on the oxygen tank, now replaced in a different wall niche, reads empty, and the crystals that Cragg brought back are glowing.

B: The experiments are either in progress or have been completed, and the crystals in the beaker have stopped glowing. The whiskey bottle is still on the shelf, much to Chuck's surprise.

G: The whiskey bottle has been opened and is partially empty, and Cragg is smoking his first cigar (the ashtray is empty, except for a single match). It looks to Chuck as if the captain's had a rough flight.

F: There are a couple of cigar butts in the ashtray. Cragg is cutting the gas-mask hose.

D: A segment of hose has been used to fix the overhead pipe. Chuck chuckles, remembering that the water pipe leaks every time Cragg takes a hot shower in orbit.

What Chuck couldn't learn from the photos was the bad news Cragg delivered the next day: The crystals are living creatures that die and thereby lose their glow of life when separated from Verdanta. The dead crystals are totally worthless.

VEFIVEFIVEFIVEFIVEFIVEFIVEFIVEFIVEFIVEFIVEFIVEFIV

97 KNIGHT TRAIN

1	6	35	20	17	4
28	19	2	5	34	21
7	36	27	18	3	16
26	29	14	11	22	33
13	8	31	24	15	10
30	25	12	9	32	23

99 I'VE GOT A SECRET

1. Marcia Baer, Painting
2. Sally Fedirka, Chemistry
3. Greg Redeagle, Algebra
4. Patrice Martin, Spanish
5. Jon Lee, Calculus
6. Gail Lotak, Botany
7. Steve Schwartz, Poetry
8. Carol Schwartz, Geometry
9. Dick Wiseman, Biology
10. Mary Redeagle, Literature
11. Bill Lotak, German
12. Marge Wiseman, Ceramics
13. Al Martin, Creative Writing
14. Debbie Lee, French
15. Paul Fedirka, Sculpture

98   DIGITITIS

Puzzle 1

```
              9889
115 ) 1137235
          1035
          1022
           920
          1023
           920
          1035
          1035
             0
```

Puzzle 2

```
              38052
29 ) 1103508
        87
       233
       232
        150
        145
          58
          58
           0
```

Puzzle 3

```
            2143009
213 ) 456460917
        426
        304
        213
        916
        852
        640
        639
        1917
        1917
           0
```

Puzzle 4

```
            91272
37 ) 3377064
       333
        47
        37
        100
         74
        266
        259
          74
          74
           0
```

102   CAN YOU THINK . . . ?

1. T
2. YRAURBEF
3. July, August
4. Yes
5. No
6. 16
7. J and V ("no" would also be an acceptable answer)
8. Seven (Ron has four and Don has two)
9. Jamaica, Japan (Jordan is also acceptable)
10. 236-9854
11. Engineer, eleven, emerge, extreme (many other answers are also acceptable)
12. 11
13. Circle "ilptu" (tulip); the others are anagrams of the names of fruits (peach, prune, grape)
14. Leave the next space blank.
15.

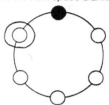

16. 70 ÷ 7 + 2 - 6 = 6
17. Finnish

Scoring
Count one point for each correct answer. Maximum score: 17.

Ratings

15-17   Whiz! Part human, part machine. Is there nothing you cannot do?
12-14   Excellent! A career in air traffic control awaits you.
10-11   Very good. A sharp head and cool wits, or something like that.
8-9   Good. You're probably more of the meditative sort …
6-7   Fair. At least you've managed to find the answer page.
Under 6   Hey, somebody has to come in last!

100   FLOATING STOCK

The objects worth taking are: the stapler (1), darts (7), exercise bicycle (8), yo-yo (11), vacuum cleaner (12), and mousetrap (15) (though the chances of catching any mice are pretty slim). Surprisingly, a candle (3) does not burn in microgravity. A ballpoint pen (10) needs gravity to keep the ink flowing (astronauts do use special ballpoints which contain pressurized liquid nitrogen to push the ink toward the point). Bathroom scales (13) measure weight, so would be of no use in a weightless environment. A pepper mill (9) will only grind when the corns are pressed by their own weight against the blades. The pendulum of a grandfather clock (5) would not swing as it should for the clock to keep time. The stylus of a record player (14) would not stay in the groove. Water in a coffee maker (6) would still be forced into the coffee grounds but would not necessarily fall through into the jug. An egg timer (4) would be no good for obvious reasons. The action of all piano keys relies on lead weights to return the keys to their original position once they are struck, so a piano (2) would not play in zero gravity.

103   ANIMAL CRACKERS

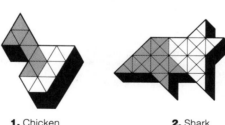

1. Chicken

2. Shark

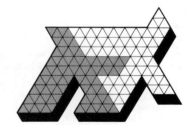

3. Elephant

4. Turtle

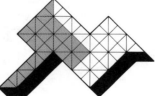

5. Seagull

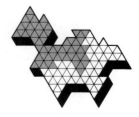

6. Camel

104 EXTRASENSORY DECEPTION

To begin with, Crispin had a highly trained memory. Wherever he went and whomever he talked to, he mentally noted whatever facts turned up; some he would be able to use, some he discarded. On arrival at the airport, he set in motion part of his standard operating procedure. He called the hotel where he been told he would be staying, to leave a phony message (see #4), but discovered he wasn't registered there. Then, pretending to be a reporter, he phoned the university seeking an interview with the psychic. Thus he learned the name of the new hotel (#3), and on further questioning got descriptions of Shillip (#1) and Judy and the news that they would both be meeting him (#2).

At the airport, Crispin called the Dorchester and left the message purportedly from his mother (#4).

Crispin took a chance on the vague phrase "on the way" (#5). If Shillip's house wasn't actually on the way to the campus, the expression could be passed over as meaning simply "while we're going"; if the house really was en route, Crispin would luck out.

When Shillip dropped Crispin off at the hotel, the psychic noted the car's odometer reading and, when he was picked up again, automatically noted the mileage to Shillip's house. Then, on the unexpected trip back to the house, Crispin made use of this information (#6).

During his 45-minute wait at the hotel bar, Crispin studied the local phone book (see #10). About ten minutes before the professor was due back, Crispin phoned Shillip's home, leaving the receiver off the hook and placing an "out of order" sign on the phone. Thus, Shillip's phone would keep ringing (#7) if he didn't have an answering machine, or, in case he did, if he had absent-mindedly forgotten to turn it on. As it turned out, the latter proved to be true. When he made the call, Crispin had planned to say to Shillip, later in the evening, "Someone has been trying for hours to reach you on the phone."

However, the unexpected trip to Shillip's house allowed Crispin to use this gambit to more dramatic effect.

While Shillip and Judy went into Shillip's house to get the check, Crispin quickly riffled through the glove compartment. Here he found an RSVP to Shillip's upcoming wedding (#8).

When Crispin was reading the newspaper during the trip from the airport, he noticed several ads for motorcycles had been circled and deduced that Shillip was looking for one (#9).

The trick at the end of Crispin's performance was simple (#10). By using dice, he limited the numbers that a volunteer could choose. The highest number that can show on three dice with different numbers is 654; the lowest, 123. Reversing either of those numbers or any number in between, and then subtracting the smaller number from the larger, can produce only five possible results: 99, 198, 297, 396, and 495. Thus the volunteer was forced to choose one of those pages in the phone book. While at the hotel, Crispin had simply checked all five pages and memorized the first phone number on each of them. Onstage, even though he was blindfolded, Crispin could see the phone book by peeking down the side of his nose. And he could tell which of the five pages had been selected by the thickness of the open directory. He deliberately muffed the first guess for dramatic effect.

Lastly, while ostensibly going to the bathroom at Shillip's house, Crispin set the clock in the professor's bedroom ahead about a half-hour (#11). At the time, he was not quite sure what use he would make of this, but he figured something would turn up. While waiting in the auditorium to go on stage, he saw a notice of a special class that Shillip was going to teach the following morning. This provided a peg for the fast clock at Shillip's home, especially when Crispin put it together with the professor's tendency to be late.

Why didn't Crispin predict the car accident? We'll let you figure that one out for yourself.

108 MY LITTLE GAMBLE

The numbers are shaded.

1	8	15	22	29	36	43
2	9	16	23	30	37	44
3	10	17	24	31	38	45
4	11	18	25	32	39	46
5	12	19	26	33	40	47
6	13	20	27	34	41	48
7	14	21	28	35	42	49

112 STATE VS. JOSEPH HILL

The correct verdict is "Not Guilty."

Mrs. Hunter can be ruled out as a suspect because she had no motive. She testified that only three people could have committed the murder.

The opportunity of the defendant Hill and Mrs. Ball *was at night,* that of Meek *in the bright morning at 7:05.*

Therefore, the murderer must have been Burton Meek. Flies and mosquitoes naturally fly toward the window when a room is darker than the outdoors (which is why indoor houseflies bounce against the window all day when it's sunny outside). As all the insects were found dead on the sill, it must have been daylight when the gas that killed Bragg was turned on.

106 PUZZLES FROM THE POLE VAULT

1. Paint Box
Since the three sections at each corner of the cube all border each other, there must be one red, one yellow, and one black section for each color—or eight sections of each color altogether.

2. Bicycle Race
Since Adam can cycle 50 kilometers in the time Bogdan can cycle 48, the two will be side by side 2 kilometers before the finish of their second race. As Adam is the faster cyclist, he will go on to win. His margin of victory, in case you're interested, will be 2 x (1-48/50) or .08 kilometers.

3. Sum Way or Other
The equation is 3548 + 2412 = 5960.

4. Eighteen Holes

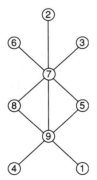

5. Follow the Folds
Cube #2 cannot be made from the pattern.

6. Puzzled Postman
The only apartments that have both doorbells and knockers are apartments 1, 3, and 5. Apartments 1 and 3 cannot be Mr. Kowalski's because their only neighbor with a doorbell is apartment 2, and Mr. Kowalski's sister lives there. Therefore, Mr. Kowalski must live in apartment 5.

7. Taking Sides
A.   5 + 3 = 8
B.   4 + 4 = 8

8. Labyrinth

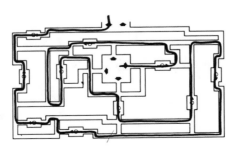

9. Tunnel Vision
Let x = length of the tunnel in meters. The man travels x meters at 45 kilometers per hour (the combined speed of the train and his walking) in the same time that the train travels x - 125 meters at 40 kilometers per hour.

The equation $x/45 = (x - 125)/40$ solves to $x = 1125$. Therefore, the length of the tunnel is 1125 meters.

10. Rank and File
Sergeant A needs 28 moves as follows:

1. B to 1	15. E to 7
2. C to 2	16. A to 11
3. D to 3	17. D to 12
4. E to 11	18. C to 6
5. F to 4	19. B to 5
6. G to 5	20. A to 1
7. H to 12	21. B to 2
8. J to 7	22. C to 3
9. A to 13	23. D to 4
10. J to 10	24. E to 5
11. H to 9	25. F to 6
12. A to 12	26. G to 7
13. G to 13	27. H to 8
14. F to 8	28. J to 9

109 ON THE ALPINE EXPRESS

M. Duval, the victim, left the dining car at 8:00; the five suspects left at 8:10, 8:20, 8:30, 8:40, and 8:50 (steward's testimony). M. Duval was killed at 8:42, and Dr. Whitneedle decided for reasons known only to himself that the person who left at 8:40 was the killer. That person was the fourth suspect to leave the dining car.

Two women left the dining car before the man in compartment No. 12: the woman in No. 15 (porter's statement) and the woman in either No. 11 or No. 13 (Mrs. Frothingham's statement). These two women were Mme. Ciandi and Miss Lindsay, who left after Mme. Ciandi (Miss Lindsay's statement).

If the man in No. 12 were the Count, then Mr. Watterson, too, left before him (Watterson's statement). In this case, the Count would be fourth—and the murderer—and Mrs. Frothingham fifth (Mrs. Frothingham's statement).

Pursuing this possibility, Mr. Watterson could have been the first or the second suspect to leave, but not the third (steward's statement). Miss Lindsay would be third and Mme. Ciandi either first or second. Since the Count in No. 12 left after Miss Lindsay, she would be in No. 13 (Miss Lindsay's statement). So, by the porter's statement, Mme. Ciandi would have to be in No. 15, but her own statement is that she is not in the rearmost compartment. Therefore the Count is not the man in No. 12; Mr. Watterson is.

Two women left before Mr. Watterson, and the Count and the other women left after him. The two women who left before him are Mme. Ciandi and Miss Lindsay, in that order; Mme. Ciandi is not in No. 15, so Miss Lindsay is. That puts the Count in No. 14 (Miss Lindsay's statement). He could not have left directly after Watterson, so he is fifth and Mrs. Frothingham is the murderer. She is in No. 13 (Watterson's statement), and Mrs. Ciandi is in No. 11.

In summary, Mme. Ciandi, in No. 11, left the dining car at 8:10; Miss Lindsay, in No. 15, left at 8:20; Mr. Watterson, in No. 12, left at 8:30; Mrs. Frothingham, in No. 13, left at 8:40 and is the murderer; and Count Zathmary, in No. 14, left at 8:50.

110 FROM THE DESK OF...

The rooms are located as shown.

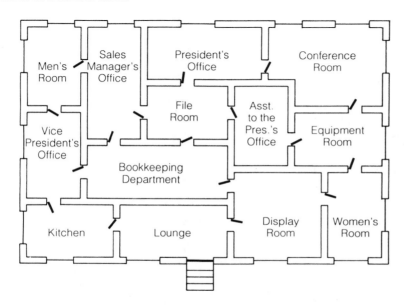

114 HIROIMONO

Our solutions:

1. Letter A   **2. Cannon**

3. Robot   **4. Armored Tank**

5. Bleachers   **6. Pinwheel**

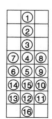

115 SAY CHEESE!

1. Whoopi Goldberg
2. David Letterman
3. Princess Di
4. Carol Channing
5. Mick Jagger
6. Groucho Marx

116 ICE CREAM, YOU SCREAM

1. a, followed by chocolate and Neapolitan
2. Most (e), least (c)
3. a
4. d
5. b
6. d
7. a (Frusen Glädjè is also produced in the U.S.)
8. Orange, pineapple, lime, lemon, raspberry
9. b
10. b
11. c
12. c
13. a
14. c
15. c
16. a
17. c
18. c
19. c
20. b
21. c
22. a
23. b
24. 1–b, 2–i, 3–h; 4–c; 5–e, 6–d, 7–g, 8–f, 9–j, 10–a

118 MEASURE FOR MEASURE

1. "Do You Know the Way to San Jose?" by Burt Bacharach and Hal David (sung by Dionne Warwick)
2. "Bridge Over Troubled Water" by Paul Simon (Simon & Garfunkel)
3. "On Broadway" by Barry Mann, Cynthia Weil, Mike Stoller, and Jerry Leiber (The Drifters, George Benson)
4. "Only the Good Die Young" by Billy Joel
5. "The Hokey-Pokey" (traditional)
6. "Day Tripper" by John Lennon and Paul McCartney (The Beatles)
7. "Send in the Clowns" by Stephen Sondheim (Judy Collins)
8. "Aquarius" by James Rado, Gerome Ragni, and Galt MacDermot (5th Dimension)
9. "The Candy Man" by Leslie Bricusse and Anthony Newley (Sammy Davis, Jr.)
10. "Mame" by Jerry Herman (Louis Armstrong, others)
11. "Return to Sender" by Winfield Scott and Otis Blackwell (Elvis Presley)
12. "Tomorrow" by Martin Charnin and Charles Strouse (Andrea McArdle, others; from the musical *Annie*)

119   SLEUTHS IN SHADOW

1. Jessica Fletcher (Angela Lansbury)
2. Charlie Chan (Sidney Toler)
3. Sherlock Holmes (Basil Rathbone)
4. Sam Spade (Humphrey Bogart)
5. Inspector Clouseau (Peter Sellers)
6. Dick Tracy (as himself)
7. Miss Marple (Margaret Rutherford)
8. Lieutenant Columbo (Peter Falk)
9. Eliot Ness (Kevin Costner)

120   SORRY, WRONG NUMBER

1. Fake (100% gold is 24K)
2. Possible
3. Fake (odd-numbered interstates run north/south)
4. Fake (packages cannot be sent by second-class mail)
5. Fake (striped balls are numbered 9-15)
6. Possible
7. Fake (zip codes begin with higher numbers the farther west one goes; all West Coast zip codes begin with 9)
8. Possible
9. Fake (numbers 70-79 are reserved for tackles)
10. Fake (all area codes have 0 or 1 as the middle digit)
11. Fake (bowling balls can weigh no more than 16 pounds)
12. Possible
13. Possible
14. Possible
15. Fake (the digit after the decimal in an FM number is always odd)
16. Possible

122   WHATCHAMACALLITS

1. B		12.	B
2. C (also called a slipcase)		13.	B
3. A		14.	B
4. A		15.	C
5. A		16.	B
6. C		17.	A
7. A		18.	A
8. B		19.	C
9. A		20.	C
10. B		21.	C
11. A			

124   SPORTS ABBREVIATED

1. Tennis
2. Football
3. Horse racing
4. Baseball
5. Figure skating
6. Decathlon
7. Soccer
8. Boxing
9. Table tennis
10. Golf
11. Rodeo
12. Jai alai
13. Auto racing
14. Bowling
15. Ice hockey

125   NUMBER, PLEASE!

The key number is 88.

A. $8 \times 3 = 24$	**J.** $6 \times 6 = 36$	**S.** $31 + 6 = 37$
B. $14 - 7 = 7$	**K.** $40 - 16 = 24$	**T.** $5 - 4 = 1$
C. $9 + 3 = 12$	**L.** $500 \div 100 = 5$	**U.** $3 \times 3 = 9$
D. $45 \div 3 = 15$	**M.** $57 \div 3 = 19$	**V.** $10 \times 5 = 50$
E. $60 \div 2 = 30$	**N.** $9 \times 3 = 27$	**W.** $9 + 7 = 16$
F. $24 - 7 = 17$	**O.** $101 - 88 = 13$	**X.** $10 \div 2 = 5$
G. $48 - 48 = 0$	**P.** $8 + 6 = 14$	**Y.** $64 \div 8 = 8$
H. $19 + 12 = 31$	**Q.** $66 - 40 = 26$	
I. $9 - 5 = 4$	**R.** $30 \div 3 = 10$	

A	B	C	D	E
24	7	12	15	30
F 17	**G** 0	**H** 31	**I** 4	**J** 36
K 24	**L** 5	**M** 19	**N** 27	**O** 13
P 14	**Q** 26	**R** 10	**S** 37	**T** 1
U 9	**V** 50	**W** 16	**X** 5	**Y** 8

126   THINKING PHYSICS

1. MAGNET CAR: (c) The force of the magnet pulling on the iron car is counterbalanced by the force of the iron car pulling on the magnet. Since the magnet is attached to the car through the boy, the two forces in effect cancel each other, and no work is done.

2. COLD BATH: (c) The weight of the water displaced by the iceberg exactly equals the weight of the iceberg. When it turns back into water, it fits exactly into the volume of water it displaced when it was an iceberg.

3. RUBBER BULLET: (a) The momentum of the aluminum bullet is transferred completely to the block, which supplies the necessary impulse to stop it. But for the rubber bullet, the block supplies not only the impulse necessary to stop it, it also provides enough additional impulse to "throw the bullet back." Depending on the elasticity of the rebound, this results in up to twice the impulse for the impact of the rubber bullet, and therefore up to twice the momentum is imparted to the block. So the rubber bullet is more likely to knock it over.

4. GOING DOWN: (b) Because water is practically incompressible, its density near the surface is the same as it is deeper down. Thus, the buoyant force needed to hold the boulder is the same regardless of the boulder's depth.

5. TURNING CART WHEELS: (a) The left wheel is the first to encounter the grass, so it is the first to be slowed. The right wheel remains at its greater speed on the sidewalk until it meets the grass. When both wheels are on the grass, they again move in a straight line.

6. BOTTLENECK: (b) Water flows faster in narrow parts and slows in wide parts, just as in a creek.

7. TOUGH NUT: (b) The screw and the nut are not completely in contact; there is a small space between them. For the very tight nut the problem is that this space is too small. How can it be increased? By heat. Heat will make everything expand: the nut, the screw, and the space between them. So to loosen the nut, heat it.

8. CAROUSEL: (b) By the time the ball reaches the other side of the carousel, Danny will have moved to the left of where the ball was thrown. Thus, it will pass to the right of him.

9. JAR OF FLIES: (c) The weight depends on the mass of the jar, and the position of the flies does not change that. Their weight in flight is transmitted to the bottom of the jar by the air currents generated by their wings.

10. CREAM IT: (a) You should add the cream right away. The hotter a body is, compared with its surroundings, the greater the rate at which it cools. (Newtons's law of cooling: a hot body cools faster, degree for degree, than a warm body.) So by adding the cream right away, you reduce the cooling rate of the coffee during the interval before drinking time. If you wait, the hot coffee will cool fast, and when you finally add the cream, you'll bring the temperature down even further.

11. TORQUE: (b) No. Attaching the rope merely increases the distance from the bolt to the location of the applied force; it doesn't increase the leverage. For more torque, Harry needs either a longer wrench or more pull.

128   WOODSTOCK RE-GENERATION

1. a
2. c
3. b
4. b: Approximately 50,000 people showed up before the concert started.
5. b
6. c
7. b
8. a: Abbie Hoffman was paid a few thousand dollars. After he jumped on stage and grabbed a microphone in the middle of The Who's set, Pete Townshend clubbed him off the stage with his guitar.
9. a
10. b
11. a: The first act scheduled to perform was Sweetwater. Because the members of the group were stuck in traffic, they were forced to perform second.
12. c
13. a: After The Who found out that The Dead were being paid up front in cash, they demanded it as well.
14. b
15. a
16. c
17. a and c: Iron Butterfly was scheduled to appear but did not show up.
18. a-3, b-6, c-4, d-1, e-2, f-5
19. a-4, b-2, c-3, d-5, e-1
20. b
21. a
22. c
23. a
24. c: According to the Town Clerk in Bethel, NY, the festival produced more trash than the town produced in one year. It took three months to clean it up.
25. c, b, a, d
    After ticket sales, film and record deals, lawsuits and legal fees, the promoters ended up losing $100,000.

130   IDENTIFYING THE ISSUES

The magazine logos were mixed up as follows:

Magazine Name:	In the Style of:
Rolling Stone	National Lampoon
National Lampoon	Sports Illustrated
Sports Illustrated	People
People	Games
Games	Mademoiselle
Mademoiselle	Gourmet
Gourmet	Time
Time	Mad
Mad	Omni
Omni	Playboy
Playboy	Esquire
Esquire	The New Yorker
The New Yorker	Reader's Digest
Reader's Digest	Scientific American
Scientific American	Rolling Stone

132 CAN YOU ANSWER THIS?

1. Fred Ott's Sneeze was the first copyrighted motion picture, filmed by Thomas Edison.
2. Alaska cost us 2¢ per acre; Louisiana cost us 3¢ per acre.
3. It indicates how the rider died: four hooves on ground, natural death; two hooves raised, killed in battle; one hoof raised, died of battle wounds.
4. For holding logs; they're andirons.
5. Strawberry.
6. To prevent their food from freezing—the refrigerator was warmer than the outside temperatures.
7. It's the only work Michelangelo ever signed. He did so after hearing sightseers credit the work to another sculptor.
8. The choice was decided by a coin toss. (History does not record who won the toss, however.)
9. He won 100,000 francs in a state lottery.
10. Iran.
11. The ostrich.
12. Your life must have been saved by a parachute. The club's name stems from the silkworms who make the silk used in parachutes.
13. Two minutes later, the temperature was +68° F.—a record temperature climb.
14. The Guinness Book of World Records
15. The Dutch boy—the tune for "The Battle Hymn" is the same as that of the Dutch national anthem.
16. Crossword tournament.
17. The famous first four notes simulate the Morse Code symbol for the letter V (dot-dot-dot-dash).
18. Chocolate cream pie. (Footnote: One key witness for the defense was Soupy Sales!)
19. Salami.
20. None. Owning a dog is illegal in Reykjavik.

EVENSEVENSEVENSEVENSEVENSEVENSEVENSEVENSEVENSEVENSEVENSEVENSEVENSEVEN

133 PATHFINDER

134 HELTER-SKELTER

1
B	E	E	L	I	N	E	S
R	C	F	L	E	A	N	T
E	N	I	A	P	O	O	A
V	A	L	I	D	A	T	E
D	D	E	R	V	I	S	H
A	P	D	E	P	O	M	O
L	A	R	A	A	R	E	A
I	T	C	H	Y	O	G	A

2

135 PENCIL POINTERS

(crossword grid)

136 A MATTER OF MINUTES

Alex asked Mrs. Featherdown what kind of clock she had seen, and she replied that it was digital.

Although Mrs. Featherdown saw 11:12 on the clock, this cannot be the true time she looked into the bedroom, because all three suspects have alibis for that time. The problem is to find out what time the murder actually occurred.

The window was on one side of the bed, and the overturned table was on the other. Peeking through the window, Mrs. Featherdown couldn't have seen the clock on the floor because the bed would have been in the way—unless, looking directly across the room, she had seen the entire scene reflected in the mirror that covered the entire opposite wall of the bedroom. She didn't have time to notice that it was a reflection because she was knocked out after getting only a glimpse of the room.

Mrs. Featherdown saw 11:12 on the reflected digital clock, which means the clock must have read 51:11. This seems to be impossible—unless the clock landed upside down on the floor when Mr. Mankos upset the bedside table. The clock actually read 11:15, and because it was turned over and reflected, Mrs. Featherdown saw it as 11:12.

If Joshua Mankos was murdered at 11:15, not 11:12, his eldest son, Igor, no longer has an alibi for the time of death. Therefore, Igor killed Joshua Mankos.

(crossword grid)

138 MARCHING BANDS

(crossword grid)

139 SIAMESE TWINS

141 STEPQUOTE

140 TRICKSTER CROSSWORD

ACROSS

1. MESS, not MESH (Vote: 11-6). Most of our voters took the pessimistic view that mixing is more likely to yield a MESS than a MESH. Dissenters felt that a MESS will *usually* occur, but *sometimes*, as the clue reads, you get a MESH.

5. HUMOR, not RUMOR (13-4). *Most* people take offense at RUMOR, which is rarely well-intentioned. But HUMOR, often meant in fun, is more likely to offend only a sensitive person.

6. SHOW, not SHOE (13-4). An improperly cast SHOE might be painful to a horse, but an improperly cast SHOW has a truly rough start.

8. NASTY, not HASTY (11-6). Being NASTY to the police is just asking for trouble, our majority felt, while HASTY answers might be attributed to nervousness. Dissenters, however, argued that HASTY responses could be even more troublesome, resulting in incorrect or incriminating statements.

9. MUGS, not JUGS (10-7). The majority of our testers felt that the host would open only one JUG at a time, so at most just one (not several) would be unfinished. Dissenters felt that partygoers would be likely to finish their own MUGS but not necessarily all JUGS.

11. HERD, not HEAD (13-4). Even to an experienced cowboy, one HEAD of cattle is likely to look pretty much like any other, from a distance. But a real buckaroo should recognize his HERD from its size and composition.

13. GUIDE, not GLIDE (15-2). Airplanes don't normally GLIDE if they're engine-powered. And we'd be more than a little nervous in a plane gliding through rough weather.

14. NEAT, not NEXT (15-2). NEATness may not be everything, but if being NEXT is all it takes to clinch a job, maybe it's not such a great job after all.

15. EGO, not EGG (11-6). All EGGs are easily broken, so it's redundant to speak of handling "one that is fragile." Or so the majority voted. Dissenters felt that it's the person, not the EGO, that's handled, and voted for EGG.

DOWN

1. MASSAGE, not MESSAGE (14-3). A good MESSAGE may make a patient happy, but to "stimulate" a patient—that is, bring blood and oxygen to tired muscles—only a MASSAGE will do.

2. SHOUT, not SCOUT (16-1). There's no "wrong time" for a SCOUT to warn of danger. A SHOUT, on the other hand, has to come at the right time to have a warning effect.

3. SUN, not FUN (14-3). Most people go to the beach for the SUN and would be disappointed by an overcast day. But there are plenty of ways to have FUN even under cloudy skies.

4. DRESS, not PRESS (15-2). If the starlet's legs are indeed famous, it's unlikely that the PRESS would "hardly" cover them. By the same measure, she would probably make special efforts to wear a DRESS that hardly covers them.

7. OUTLIVE, not OUTLINE (9-8). By a slim margin, we felt that nearly all candidates OUTLINE their campaign promises, but only "many" candidates OUTLIVE them. Dissenters said the opposite was true.

10. NIGHT, not FIGHT (10-7). The majority felt that soldiers would consider deserting during the NIGHT instead of the heat of the FIGHT, when there's little time for any kind of reflective thinking. Dissenters argued that soldiers' fears during battle would be more likely to make them think of deserting.

11. HOSE, not HOME (11-6). Although both are true, our majority selected HOSE because the relative reduction in its value is greater than that of a HOME that leaks. Dissenters said that, dollar for dollar, a HOME with leaks costs much more to repair than replacement of a leaky HOSE.

12. DICE, not DIME (11-6). It's unlikely, we thought, that a gambler would have started on the road to ruin with a single DIME, especially in these inflationary times. The minority felt that the word "this" in the clue was more apropos for the singular answer DIME than the plural DICE.

142 LOVE LETTERS

143 THREE-WAY

143 ORNERY CROSSWORD

B	O	O	K	S	S	O	L	I	D		S	O	D	S		B	A	T	H	T	O	W	E	L
I	N	V	E	T	E	R	A	T	E		E	U	R	O		O	T	H	E	R	S	H	O	E
R	E	A	R	R	A	N	G	E	S		A	R	E	S		B	A	R	B	I	C	A	N	E
	F	E	T	A		M	I	S	C	H	A		C	A	R		E	T	A	T
C	U	M		G	A	Y	E		T	H	E	M	O	O	N	I	S		A	R	H	A	T
A	N	E	M	I	C		C	O	M	E	A	R	O	U	N	D		L	I	P	S	A	R	E
S	I	L	A	S		M	O	V	I	E	S	O	N	T	V		T	I	S	H		V	E	L
A	T	O	N		F	E	N	E	T	R	E		P	O	M	A	D	E		G	E	N	L
B	A	T	T	L	E	D	O	R	E	S		G	A	L	L	O	P	I	N	G	A	W	A	Y
A	S	T	R	O	N	O	M	E	R		G	O	T	O	U	T	I	N	T	I	M	E
	A	B	C		I	N	S		A	B	E	T	T	O	R	S		N	O	H	I	T
P	U	S	S		I	S	E	D		S	M	E	L	T	E	R		I	D	S	W	E	A	R
H	H	H		N	H	S		T	I	E	T	I	E	S		F	D	A		R	T	E
D	U	R	A	N	G	O		W	I	D	O	W	E	D		W	I	E	N		M	E	E	K
S	H	E	B	A		W	H	O	M	E	V	E	R		I	A	N		I	D	A
	W	E	S	T	P	Y	R	E	N	E	E	S		O	L	G	A	K	O	R	B	U	T
M	I	D	D	L	E	E	A	S	T	E	R	N		V	O	T	E	G	E	T	T	E	R	S
E	R	O	S		H	O	M	E	E	C		L	A	T	E	R	A	N		E	A	S	E
D	I	P		R	E	P	S		S	K	I	R	E	S	O	R	T	S		O	N	D	I	T
O	N	E	R	E	E	L		S	T	E	R	E	O	H	I	F	I		I	B	S	E	N	S
C	A	R	E	T		E	X	P	E	D	I	E	N	T		P	H	N	O		D	E	E
	A	M	I	A		T	E	D		D	R	A	I	N	S		O	S	I	P
A	N	T	A	R	C	T	I	C		S	I	A	M		O	H	A	W	I	S	E	G	U	Y
L	O	O	S	E	T	A	L	K		O	U	S	E		M	A	G	I	S	T	R	A	T	E
P	A	R	K	S	I	T	E	S		U	M	E	S		S	W	E	E	T	S	U	S	A	N

146 PETAL PUSHERS

148 HEX SIGNS

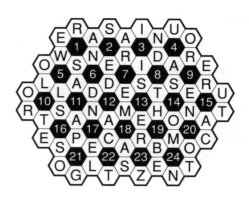

The complete sentences are:

1. The techniciANS WERe working with a saltwater solution.
2. The spoiled child held the bowls and silverwARE, NAStily refusing to share.
3. On my movie scale, *Gandhi* is the kIND I RAte a four-star film.
4. In the desert stood a long saguARO UNDer a circling vulture.
5. Zack's unusuAL LOW Spirits were a result of his failing to get any college grants.
6. The company chemistS ADD ENough indigo to make blue dye.
7. I didn't have to wait long for the razor blaDES I REquested at the drugstore.
8. Overwork makeS A DISTrict attorney become a cruel fellow.
9. Whenever I hear *Que sERA SERa*, it eliminates my sorrows.
10. After riding a faST ROLLer coaster, it may seem great just to walk.
11. That loafer's cousin is a nice guy, wartS AND ALl.
12. The self-maDE MAN Derived his income from his mail-order business.
13. The king's subjects sang the national anTHEM ESpecially loud on his birthday.
14. The combo included two saxopHONES, Three trombones, and an upright piano.
15. A host who is of good character will serve soup iN A TUREen.
16. Some health sPAS TESt their patrons' agility with pogo sticks.
17. For a dinner that's truly romantiC AN APEritif is just the thing to whet the appetite.
18. The youngest Brownie beCAME RAttled when she was separated from the troop.
19. A fellow for wHOM BREathing is difficult should see a doctor.
20. You'd be crazy to bet the farM ON A COlor at roulette where much so gambling is done.
21. To tell the truth, I prefer to forGO SPELling bees if possible.
22. The police broadCAST LEd to the arrest of the man who tried to rook me.
23. The toy animals were made of bronZE, BRASs, and tin.
24. WhEN TOMBoys get dolls, they're more likely to bury them than play with them.

147 AMAZEMENT

The shading shows the path from 1-Across to 126-Across using only the letters of LABYRINTH (69-Across).

149 LETTER DROPS

M	Y	T	O	U	G	H	E	S	T	F	I	G	H	T	W	A	S
W	I	T	H	M	Y	F	I	R	S	T	W	I	F	E	A	L	I

150 ARTHUR WYNNE TRIBUTE

152 THE SPIRAL

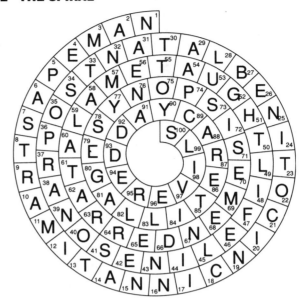

GHTEIGHTEIGHTEIGHTEIGHTEIGHTEIGHTEIGHTEIGHTEIC

NINENINENINENINENINEN

155 SCORE FIVE

Move diagonally to the 6. This forces the next move for both your opponent and yourself, a 4 and a 1, bringing the running total to 127. Your opponent has a choice of 4 or 9; whichever he chooses, take the other to bring the total to 140, adding this score to your side. You can prevent your opponent from scoring further by making moves that bring the running total to a multiple of five whenever possible.

156 NAMYSTICS

(Names of contributors appear in parentheses)
1. Johnny Carson (Marty Harold, Lafayette, IN)
2. Candy Land (Barb Wielfaert, Riga, MI)
3. *David Copperfield*
4. Lee Iacocca (Hy Williamson, Charlottesville, VA)
5. Los Angeles
6. *Titanic* (S.W. Waugh, Midwest City, OK)
7. The Rolling Stones
8. Alfalfa Sprouts
9. Santa Claus
10. Chinese Checkers

154 STACKING THE DECK

The value of the top card on the third stack is the same as the number of cards in your hand.

159 THE BEADLESS ABACUS

1. To give a total of the operations in any three cells in a row, perform the operation in the next cell beyond the row of three, at either end of it, and subtract the result from 34.
   If a row has *only* three cells, do the following: for the third from the top, simply subtract the result of the operation in the *bottommost* cell of the abacus from 34. For the third row from the bottom, subtract the result of the operation in the *topmost* cell from 34.
2. A row of four is even easier: Its total will *always* be 34.
3. All you need to do is glance at the operation in the central cell of the cluster, perform it, and subtract that answer from 68. The result will be the sum of the operations in all seven cells.

162 LUCKY LADY

The queen is between two cards whose sum is 7. Note, too, that this is the only pair of adjacent cards that add up to this total.

163 HEADCRACKER

The greatest number of sections that can be colored without any two colored sections touching is 16. Daniel Johnson, a reader from Terre Haute, Indiana, sent us an elegant proof. He divided the skull into 16 regions, as shown below, so that every area touches every other area in its region. For example, in the lower left, PHILOPROGENITIVENESS, CONJUGAL LOVE, and AMATIVENESS all touch each other. Thus, only one of these can be colored. Likewise, only one area can be colored in each of the other 15 regions. One possible solution with 16 colored sections is shown.

158 CREASED LIGHTNING

The diagrams below show the location of cuts (solid lines) and folds (dotted lines) in each paper sculpture. Dimensions, where important, are indicated.

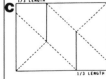

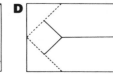

164 LOGIQUIZ

1. MIAMI (synonyms)
(M) mournful, morose; (I) innate, inherent; (A) ancient, archaic; (M) mean, malicious; (I) infuriated, irate.
2. TULSA (antonyms)
(T) short, tall; (U) ugly, beautiful; (L) early, late; (S) fast, slow; (A) plain, fancy.
3. OMAHA (rhymes)
(O) cost, tossed; (M) claim, blame; (A) waist, paste; (H) loathe, clothe; (A) bald, called.
4. TUCSON (homophones)
(T) weight, wait; (U) taut, taught; (C) chaste, chased; (S) least, leased; (O) rowed, road; (N) new, gnu.
5. NEWARK (synonyms)
(N) modern, new; (E) naked, nude; (W) shrewd, wily; (A) crazy, insane; (R) afraid, scared; (K) skinny, lank.
6. DALLAS (phrases containing names of metals)
(D) gold digger; (A) brass tacks; (L) platinum blonde; (L) aluminum foil; (A) lead balloon; (S) silver spoon.
7. ATLANTA (Presidents' names)
(A) James Madison; (T) Theodore Roosevelt; (L) Millard Fillmore; (A) Harry Truman; (N) Andrew Jackson; (T) Chester Arthur; (A) Ronald Reagan.
8. TRENTON (phrases starting with ordinal numbers)
(T) *Twelfth Night*; (R) Third World; (E) nineteenth hole; (N) seventh heaven; (T) Fifth Amendment; (O) fourth dimension; (N) second hand.
9. SEATTLE (phrases starting with possessives)
(S) chef's salad; (E) baker's dozen; (A) busman's holiday; (T) teacher's pet; (T) catcher's mitt; (L) plumber's helper; (E) dealer's choice.

166 MEASURING UP TO MENSA

1. (c)
2. MAIN
3. (b) The position of each black square is moved one box at a time in a straight line, disappears at the end of the square, and then starts again in the same direction.
4. (c) There are two alternating series. Every other number, starting with 2, is increased by one, then by two, then by three, etc. The second series, starting with the 8, is decreased by one.
5. Bolt
6. (a) The lines are at right angles to the edges of the preceding figures.
7. (d)
8. Blossom
9. (b)
10. 30
11. ANT
12. (a) Alarming is an anagram of marginal; enraged is an anagram of angered.
13. (c) 8:30 is half an hour earlier than 9:00
14. SMART
15. Four boys and three girls
16. (a)
17. 24
18. (b) It's the area where the three figures overlap.
19. 12   **20.** (c)
21. (a)   **22.** (b)
23. 40 seconds   **24.** (a)
25. 6
26. (b) The arrow appears at the left edge of the circle every time.
27. $1,000 profit
28. $2.00. "Worsted" contains the letters TWO, as each of the other words contains the letters of its corresponding number.
29. (c) The two numbers are 6 and 12.
30. V   **31.** (d)
32. $45   **33.** (d)

165 KNIGHT MOVES

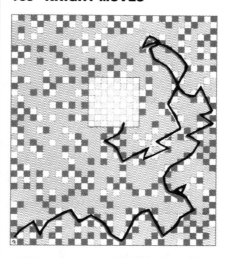

169 ABC CRYPTIC

A	L	A	B	A	M	A	S	T	A	G	G
J	I	N	X	B	O	U	T	I	Q	U	E
A	N	N	A	L	S	P	R	O	U	S	T
X	G	E	S	E	Q	U	I	N	A	H	S
F	O	X	H	O	U	N	D	A	R	E	A
O	C	E	A	N	I	C	E	C	T	R	W
L	Z	S	Y	A	T	H	E	R	E	S	A
L	A	Z	E	S	O	D	D	E	N	L	Y
O	R	E	S	T	E	R	E	O	S	O	Y
W	I	N	C	E	S	U	R	S	I	N	E
E	N	V	I	R	O	N	S	S	L	E	W
R	A	Y	O	N	S	K	E	W	E	R	S

1. Area (NeAR EAstern) **2.** Yews (use)
3. Jinx (J + in + X) **4.** Able (sable - s)
5. Envy (E + navy - a) **6.** Ajax (A + A + J + X)
7. Laze (leis) **8.** Erse (seer) **9.** Aqua (a + qua) **10.** Slew (2 meanings) **11.** Rayon (ray + on) **12.** Lingo (l + in + go) **13.** Loner (or Len) **14.** Stagg (waS TAGGed)
15. Nacre (N + acre) **16.** Hayes (haze) **17.** Winces (wines + C) **18.** Annals (mANN ALSo) **19.** Ursine (insure) **20.** Proust (stupor) **21.** Sequin (use in + Q) **22.** Stride (st + ride) **23.** Stereo (store + e) **24.** Astern (a + stern) **25.** Skewers (k + sewers) **26.** Alabama (lab + a + AMA) **27.** Oceanic (cocaine) **28.** Czarina (car + in + z + a) **29.** Gushers (hers + G + US) **30.** Theresa (there's a) **31.** Annexes (sex + Anne) **32.** Tensile (eel isn't) **33.** Environs (in one RV's) **34.** Boutique (bout + Que) **35.** Follower (flower + O + I) **36.** Gets away (waste +gay) **37.** Soddenly (send old + y) **38.** Foxhound (found + ox + h) **39.** Mosquitoes (Moses + Quito) **40.** Punch-drunk (Dr + pun + chunk)

170 OUTRAGEOUS FORTUNE

The cards were arranged as follows.
Top row, left to right: Queen of Wands, Justice, Moon
Middle row: Knight of Pentacles, Two of Swords, Page of Cups
Bottom row: High Priestess, Ace of Swords, Magician

168 STAR HOPPING

While nine-jump solutions are possible starting with any of the circles empty, the answer below begins with circle 16 empty and ends with a remarkable six-step multiple jump.
 1. Jump 6 to 16.
 2. Jump 10 to 12.
 3. Jump 1 to 11.
 4. Jump 6 to 16.
 5. Jump 7 to 5.
 6. Jump 4 to 6.
 7. Jump 5 to 15.
 8. Jump 2 to 12.
 9. Jump 13 to 6 to 4 to 11 to 16 to 6 to 1.

171 500 RUMMY

Words							Points
A	N	G	U	I	S	H	
2	3	4	A	A	A	A	13
A	N	G	U	L	A	R	
2	3	4	Q	Q	Q	Q	49
B	R	U	S	Q	U	E	
K	K	K	10	J	Q	K	70
C	O	R	S	A	G	E	
10	J	Q	4	4	4	4	46
D	Y	N	A	S	T	Y	
6	7	8	9	9	9	9	57
E	A	R	T	H	E	N	
J	Q	K	8	8	8	8	62
E	N	T	H	U	S	E	
8	8	8	8	3	4	5	44
G	L	I	S	T	E	N	
4	5	6	7	8	8	8	46
H	E	A	R	S	A	Y	
10	J	Q	K	9	9	9	67
H	E	A	R	T	E	N	
10	J	Q	K	8	8	8	64
H	E	A	T	H	E	N	
10	J	Q	8	8	8	8	62
S	H	E	L	T	E	R	
2	3	4	5	5	5	5	29
S	K	Y	W	A	R	D	
7	7	7	7	4	5	6	43
S	T	A	R	L	E	T	
7	8	9	5	5	5	5	44
S	T	A	R	T	L	E	
7	8	9	5	5	5	5	44
S	T	A	U	N	C	H	
7	8	9	3	3	3	3	36
S	T	Y	L	I	S	T	
9	9	9	5	6	7	8	53
T	H	E	A	T	E	R	
9	10	J	Q	5	5	5	54
U	N	U	S	U	A	L	
A	2	3	4	Q	Q	Q	40
Total Score							923

INDEX